FROM CREATION
TO NEW CREATION

OVERTURES TO BIBLICAL THEOLOGY

Old Testament Perspectives

FROM CREATION TO NEW CREATION

Bernhard W. Anderson

⅃ FORTRESS PRESS   **Minneapolis**

Library of Congress Cataloging-in-Publication Data available
ISBN 0-8006-2847-0

Manufactured in the U.S.A.   AF 1-2847
98   97   96   95   94   1   2   3   4   5   6   7   8   9   10

Contents

Editor's
Foreword

The place and function of creation in biblical theology is presently undergoing a major revision. The "eclipse" of creation in Old Testament studies has been largely determined by the categories of Gerhard von Rad, who, at least in his early writings, made creation subordinate to salvation history. In his latest work, however, even von Rad was changing his mind about the matter in significant ways.

One may identify at least four facets of this emerging new perspective:

First, with the collapse of positivism as a convincing intellectual stance in both science and theology, there is now a chance for a new way of understanding useful interaction between the two enterprises, at the meeting point of "creation." It is now possible to see that theology as well as science is not a descriptive work but is an imaginative construal, seeking to make sense out of reality. This recognition of common work done in two quite different modes means that theological interpretation need not be embarrassed in the face of science, nor flee from it to private and personal dimensions of life, but can be engaged with a common effort at imaginative construal.

Second and more immediately practical, the ecological crisis means that we are both permitted and required to ask different questions of the text than we have asked heretofore, and to notice claims in the text that we had not noticed before. Given that crisis as a new interpretive context, we notice how much the Bible addresses these issues that come under the general concern for creation.

Third, the awkward conflict of "creationism versus evolution," a subset of the above two items, has invited a reconsideration of the modes of discourse, the contexts, and the intention of creation texts in the Bible. This conflict evidences (on both sides) how the character of the text itself has been distorted either in scholastic or in modernist ways, both of which miss the point of the text. That is, neither creationism nor evolution has taken seriously that the creation texts are doxological voices engaged in offering an "alternative" world in which to live and work and trust.

Fourth, many people believe that Karl Barth's magnificent *Church Dogmatics* represented a peculiar season in the life of the church in which Barth, for practical and contextual reasons, accented Christology to the minimizing of other important interpretive matters. While Barth himself attended at some length to "creation faith," the Barthian program was widely perceived and was thought to neglect the theme of creation. Now in a changed context, away from the Eurocentrist issues that preoccupied Barth, scholars are devoting a great deal of energy either to moving beyond Barth (even if in a Barthian posture, witness Jürgen Moltmann, *God in Creation: A New Theology of Creation and the Spirit of God* [trans. Margaret Kohl; San Francisco: Harper & Row, 1985; Minneapolis: Fortress Press, 1993]), or to "rediscovering" in Barth neglected themes.

All of these factors mean that there is important new impetus to reassert the cruciality of creation for framing and shaping biblical faith. This ferment may be seen in the work of a host of scholars including James Barr, Terence Fretheim, Rolf Knierim, Jon Levenson, Hans Heinrich Schmid, Claus Westermann, and, in a different way, Klaus Koch.

The present volume from Bernhard Anderson is of signal importance in this recent development because (as this collection makes clear) it has been Anderson who has spent his long and distinguished career reflecting upon the creation texts, keeping alive the potential of creation theology in the long period of scholarship when creation was neglected and when biblical theology as a whole suffered a pronounced malaise. This collection is welcome and important because it provides entry into a long-term chronicle of Anderson's thinking, as he remained constant with the theme but decidedly contextual and contemporary in his interpretation, always knowingly "on location."

One may identify four facets of Anderson's work that have made him peculiarly influential in the more recent work of biblical interpretation:

1. Anderson is consistently a sensitive and discerning reader and interpreter of specific texts. In each of these papers, but especially in his discussion of the flood narrative (chapter 9) and Gen. 11:1-9 (chapter 10), his capacity to rethink the text and show it to us afresh is exquisite. In the end, faithful theological interpretation depends upon the specificity of par-

ticular texts and proceeds one text at a time. Anderson models the best in such method.

2. Anderson early on was attentive to the ancient Near Eastern context of Israel's creation faith and the mythopoeic dimension of the creation accounts, as is known in various textual traditions and as it is particularized in Israel's text. He understands how the speech of faith works and thus lets one see why and how creation faith cannot be pocketed in the traps of either "science and religion" or "creationism versus evolution." In all of these essays but especially in chapters 5, 13, and 14, Anderson makes clear why doxological language situates creation faith in worship.

3. Because he is a knowing historian, Anderson attends to the issues present in the ancient text. But he is also a contemporary man as believer and citizen, and so he regularly permits the text to voice for us its inescapable contemporaneity. This is evident especially in his recent articles on the ecological crisis, but his work is alive to the ways in which issues such as violence, pluralism, and the arms race are within the horizon of a rightly read ancient text.

4. It is this capacity of Anderson to move back and forth between ancient text and present interpretive circumstance that has established him as one of the most suggestive and faithful theological interpreters of his generation. With the stalemate between Eichrodt and von Rad, and the collapse of the biblical theology movement, Old Testament theology has languished and until recently seemed to lack any vitality. Through all of that time, however, Anderson has insisted upon the legitimacy and worthwhileness of theological interpretation. Both the church community and the scholarly community owe him a great debt for his refusal to back off from the theological task, the gains of which are richly evident in this book.

As early as 1967 in *Creation versus Chaos: The Reinterpretation of Mythical Symbolism in the Bible* (Association Press), Anderson in a programmatic way sounded the themes that were to define his continuing scholarly work. The reissuance of the book in 1987 (Fortress Press) indicates that it has become something of a classic with an enduring freshness. This book, together with *Creation in the Old Testament,* which he edited in 1984 (Fortress Press), make Anderson the reference point for the most important work of the past generation on the theme of creation, and the beginning point for the new season of work just now emerging. That new work will no doubt go beyond the achievements of Anderson and in directions he himself might not go. But all of the newer work is and will be informed by and indebted to his work.

It is a delight to offer these essays to a broader public and to express our shared gratitude to Anderson for his major contribution to our common work, and for the model he has been and is of careful and imaginative reading, faithful to the text and immediately present to his own time and place.

Walter Brueggemann

Author's Note and
Acknowledgments

I wish to thank my daughter, Carol Hanawalt, and my granddaughter, Gwyndeth Catlin, for their indispensable editorial assistance in the preparation of these essays for publication. Also, my thanks go to Walter Brueggemann, the editor of this series, and the staff of Fortress Press, especially David Lott, for their encouragement and help.

Translations of biblical passages are my own unless otherwise indicated. I gratefully acknowledge the following for granting permission to republish the material in this book:

Chapter One, "The Earth Is the Lord's," first appeared in *Interpretation: The Journal of Bible and Theology* 9 (1955): 3–20; the present revised version first appeared in *Is God a Creationist? The Religious Case against Creation-Science*, ed. Roland Frye (New York: Charles Scribner's Sons, 1983).

Chapter Two, "Biblical Perspectives on the Doctrine of Creation," first appeared as "Creation" in *Interpreter's Dictionary of the Bible* (1962); the present revised version first appeared in *Cry of the Environment: Rebuilding the Christian Creation Tradition*, ed. P. N. Joranson and Ken Butigan (Santa Fe: Bear & Co., 1984).

Chapter Three, "The Priestly Creation Story: A Stylistic Study," first appeared as "A Stylistic Study of the Priestly Creation Story" in *Canon and Authority: Essays in Old Testament Religion and Theology*, ed. George W. Coats and Burke O. Long (Philadelphia: Fortress Press, 1977).

Chapter Four, "The Flood Story in Context: From Analysis to Synthesis," first appeared in *The Journal of Biblical Literature* 97 (1978): 23–39.

Chapter Five, "Mythopoeic and Theological Dimensions of Biblical Creation Faith," first appeared in *Creation in the Old Testament,* ed. Bernhard W. Anderson (Philadelphia: Fortress Press, 1984).

Chapter Six, "Theology and Science: Cosmic Dimensions of the Creation Account in Genesis" was given as the Carl Michalson Memorial Lecture in 1985 at Drew University and first appeared in the *Drew Gateway* 56 (1986): 1–13; the same version was reprinted as a postscript in *Creation versus Chaos: The Reinterpretation of Mythical Symbolism in the Bible* by Bernhard W. Anderson (Philadelphia: Fortress Press, 1987).

Chapter Seven, "Human Dominion over Nature," first appeared in *Biblical Studies in Contemporary Thought,* ed. Miriam Winter (Winchendon, Mass.: Greeno, Hadden & Company, 1975).

Chapter Eight, "Relation between the Human and Nonhuman Creation in the Biblical Primeval History," first appeared as "Creation and Ecology" in *American Journal of Theology and Philosophy* 4 (1983): 14–30; the same version appeared in *Creation in the Old Testament,* ed. Bernhard W. Anderson (Philadelphia: Fortress Press, 1984).

Chapter Nine, "Creation and the Noachic Covenant," first appeared in *Cry of the Environment: Rebuilding the Christian Creation Tradition,* ed. P. N. Joranson and Ken Butigan (Santa Fe: Bear & Co., 1984).

Chapter Ten, "The Tower of Babel: Unity and Diversity in God's Creation," first appeared in *Concilium* 121 (1977): 89–97; the present revised version first appeared in *Currents in Theology and Mission* 5 (1978): 69–81.

Chapter Eleven, "'The Lord Has Created Something New': A Stylistic Study of Jeremiah 31:15-22," first appeared in *Catholic Biblical Quarterly* 40 (1978): 463–78.

Chapter Twelve, "The Slaying of the Fleeing, Twisting Serpent: Isaiah 27:1 in Context," first appeared in *Uncovering Ancient Stones: Essays in Honor of H. Neil Richardson,* ed. Lewis M. Hopfe (Winona Lake, Ind.: Eisenbrauns, 1994).

Chapter Thirteen, "Creation Faith in Its Setting of Worship," first appeared as "Creation and Worship" in *Creation versus Chaos: The Reinterpreta-*

tion of Mythical Symbolism in the Bible by Bernhard W. Anderson (Philadelphia: Fortress Press, 1987).

Chapter Fourteen, "Creation and New Creation," first appeared as the J. Clyde Wheeler Lecture at Phillips Graduate Seminary, Tulsa, Oklahoma, January 1993.

Abbreviations

AB	Anchor Bible
AnBib	Analecta biblica
ANET	*Ancient Near Eastern Texts Relating to the Old Testament*, ed. J. B. Pritchard, 3d ed. 1969
ARW	*Archiv für Religionswissenschaft*
ATD	Das Alte Testament Deutsch
BA	*Biblical Archaeologist*
BASOR	*Bulletin of the American Schools of Oriental Research*
BAT	Die Botschaft des Alten Testaments
BHK	*Biblical Hebraica*, ed. Rudolf Kittel
BibOr	Biblica et orientalia
BSac	*Bibliotheca Sacra*
BWANT	Beiträge zur Wissenschaft vom Alten and Neuen Testament
CBQ	*Catholic Biblical Quarterly*
CBQMS	Catholic Biblical Quarterly—Monograph Series
Ebib	Etudes bibliques
HAT	Handbuch zum Alten Testament
HKAT	Handkommentar zum Alten Testament
HSM	Harvard Semitic Monographs
HTR	*Harvard Theological Review*
IB	*Interpreter's Bible*, ed. G. A. Buttrick
IDB	*Interpreter's Dictionary of the Bible*, ed. G. A. Buttrick, 4 vols., 1962
IDBSup	Supplementary volume to *IDB*, ed. K. Crim, 1976
Int	*Interpretation*
IRT	Issues in Religion and Theology
JB	Jerusalem Bible
JBL	*Journal of Biblical Literature*
JPSV	Jewish Publication Society Version (1988)

JSOTSup	Journal for the Study of the Old Testament—Supplementary Series
KAT	Kommentar zum Alten Testament
KB L.	Koehler and W. Baumgartner, *Lexicon in Veteris Testamenti libros*
KJV	King James Version
KTU	*Die keilalphabetischen Texte aus Ugarit,* ed. M. Dietrich, O. Loretz, and J. Sanmartin, 1976
LUÅ	Lunds universitets årsskrift
LXX	Septaugint
MT	Masoretic Text
NAB	New American Bible
NCB	New Century Bible
NEB	New English Bible
NIV	New International Version
NRSV	New Revised Standard Version
OBT	Overtures to Biblical Theology
OTL	Old Testament Library
PG	*Patrologia graeca,* ed. J. Migne
PL	*Patrologia latina,* ed. J. Migne
PTMS	Pittsburgh Theological Monograph Series
REB	Revised English Bible
RSV	Revised Standard Version
SBT	Studies in Biblical Theology
TDOT	*Theological Dictionary of the Old Testament,* ed. G. J. Botterweck and H. Ringgren
TQ	*Theologische Quartalschrift*
TToday	*Theology Today*
TZ	*Theologische Zeitschrift*
USQR	*Union Seminary Quarterly Review*
UT	C. H. Gordon, *Ugaritic Textbook*
VTSup	Vetus Testamentum, Supplements
WBC	Word Biblical Commentary
ZAW	*Zeitschrift für die alttestamentliche Wissenschaft*
ZKT	*Zeitschrift für katholische Theologie*
ZTK	*Zeitschrift für Theologie und Kirche*

CHAPTER 1

The Earth Is
the Lord's

To understand creation biblically one must abandon the premise on which the "science-versus-religion" battle has been waged: the notion, still popularly held, that the biblical view of creation is either bad science or good science, depending on which side one takes in the controversy. To be sure, the creation faith does have radical implications for the scientific enterprise, as it does for any phase of human activity. This doctrine is a clear warning against assigning any form of human activity—whether science, politics, economics, education, or art—to a special reservation where it has a supposedly autonomous role. To say that "the earth is the Lord's and the fullness thereof" is to affirm that no area of life escapes the unconditional religious concern that informs our creaturely existence. Nevertheless, the biblical view of creation is not an effort at primitive science. Its primary concern is not the speculative question of the origin and genesis of the earth, a question that lies properly in the domain of natural science. Whatever "science" is found in the biblical creation narratives is a legacy from the cosmological speculation of Israel's neighbors and has been outmoded by the *Weltbild* or world-picture that modern science has brought to view.

This does not mean that the biblical doctrine is irrelevant to our scientific culture. Actually, the doctrine speaks to our condition with greater relevance, since it is not dealing with a speculative question but with *human life here and now*. The affirmation that God is Creator arose originally out of the worship experience of Israel, not out of the reflections of a systematic theologian or a philosopher. That the Genesis creation story reaches its climax in the observance of the Sabbath is clear witness to the existential foundation of the creation faith in the Israelite cultus. The atmosphere pervading the first chapter of Genesis is that of the community of worship. The language, which moves in the majestic cadenzas of Priestly prose, is the language of faith—not that of speculative thought or prescientific reasoning. Therefore, our task is to go beyond the *doctrine* to the *experience* of worship out of which has come the affirmation that "the earth is the Lord's" (Ps. 24:1). In the Bible, creation refers not to a distant event that belongs in the field of astrophysics but to an event that now—in this moment of worship—is celebrated in cultic participation, especially in connection with annual religious festivals.

My method of study will involve, of course, special attention to the first two chapters of Genesis. Literary criticism has singled out two different accounts of creation in these chapters: one (2:4b-25) belonging to the Old Epic (Yahwistic or J) narrative, written in the time of the united monarchy about 950 B.C.E., and the other (1:1—2:3) to the so-called Priestly writing (P), which is dated in the postexilic period about 500 B.C.E. To assign dates to these chapters in terms of the literary history of the Pentateuch, however, is not necessarily to indicate the age of the traditions that were written down at these particular times. Both chapters embody traditions that are much older than the time of their literary composition. Indeed, belief in divine creation is one of the oldest elements of Israel's faith and is attested in many biblical passages, not only in historical books (for example, Gen. 14:19; 1 Kings 8:12 [Septuagint]) but in Israel's hymns (such as Psalms 8, 19, 24, and 104). My study therefore must range beyond Genesis 1 and 2 and cannot conclude without at least a brief treatment of the New Testament.

Today some interpreters advocate demythologizing the biblical language concerning creation, that is, disengaging the essential content of meaning from the language in which it is expressed—a prescientific language that is obsolete in terms of the modern scientific outlook.[1] To attempt such a translation into the modern idiom is an important aspect of the apologetic task of the community of faith, which must ever seek a point of contact in secular life and thought in order that the gospel may be communicated to the world. In the last analysis, however, it is questionable whether one can abstract the content of the creation faith from the biblical form in which it is expressed. Instead of dispensing with the biblical language the interpreter should seek to understand it from within, that is, from within the worshiping community of Israel. The problem of demythology is put into a new light when at the outset one recognizes that the biblical language concerning creation does not purport to give knowledge about nature, such as can

---

1. See the stimulating essay by Rudolf Bultmann in *Kerygma and Myth* (ed. H. W. Bartsch; trans. R. H. Fuller; London: Society for the Promotion of Christian Knowledge, 1953).

be acquired through science and expressed in scientific terms. Rather, it affirms something about human existence itself—about the scientist as a person involved in the drama of history, about the life of any person regardless of the culture in which that person lives. It affirms something about my life and your life that no amount of scientific knowledge could ever disclose. It speaks to the person who is immersed in history and for whom the status of a detached observer is out of the question.

CREATION AND MEANING

In the first place, the creation faith affirms that God alone is the author of the meaning that supports all human history and the natural world, which is the theater of the historical drama. Human history and nature do not generate their own meaning. Rather, God's revelation creates the meaning that undergirds all existence. God's creative word is the source of all being. Thus the psalmist affirms:

By the word of the Lord the heavens were made,
    and all their host by the breath of his mouth. (Ps. 33:6, NRSV)

It is folly for peoples and nations to act as though their plans determined the meaning of life. Rather:

Let all the earth fear the Lord,
    let all the inhabitants of the world stand in awe of him!
For he spoke, and it came to be;
    he commanded, and it stood firm. (Ps. 33:8-9, NRSV)

With the same kind of universal vision the psalmist expresses the conviction found in Genesis 1, that all existence is grounded in the meaning disclosed by God's word.

Both stories of creation are characterized by this universal view—one that includes the heavens and the earth and all humankind. It is noteworthy, however, that in both cases creation faith presupposes election faith, that is, the conviction that God has chosen the history of Israel as the special medium of divine revelation. This is clear in the Old Epic (J) narrative, where the movement of primeval history (Genesis 2–11) is toward the decisive moment related in Genesis 12: the call of Abraham and the divine promise that in him and his seed all the families of human-kind would be blessed. It is also true in the Priestly (P) scheme, where everything points toward the singling out of the holy community, Israel, and God's revelation of the Torah at Sinai. In neither the Old Epic nor the Priestly tradition does creation stand by itself. It is integrally related to the special history of Israel within which God chose to make known certain "mighty acts" of salvation. Thus the place of the creation stories in the narrative sequence indicates that the primary concern is about the meaning of history, especially Israel's history in relation to the histories of other peoples. To speak of the "first things" in this context is not to reflect on ancient origins but to say something about the source and foundation of the meaning discerned within Israel's history. As Ludwig Köhler observes:

> The Old Testament story of creation does not answer the question "How did the world come into being?" with the answer: "God created it," but answers the question "From where does the history of God's people derive its meaning?" with the answer: "God has given the history of His people its meaning through creation."[2]

When one opens the Bible and begins reading from creation toward the call of Israel, one is really reading the story backward. Israel came to believe that the word of God created a historical community, a social order (Exod. 15:16, "the people whom thou hast created"; echoed in Isa. 43:1-2), before Israel affirmed that "by the word of the Lord were the heavens made." The earlier Old Epic (J) creation story and the later Priestly (P) version are both secondary to the ancient Israelite witness, which pointed to Yahweh's saving deeds in the exodus, the wilderness wandering, and the conquest of Canaan. Israel's early credo, as preserved in the little liturgy found in Deut. 26:5-10, makes no reference to the creation but rehearses the mighty acts of the Lord, beginning with the deliverance from Egypt. This silence about the creation is striking,[3] and even suggests that in Israel's faith redemption was primary, creation secondary, not only in order of theological importance but also in order of appearance in the Israelite tradition. In the early stage of Israel's faith attention focused on what Yahweh had done in history, especially in the crucial event of the exodus, when Israel was, so to speak, created out of nothing (that is, out of a mass of slaves who were regarded as a historical nonentity in the ancient world). In this event the word of God, spoken through Moses and actualized in concrete events, created meaning and order out of desolation. God's word made history; it created a new people. Israel could have said with Paul: "God chose what is low and despised in the world, things that are not, to reduce to nothing things that are" (1 Cor. 1:28, NRSV). Later prophets rightly pointed back to the exodus as the time of Israel's beginning (Amos 3:1-2; Hos. 11:1; 12:9[10]; 13:4).

2. Ludwig Köhler, *Old Testament Theology* (trans. A. S. Todd; Philadelphia: Westminster, 1957) 87.
3. See also the longer summary found in Joshua 24, which, again, does not refer to the creation.

Israel's early faith, while concentrating on Yahweh's redemptive acts in history, did not ignore Yahweh's lordship over nature. According to the tradition, Yahweh commanded the plagues in the land of Egypt, was victorious in the cataclysm of the Reed Sea, and graciously provided the pilgrim people with food and water in the wilderness. The Song of Deborah (Judges 5) describes Yahweh's coming on the storm to rescue the embattled "people of Yahweh" at Megiddo and portrays the heavenly host—"the stars in their courses"—joining battle in the defeat of Sisera's army. Nature was not removed from Yahweh's sovereignty but was the servant of Yahweh's historical purpose. The Old Epic (J) tradition makes the impressive claim that the whole earth belongs to Yahweh (Exod. 19:5). According to Israel's early faith, Yahweh's sway was plainly as high as the heavens and as wide as the whole earth (see also Josh. 10:12; Gen. 49:25; Exod. 15; Deut. 33:13-16). These tremendous affirmations, however, were made from the standpoint of a community that remembered and celebrated the saving deeds of Yahweh in history. The first thing that Israel said was not "In the beginning God created the heavens and the earth," but rather, "In the beginning Yahweh created Israel to be his people and gave us a task and a future in his purpose."

During the first generations of Israel's historical career there was little motive to view the meaning of the exodus, the call of Israel, within a universal or cosmic design. As Israel was pressed on every hand by foes that threatened to annihilate them, the burning issue was the meaning of what was happening in the history of *this* people, not the question of Israel's relation to the nations or to the cosmos. When historical tensions relaxed and Israel achieved some measure of security in the Palestinian corridor, however, the time was ripe to affirm that the meaning revealed in Israel's history was actually the meaning undergirding the history of all peoples and the whole creation.

The time for this widening historical vision was, above all, the glorious era of nationalism under David and Solomon. Whatever tendencies may have existed in this direction during the earlier period, it was the great political achievements of these kings, especially David, that widened the political and cultural horizons of Israel. With this expanding national view went also an expanding view of Yahweh's lordship over the world, as expressed preeminently in the Old Epic or Yahwist narrative that, in its written form, probably dates from the reign of Solomon. This comprehensive history, which extends from the creation (Genesis 2–3) to at least the eve of the conquest of Canaan, reviewed the whole past in the light of the exodus faith and the special history whose theme was the saving deeds of Yahweh. Especially significant for the subject of this essay was the prefacing of the traditions dealing with primeval history (Genesis 2–11) to the stories concerning God's dealings with Israel (Genesis 12 through Joshua).

According to Gerhard von Rad, the Yahwist's most original contribution was the incorporation of these traditions into a comprehensive history so that the creation is now seen in the light of Israel's exodus faith.[4]

Thus a line was traced from where Israel stood in history right back to the remotest beginnings of human history, using the traditional stories that were available. The result of this broadening of the narrative scope was a vision of the whole range of history in the light of the meaning that was revealed within Israel's history. The narratives of Genesis 2–11 do not deal particularly with Israel but with all peoples. *'Ādām* is neither a Hebrew nor an Israelite, but human being (humankind) generically, including both "male and female," as explicitly stated in Gen. 1:26-27 (note the alternation of singular and plural forms of speech). This typical or representative role is further exemplified in the paradise story in Genesis 2–3, where the human situation is portrayed in the primeval parents, the man and the woman—Adam and Eve. This universal perspective is evident throughout the primeval history (Genesis 1–11). In the story of the flood we learn that Noah is not an Israelite but the ancestor from whom sprung the major ethnic groups, of which the Semites are one. Genesis 2–11, then, claims that Yahweh, who spoke to Moses and delivered Israel from Egypt, is none other than the God of primeval times.[5] The One who created the community Israel is the Creator of humankind. In this way the Yahwist expands and universalizes the meaning that was revealed to Israel in its unique historical experiences. In a similar manner, but with less concern for the dynamic movement and conflict of history, the Priestly writer affirms that Israel's cultic history is given meaning by the God of the whole creation.

To speak of God as creator, then, is not to make an affirmation about the manufacture of nature. Were this the case, the doctrine of evolution could rationally replace the old oriental myths that portray the birth of the gods out of the previously existing stuff of chaos, and describe one of these gods making the world in a great battle with the powers of chaos.[6] But the biblical creation faith deals primarily with *the meaning of human history*. The great affirmation of the Bible is that the meaning of human history, first disclosed in the events of Israel's history, is the meaning upon which the world is founded. The redemptive word, by which

---

4. Gerhard von Rad, *Genesis* (trans. John H. Marks; OTL; rev. ed.; Philadelphia: Westminster, 1972) 13–28.

5. This is made explicit in the J narrative by the usage of the special divine name, Yahweh, throughout Genesis and by the claim that people began to worship Yahweh in the antediluvian period; cf. Gen. 4:26.

6. The Babylonian myth of creation, *Enuma Elish,* begins with a theogony. See the translation by E. A. Speiser in *ANET,* 60ff. See also my *Creation versus Chaos: The Reinterpretation of Mythical Symbolism in the Bible* (New York: Association, 1967; repr. Philadelphia: Fortress Press, 1987), 11–42.

Israel was created as the people of God, is none other than the creative word, by which the heavens were made. The point bears reemphasis that in the Bible creation is not an independent doctrine but is inseparably related to the basic story of the people in which Yahweh is presented as the actor and redeemer. Salvation and creation belong together (cf. Isa 43:14-19; 51:9-10). To proclaim God as creator is therefore, as so often in the Psalms (cf. Psalms 29, 33, 104), a call to worship. It is a summons to acknowledge *now* the foundation and source of the meaning of our history.

CREATION AND CONTINUITY

Closely related to what I have been saying about historical meaning is a second facet of the doctrine of creation: the total dependence of the world upon God. The earth is the Lord's; it is not self-sustaining. Everything in it, including human life, partakes of creaturely finitude. Were it not for the fact that the Creator sustains the world, it would lapse back into primeval chaos.

To acknowledge the infinite distance between the Creator and the creature is difficult for people in the modern world who are prone to identify God with some aspect of human consciousness, perhaps the Intelligence that our minds perceive in the cosmos, or the natural processes in which human history is involved, or even "the best in human nature." But the God of the Bible is not identified with any phenomenon in the world. The God who claims Israel and whom Israel worships is "God and no mortal, the Holy One in your midst," as the prophet Hosea proclaimed (Hos. 11:9, NRSV). Although we must seek analogies from human experience to witness to the presence of the Holy God in the human world, the great blasphemy is to identify the image with the One to whom the image points. The doctrine of creation, which stresses the dignity and supremacy of humankind in God's creation (Ps. 8:3-8[4-9]), also draws the sharpest line between the Creator and the creature (Job 38:2-7).

At first glance this distinction does not seem to be true of the Old Epic story in Genesis 2, which portrays Yahweh in vividly human terms as he forms man, then the animals, and finally a woman. But despite the naïveté of the language there is no doubt about Yahweh's sovereignty. Two divine prerogatives, symbolized by two trees, separate creatures from their Maker: the knowledge of good and evil (i.e., the capacity for responsible decision) and deathless life. To grasp for these prerogatives, and thereby overstep the bounds of humanity, is an act of rebellion against the Lord God. Lest the eating of the fruit of the first tree should tempt the human being to "reach out his hand and take also from the tree of life, and eat, and live forever" (Gen. 3:22, NRSV), the couple is driven out of the garden. Human beings can assert their independence from their Creator, but they cannot escape being who they are: creatures who exist in relation to God and who are exposed to God's grace and judgment. This theme is developed further in the Old Epic (J) stories dealing with Cain and Abel (4:1-16), the flood (chaps. 6–8), and the Tower of Babel (11:1-9).

That God alone is sovereign is affirmed emphatically in the Priestly creation story in Genesis 1. According to this chapter, the creation depends totally on the will of the transcendent God. Here there is not the slightest suggestion that the Creator is identified with any power immanent in nature, as was the case in the nature mythologies of antiquity. God is completely independent from the primeval watery chaos, out of which the habitable world is created. The imperative of the Creator's word is the only connection with the works of creation. Perhaps the belief in "creation out of nothing," implying that even the primeval chaos was created by God, is too sophisticated for Israel's faith; for the primary concern of this chapter is to express the total dependence of everything upon God's ordaining will rather than to answer the question of the origin of the stuff of chaos. It is noteworthy, however, that the Old Testament uses the verb *bārā'* ("create"), which appears in the preface to the creation epic (v. 1) and again emphatically in the case of the creation of animal life (v. 21) and human life (v. 27), exclusively to refer to effortless divine creation that brings into being something absolutely new. This language comes as close to creation *ex nihilo* as one can without actually using the expression, which is first found in the late Jewish book, 2 Maccabees (7:28).[7] In any case, the Priestly creation story affirms the unconditional sovereignty of God and the complete dependence of creation upon God's transcendent will, an affirmation that is only further underscored by later discussions in which creation *ex nihilo* was made explicit.

Once again one must remember that this emphasis on God's sovereignty over creation belonged to the present experience of the worshiping community, Israel. The unforgettable events of Israel's history, chiefly the deliverance from Egyptian bondage and the giving of the covenant, were impressed upon the people's experience as signs of Yahweh's lordship over them. The covenant itself was not a parity relationship but a covenant between unequals: the sovereign and the vassal people. Israel was dependent for its very life upon the will of the One who had taken the initiative to deliver this people and bring them into covenant relationship (Exod.

---

7. For a defense of creation *ex nihilo* in Genesis 1, see Walther Eichrodt, "In the Beginning: A Contribution to the Interpretation of the First Word of the Bible," in *Israel's Prophetic Heritage: Essays in Honor of James Muilenburg* (ed. Bernhard W. Anderson and Walter Harrelson; New York: Harper & Row, 1962) 1–10; repr. in *Creation in the Old Testament* (ed. Bernhard W. Anderson; IRT 6; Philadelphia: Fortress Press, 1984) 65–73; idem, *Theology of the Old Testament* (trans. J. A. Baker; OTL; 2 vols.; Philadelphia: Westminster, 1961–67) 2.101–6.

19:4-5). The basic motif of Israelite worship is the confession that Yahweh is Lord.

From this standpoint of present faith Israel looked back to the creation and affirmed that the world itself depends on the same sovereign will, the same Lord of the covenant. All polytheism is excluded from the creation because Israel depends on only one sovereign will. The regularities of nature are not regarded as natural laws but as expressions of the same faithfulness that characterized Yahweh's relation to the covenant people (cf. Gen. 8:22). Even as Israel would fall prey to the enemies that constantly threatened, were it not for Yahweh's sustaining power, so also the world is maintained only by its relationship to God. Apart from the power of the Creator the earth would return to the watery chaos from which it was created.

One of the curious aspects of the biblical doctrine of creation is the portrayal of the earth as being established upon the primeval sea (Ps. 24:1). In one sense, this is only an expression of the world-picture that Israel inherited from its cultural neighbors: the view of the earth as a flat surface, resting upon subterranean waters and overarched by the solid firmament that upholds the heavenly ocean. From our perspective, this is obviously not good science. Since the creation faith does not pretend to deal with natural science, however, the more important issue is whether this mythopoeic language communicates an understanding of the depth of human existence that is ignored in the modern scientific outlook.

The Priestly (P) creation story begins with a description of the earth in an uninhabitable stage: "the earth was a formless void and darkness covered the face of the deep" (Gen. 1:2, NRSV). As in the preface, so in the rest of the Priestly story creation is seen in relation to chaos. By the command of God light is separated from the primeval darkness, a firmament is placed in the midst of the waters to separate the waters (above) from the waters (below), and the waters under the heaven are gathered together into one place so that dry land appears. In this view the watery chaos is not destroyed; rather, the primeval sea surrounds the habitable earth on every hand. Were it not for the Creator's power, by which the firmament was created and the sea assigned boundaries, the earth would be engulfed by the flowing together of the waters and would return to primeval chaos (cf. Gen. 7:11; 8:2). No language could express more forcefully the utter dependence of the world upon the Creator.

This imagery recurs throughout the Old Testament.[8] The psalmist who

---

8. Many passages in the Old Testament allude to the ancient myth of the battle with chaos (Tiamat in Babylonian mythology) portrayed as a dragon or serpent. See Isa. 27:1; 51:9; Ps. 89:9-10 (10-11); Job 9:13; 26:12. In Gen. 1:2 *tĕhôm* ("deep") is linguistically related to Babylonian Tiamat, but there is no suggestion of a mythological struggle.

exclaims that "the earth is the Lord's" also marvels that Yahweh has established the earth firmly on the primeval deep.

> The earth is the Lord's and all that is in it,
>   the world, and those who live in it;
> for he has founded it on the seas,
>   and established it on the rivers. (Ps. 24:1-2, NRSV; cf. 136:6)

Other texts state that God has made firm the firmament above and has assigned boundaries to the sea (Prov. 8:27-29; Ps. 104:7-9; Jer. 5:22). God watches over the sea (Job 7:12), and if the waters lift themselves up, God rebukes them and they flee (Pss. 77:16[17]; 18:15[16]; etc.). God has established the foundations of the earth in the depths of the sea, and when the earth shakes with the roaring of the waters, God holds its pillars firm (Pss. 75:3[4]; 46:1-3[2-4]). Ancient peoples knew, perhaps in a more immediate sense than those who live in the modern scientific era, that the goodness and order of human life are constantly threatened by the powers of chaos. Jeremiah could envision God's judgment bringing about a return to primeval chaos in a powerful poem that uses the same phrase (*tōhû wābōhû*) that occurs in Gen. 1:2.

> I looked upon the earth, and lo, a chaotic waste [*tōhû wābōhû*],
>   and unto the heavens, and their light was gone.
> I looked on the mountains, and lo, they were quaking,
>   and all the hills were trembling.
> I looked, and lo, there was no human being,
>   and all the birds of the sky had vanished.
> I looked, and lo, the fertile land was wilderness,
>   before Yahweh, before his burning wrath. (Jer. 4:23-26)

In another poem a psalmist, near to death, speaks of being cast into the waters of the primeval deep (Jonah 2). Were it not for the Creator's sustaining power the waters of chaos would break in upon the earth, destroying all meaning and order. God's work of creation, then, is also God's work of salvation. Moment by moment the creation is supported solely by the will of the Creator. In this perspective, to affirm that God is Creator is to acknowledge utter dependence on the One who is our refuge and our strength.

> Therefore we will not fear, though the earth should change,
>   though the mountains shake in the heart of the sea;
> though its waters roar and foam,
>   though the mountains tremble with its tumult. (Ps. 46:2-3, NRSV)

Clearly one cannot quickly dismiss this biblical language as the expression of an outmoded cosmology. In describing the earth as resting on the sea, Israel had in mind something other than the chemistry of water (H_2O), just as the author of Revelation likewise had something different in view in his vision of the new heaven and the new earth where the sea would be no more (Rev. 21:1). Is it not true that human life indeed rests upon and is surrounded by elemental chaos that constantly threatens the goodness and orderliness of the world? The "chaos and desolation" of Gen. 1:2 is not just a statement about primeval times; it is a statement about a present possibility. Commenting on this verse, Gerhard von Rad observes that human beings have always had a haunting awareness "that behind all creation lies the abyss of formlessness; that all creation is always ready to sink into the abyss of the formless; that the chaos, therefore, signifies simply the threat to everything created. This suspicion has been a constant temptation" to faith.[9]

Today, more than ever, people are becoming aware of this depth, this abyss. The threat of "nonbeing," the anxiety over the possible meaninglessness of life, the fear of chaotic forces that threaten to overwhelm our secure world—this experience has found expression in modern language that has striking affinity with the creation imagery of the Bible. The truth of the matter is that existence is not self-sustaining. The world and all creatures in it are radically dependent on God. For it is by God's command that order is created and sustained in the midst of the surging forces of the deep that threaten to burst beyond their assigned boundaries and plunge the world into chaos.

CREATION AND ORDER: THE *IMAGO DEI*

Third, the doctrine of creation affirms that every creature is assigned a place in God's plan in order that it may perform its appointed role in serving and glorifying the Creator. This is magnificently portrayed in the Priestly creation story. God "calls" each thing by its name, that is, God exercises sovereignty by designating the peculiar nature and function of each creature. For instance, the heavenly bodies are not celestial beings who control human life, as the astrological cults of antiquity supposed; rather, they are servants of God whose appointed function is to designate the seasons and to separate the day from the night. Every creature of heaven and earth participates in the "liturgy," the divine service of which the Sabbath is the climax. "Nature is the order decreed by God in which each part is called to worship."[10] Hence the psalmist says that the heavens are joining in an inaudible anthem to the Creator (Ps. 19:1-4).

9. Von Rad, *Genesis*, 51.
10. Wilhelm Vischer, *The Witness of the Old Testament to Christ* (trans. A. B. Crabtree; London: Lutterworth, 1949) 46.

It is human beings, however, who occupy a special place in the liturgy of creation. In the Priestly creation story the creation of *'ādām,* consisting of "male and female" (Gen. 1:27), is the last of God's works; therefore humankind constitutes the crown of the creation. That human beings are created on the same day as the animals is an important testimony to the intimate relation between the human and nonhuman creatures. But humankind is accorded a place of dignity far above the animals; human beings are given a special divine blessing and are commissioned to have dominion over the nonhuman creatures. Their task is to glorify God by filling the earth and subduing it, thereby acting as the appointed representatives of the Creator.[11]

The Old Epic (J) creation story presents the same view in more picturesque language. This story places *'ādām* in the natural environment that the Lord God has provided. This earthly being is intimately related to the animals, the narrator says, for like them *'ādām* is a "living creature" (*nepeš ḥayyâ:* 2:19; cf. 2:7) who is made from the dust (2:7) and returns to it (3:19) at death. But *'ādām* is more than a natural animal, as evidenced by the sovereign power to give the animals names (2:20) and by the special kind of partnership between man and woman (2:21-24). Above all, these human beings, unlike the animals, stand in an "I and thou" relation with their Maker and can be obedient, or disobedient, to the task that is given: to dress and keep the garden as faithful stewards of God's estate (cf. 2:15).

Again one must remember that these two creation stories derive their meaning from the faith of the covenant community, Israel. The purpose of Israel's deliverance from Egypt, according to Exod. 3:12, was that Israel should "serve God" at the sacred mountain. Although the nature of Israel's God-given task was more profoundly understood in later times, especially in the poems of Second Isaiah (Isaiah 40–55), the consistent witness of Israel's tradition is that Yahweh's gracious deeds bound the people to their God in the obligation of service. Israel was beholden to its Creator and Redeemer. Its calling was for a task: to be obedient to what Yahweh requires (Mic. 6:8). Accordingly, Joshua is represented as rehearsing the story of Yahweh's benevolent deeds and summoning the people assembled at Shechem to covenant decision: "Now therefore revere the Lord [Yahweh] and serve him in sincerity and in faithfulness. . . . Choose this day whom you will serve" (Josh. 24:14-15, NRSV). This emphasis on volitional response with one's whole being to the gracious overture and sovereign claim of God is characteristic of Israel's faith and was an indispensable basis of the experience of worship.

In the creation stories this view of the relationship between God and people is projected back to the very beginning of history. Thus the claim is

11. See chap. 7 below.

made that the *role of humankind*—not just the role of Israel—is to perform
the task given by the Creator. The uniqueness of human beings among
other earthly creatures is that they are persons whom God addresses, the
"thou" with whom God enters into personal relationship. Human beings
are not bound within the order of nature, experiencing no greater demand
upon them than to adjust harmoniously to the rhythms of nature. They are
decisional creatures, summoned into dialogue with their Creator. Unlike
the animals, who are bound only to the earth, human creatures are historical beings who live vis-à-vis the God who gives them a task. Since God's
word, when responded to, frees humans from the cycles of nature and sets
their face toward the future, the creation is truly the beginning of history.
Though the Yahwist and Priestly traditions differ from each other in
important respects, both agree in regarding the creation as the inauguration
of a historical drama in which human beings must reckon with the sovereign power and purpose of the God who is Creator and Lord.[12] History is
not a natural process of growth and development; it is the realm of inter-
personal relationships (political, economic, social) where peoples and
nations cannot escape the sovereign voice: "Let be then: learn that I am
God" (Ps. 46:10, NEB).

The natural world, however, is the sphere within which this historical
drama unfolds. The creation narratives of Genesis give no hint that the
natural environment is intrinsically an evil, material realm from which one
should seek escape into a sphere that is presumed to be "higher" and
"more spiritual." In the Priestly creation account the world of God's creation is called "exceedingly good" (Gen. 1:31). This verdict of divine
approval is not simply an aesthetic judgment, like that of an artist who
looks with satisfaction on a finished painting; more than that, the approving judgment signifies that every creature in the created world corresponds
to God's intention, fulfills the function for which it was created, and performs its task as part of the larger whole. The Priestly creation account
(Gen. 1:1—2:3), though supplemented with the story of paradise lost (Gen.
2:4—3:24), lacks any trace of creaturely rebellion against the Creator that
mars the goodness of the creation. This creaturely flaw is mentioned only
briefly in Psalm 104 (see the concluding reference to wicked people in v.
35), a psalm that otherwise provides a poetic parallel to the Priestly creation story. Even in the Old Epic traditions about paradise, Cain and Abel,
the flood, and the Tower of Babel (Genesis 2–11), however, the flaw in
God's creation lies in the *human will* (freedom), not in the natural or
cosmic environment.

---

12. See Eichrodt, "In the Beginning," 8–9, for comments on "the inner connection" between
creation and "the working out of salvation."

This positive view toward "nature" (the environment provided by the Creator) is given poetic expression in the magnificent creation hymn, Psalm 104. The poet urges Yahweh to "rejoice in his works" (v. 31): the gushing springs, the growing grass, the nocturnal habits of the animals, the daytime activities of human beings, the teeming creatures of the sea— even Leviathan, the dread monster of the deep (v. 26) that figures in Melville's *Moby Dick*. Everything has a role in relation to Yahweh's purpose and joins in the anthem of praise to the Creator that the poet verbalizes. The human body, too, shares in the goodness of God's creation. The biblical view of creation provides no basis for a negative attitude toward sex, eating and drinking, and physical enjoyment (see Ps. 104:15). The world of "nature" is the God-given habitat in which human beings are to find *joy* in performing their task in the service of the Creator.

This view of the task of creatures to serve and glorify God helps one to understand more clearly the crucial statement in the Genesis creation story about "the image of God."

> Then God said: "Let us make human beings ['*ādām*] in our image, after our likeness, and let them have dominion over the fish of the sea, the birds of the sky, the cattle and all wild beasts, and everything that moves upon the earth."
>
> So God created humanity ['*ādām*] in his own image, in the image of God he created it; male and female he created them. (Gen. 1:26-27, au. trans.)

One should take the word translated "image" (*ṣelem*) much more concretely than is often done by those who attenuate its meaning to the "spiritual" part of human nature, or, in Greek fashion, to the "soul" as distinguished from the "body." Elsewhere the Hebrew word refers to something concrete and visible, for instance, a picture drawn on a wall (Ezek. 23:14) or a statue of a god (2 Kings 11:18; Dan. 3:1). Such concreteness characterizes the usage of *ṣelem* in Gen. 1:26-27, although the explanatory addition of "likeness" (*dĕmût*) moves in the direction of greater abstraction.[13] The view in the Priestly account is apparently that '*ādām*, regarded as a total bodily whole (a psychosomatic unity, as we would say), is fashioned after the heavenly beings of God's council who are addressed in the plural pronouns of Gen. 1:26 ("us," "our"). In this interpretation, '*ādām* is made in the image of the heavenly beings ("angels"; see Ps. 8:5 LXX) who surround God and are members of the heavenly council referred to in Micaiah's vision (1 Kings 22:19-23) and in the prologue to the book of Job (Job 1:6). But the main import of the statement about the *imago Dei* is not just to define human *nature* in relation to God but to accent the special

---

13. Notice, however, that the explanatory *dĕmût* does not appear in Gen. 1:27 or 9:6.

function that God has assigned human beings in the creation. Human beings, male and female, are designed to be God's representatives, for they are created and commissioned to represent or "image" God's rule on earth. To be made in the image of God is to be endowed with a special task. Gerhard von Rad puts it this way:

> Just as powerful earthly kings, to indicate their claim to dominion, erect an image of themselves in the provinces of their empire where they do not personally appear, so man is placed upon earth in God's image as God's sovereign emblem. He is really only God's representative, summoned to maintain and enforce God's claim to dominion over the earth. The decisive thing about man's similarity to God, therefore, is his function in the nonhuman world.[14]

Hence the statement about the *imago Dei* is appropriately followed immediately by the further announcement that God confers a special blessing on human beings and commands them to exercise dominion over the earth.

The dignity of humankind is not based on something intrinsic to human nature, such as "the infinite value of the human personality." The worth of human beings lies in their relation to God. They are persons whom God addresses, visits, and is concerned about. But above all they are "crowned" as kings and queens to perform a special task in the Creator's earthly estate. This special dignity of human beings in God's creation excites the wonder and praise of a psalmist:

> When I survey your heavens, your finger-works,
>   the moon and the stars that you have established,
> what are human beings that you remember them,
>   human persons that you seek them out?
> Yet you have placed them slightly below heavenly beings,
>   and with honor and majesty have crowned them.
> You have given them dominion over your handiwork,
>   everything you have put in subjection to them. (Ps. 8:3-6[4-7], au. trans.)

This passage is extraordinarily interesting because it is the only one in the Old Testament, aside from Priestly passages in Genesis (1:26-27; 5:3; 9:6), that mentions the divine image—a rather striking fact in view of the importance of the *imago Dei* in Christian theology. Psalm 8 provides a commentary on Gen. 1:26-28. The psalmist affirms that God "has caused humankind to lack a little less than God," or perhaps, "than the angels" (LXX). As in the Genesis creation story, this high status endows human beings with a function given to no other creature: to have dominion over the nonhuman creation. Human dominion on earth, then, is to be exercised

14. Von Rad, *Genesis*, 60. In the above discussion I am indebted to von Rad's insights at a number of points.

within the sovereign rule of God. The "glory and honor" of human beings is the task that God has given them.

NEW CREATION

In this essay I have pointed to three aspects of the creation faith, all of which derived from the worship experience of the covenant community, Israel. The affirmation that God is Creator is actually a corollary of the primary knowledge of God as the Lord of history: the God whose acts gave meaning to Israel's history, bound Israel in dependence upon the Lord of the covenant, and gave Israel a task in the divine plan. From this faith situation Israel looked back to the primordial beginning, interpreting all history and nature in the light of the word of God that had been spoken to Israel.

Israel's backward view to the beginning has its counterpart in Israel's forward view to the end when God's purpose will be fulfilled. God is the Lord of time, for

Before the mountains were brought forth,
  or ever you had formed the earth and the world,
  from everlasting to everlasting you are God. (Ps. 90:2, NRSV)

It is significant that the Priestly creation story is articulated in the time sequence of a week. The week is governed not by an abstract principle of Time but by the will of God, which gives each day its meaningful content. In Israel's faith time does not move in a circle; it moves toward the culmination of the Creator's intention, just as the week of creation moves toward the Sabbath rest. Thus the creation faith is eschatological. The affirmation "in the beginning" is incomplete without the related affirmation "in the end."[15]

The eschatological aspect of the creation faith is more evident in the Old Epic (J) tradition and in the prophetic message than in the Priestly writing of the Pentateuch, which lacks the story of Adam's rebellion against the Creator. While the priest emphasizes God's upholding the order of the present world, the prophet sees the present under the stigma of divine judgment. Because '*ādām,* whose imagination of the heart is only evil continually (Gen. 6:5; 8:21), mars the goodness of the creation, he thereby provokes the Creator to act in judgment to cleanse the earth of corruption and violence. The contrast between God's original intention for the creation and the sorry reality of the present world is so sharp that, according to Israel's prophets, God wills to act, bringing judgment upon the world order so that there may be a new beginning, indeed a new creation.

15. See Köhler, *Old Testament Theology,* 86–87.

The theme of the new creation is most clearly emphasized in the poems of so-called Second Isaiah (Isaiah 40–55), who understood himself to be standing just beyond the shadow of divine judgment that fell severely upon Israel and on the threshold of the new age. Not only is Yahweh the Creator of the cosmos, who numbers and names the myriads of stars (40:26), but also Yahweh's redemptive work in history is creative. Yahweh is Israel's Creator and Redeemer (43:1; 44:1-2; 45:11-12). Even now, says this prophet, Yahweh is beginning a new work of creation in this historical community (41:17-20; 42:9; 43:19; etc.)—a creative/redemptive beginning that will shed blessing and light on the whole world of humanity and nature. Later prophetic voices in the Isaianic tradition spoke in more apocalyptic terms of a cosmic re-creation: a "new heaven and a new earth" (Isa. 65:17; 66:2).

The New Testament doctrine of creation, treated here all too briefly, presupposes the view of creation set forth in the Old Testament. Contrary to the second-century radical Marcion, who wanted to make a sharp separation between creation and redemption and even to repudiate Israel's creation faith, it is clear in the pages of the New Testament that the God who acts redemptively in Jesus Christ is none other than the Creator of heaven and earth. In the New Testament, however, the theme of creation is reinterpreted, especially under the influence of the prophetic/apocalyptic stream of tradition.

Paul, the great theologian of the early church, understood the resurrection of Jesus to be the beginning of the new age, the new creation that would ultimately be consummated in the transformation of the whole world and even the cosmos. God's act of redemption in the life, death, and resurrection of Jesus Christ begins to actualize not only God's saving purpose manifest to Israel but also the intention of the creation "in the beginning" (2 Cor. 4:6). Jesus Christ is the eschatological new Adam who is "the likeness of God" (2 Cor. 4:4), "the image of the invisible God, the firstborn of all creation" (Col. 1:15)—language that clearly recalls the creation story of Genesis. Therefore he is the beginning of a new humanity, a new history; for "if any one is in Christ," says Paul, that one "is a new creation; the old has passed away, behold, the new has come" (2 Cor. 5:17, RSV; cf. Gal. 6:15). The new community, the church, is the sphere where God's new act of creation/redemption has begun; but the whole creation, human and nonhuman, is also involved, waiting longingly for the finishing of God's new creation (Rom. 8:19-23).[16] Through Christ, persons

---

16. See the illuminating book by J. Christiaan Beker, *Paul the Apostle* (Philadelphia: Fortress Press, 1980). He shows that Paul's message belongs in the prophetic/apocalyptic context. On the "new creation" (2 Cor. 5:17) he writes (p. 310): "To be 'in Christ' is indeed a 'new act of creation,' but this creation must still wait for its future completion in the liberation of the whole creation (Rom. 8:21), when 'we shall always be with the Lord' (1 Thess. 4:17)." See also pp. 101, 152, 191, *et passim*.

may be invested with "the new nature, which is being renewed in knowledge after the image of its creator" (Col. 3:10, RSV). These passages and others testify that God's work in Christ has in view the restoration of the original intention of the creation, and therefore is a foretaste of the final consummation when all things will be made new.

In the New Testament, God's original creation is often understood christologically. Just as in the Old Testament the creation is viewed in the perspective of the exodus faith of the covenant community, so Christian interpreters view the whole span of the biblical story—from beginning to end—from the standpoint of God's self-disclosure in the life, death, and resurrection of Jesus Christ. In the light of this revealing event, the community of faith looks backward to the original creation, as in the prologue to the Fourth Gospel, which echoes the words of Genesis: "In the beginning" (John 1:1). Similarly the Epistle to the Colossians views the creation christologically:

> In him all things in heaven and on earth were created, things visible and invisible, whether thrones or dominions or rulers or powers—all things have been created through him and for him. He himself is before all things, and in him all things hold together. (Col. 1:16-17, NRSV)

Here again we see that in the Christian view the doctrine of creation cannot be separated from its larger narrative context: the whole drama that unfolds from creation to consummation and has its climactic center in Jesus Christ. The whole of human history and all of nature stand under God's signature in Christ. In Christ is laid bare the meaning that undergirds all existence; through him people acknowledge the God upon whom they depend completely; from him they hear anew the summons to a task within God's plan. From this standpoint of faith the Christian community traces the purpose of God backward to the beginning, saying that "in Christ all things were created"; and it traces the purpose forward to the consummation of history, saying that "God will sum up all things in Christ."

CHAPTER 2

Biblical Perspectives
on the Doctrine
of Creation

In the Bible the doctrine of creation presupposes and builds on the mythopoeic views of divine creation found in the ancient Near East, particularly Babylonia, Egypt, and Canaan. In the Old Testament, however, the inherited views were reinterpreted in the light of Israel's worship of Yahweh, the Holy God, whose saving power and commanding will were revealed in crucial historical experiences, preeminently the exodus and the Sinai covenant. In the New Testament, faith in God the Creator, mediated to the church through the canonical Scriptures of Israel, was reinterpreted christologically, that is, in the light of God's revelation in Jesus Christ and the "new creation" that through him has already begun in history. In both Testaments, the doctrine stresses the transcendence and freedom of God, the complete dependence of the whole creation upon the Creator, the reverence for all forms of life, especially human beings, who are elevated to a supreme purpose of God that undergirds the whole earthly drama from beginning to end and that endows the cosmos, and everything in it, with ultimate meaning.   .

CREATION AND THE ANCIENT WORLDVIEW

The New Testament inherits and transforms the Old Testament faith that God created all things (Acts 4:24; 14:15; 17:24; Eph. 3:9; Rev. 4:11; 10:6). Likewise the Old Testament creation faith, as expressed consummately in the creation stories of Genesis, the message of Second Isaiah (Isaiah 40–55), various psalms of the Psalter (e.g., Psalms 8, 19, 104), and Israelite wisdom literature (especially Job), both presupposes and modifies the cosmological views of antiquity. The Old Testament affirms that Yahweh, the God known and worshiped in Israel, is the creator of heaven and earth. Since the meaning of God's personal name (identity) was given to Israel in historical experiences as interpreted by a series of prophetic figures beginning with Moses, Israel understood Yahweh's creative work in a different sense from the prevalent creation beliefs among Babylonians, Egyptians, or Canaanites.

ANCIENT COSMOLOGY AND MYTHOLOGY

In a formal sense Israel's creation faith and the cosmological views of antiquity have numerous points of contact. The Bible takes for granted a three-storied structure of the universe: heaven, earth, and underworld (Exod. 20:4). According to this *Weltbild,* the earth is a flat surface, corrugated by mountains and divided by rivers and lakes. Above the earth, like a huge dome, is spread the firmament that both holds back the heavenly ocean and supports the dwelling place of the gods (Gen. 1:8; Ps. 148:4). The earth itself is founded on pillars that are sunk into the subterranean waters (Pss. 24:2; 104:5), in the depths of which is located Sheol, the realm of death. In this view, the habitable world is surrounded by the waters of chaos, which, unless held back, would engulf the world, a threat graphically portrayed in the flood story (Gen. 7:11; cf. 1:6) and in various poems in the Old Testament (e.g., Pss. 46:1-3[2-4]; 104:5-9). (See figure 1.)

In various ways ancient peoples affirmed that the world emerged out of primordial chaos. In Babylonian mythology the origin of the three-storied universe was traced to a fierce struggle between divine powers that emerged from uncreated chaos—Marduk the god of order and Tiamat the goddess of chaos. Victorious in the struggle, Marduk split the fishlike body of the monster down the middle, thus making a separation between the upper and lower parts. In Canaan there was a similar myth of the victorious struggle of Baal, the god of storm and fertility, against *Yamm* ("Sea"), the god of chaos. Canaanite mythology apparently does not deal with creation in the cosmic sense but with the maintenance of the created order in the face of the periodic threats of chaos. The gods and goddesses, whose loves and wars dramatize the conflicts of nature and the cyclical movement of the seasons, are personifications of natural forces.

The Old Testament contains reminiscences of these ancient myths of creation against chaos.[1] We hear of Yahweh's primordial battle with sea

---

1. See Hermann Gunkel, "The Influence of Babylonian Mythology upon the Biblical Creation Story" (trans. Charles A. Muenchow), in *Creation in the Old Testament* (ed. Bernhard W. Anderson; IRT 6; Philadelphia: Fortress Press, 1984) 25–52; also *Creation versus Chaos: The Reinterpretation of Mythical Symbolism in the Bible* (New York: Association, 1967; repr. Philadelphia: Fortress Press, 1987) 11–42.

Figure 1

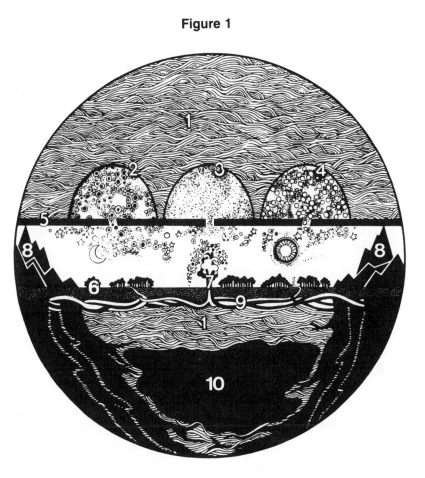

The Ancient Pictorial View of the Universe

1. The waters above and below the earth
2–4. Chambers of hail, rain, snow
5. The firmament with its "sluices"
6. The surface of the earth
7. The navel of the earth: "fountain of the great deep"
8. The mountain pillars supporting the firmament
9. Sweet waters (rivers, lakes, seas) on which the earth floats
10. Sheol, the realm of death (the "pit")

monsters named Rahab or Leviathan (Job 9:13; Pss. 74:13-14; 89:10[11]; Isa. 27:1; 51:9) and of Yahweh's action in "dividing" the upper and lower waters (Gen. 1:6-8) and in setting bounds for the sea (Ps. 104:7-9; Prov. 8:27-29). But these are distant echoes. Although the Bible takes for granted the contours of ancient cosmology, it has demythologized ancient cosmological views. The Old Testament contains no theogony, no myth that traces the creation to a primordial battle between divine powers, no ritual that enabled people to repeat the mythological drama and thereby ensure control over the conflicting forces of the natural world. Mythological allusions have been torn out of their ancient context of polytheism and nature religion, and have acquired a new meaning within the historical syntax of Israel's faith. The pagan language survives only as poetic speech for the adoration of Yahweh, the creator of the world and the ruler of history (Psalm 33).

THE ORIGIN OF ISRAEL'S CREATION FAITH

One must consider the creation stories of Genesis 1 and 2 not only in terms of the date of their literary composition but also in terms of the age of the tradition they preserve. The Old Epic (J) story (Gen. 2:4b-25), although it does not deal with creation in the broadest sense, dates back at least to the time of the early monarchy, probably Solomon's reign; and it is possible that its terse reference to "the day that Yahweh God made the earth and the heavens" implies a longer account of the creation of the earth that has been superseded by the Priestly (P) account (Gen. 1:1—2:3). Creation is dealt with most comprehensively and intensively in the latter story. The Priestly account is usually dated in the time of the exile (ca. 550 B.C.E.), but careful study of its form and content indicates that the present version is the end result of a tradition whose development extended over a considerable period of time.

Various biblical texts indicate that Yahweh was acclaimed as creator in the Jerusalem Temple during the period of the monarchy. Although the date of Genesis 14 is uncertain, it is noteworthy that in this passage, which is placed in a pre-Davidic Jerusalem setting, the title *'ēl 'elyôn*, "Maker [*qōnēh*] of heaven and earth," is applied to Yahweh (vv. 19, 22). The title has been appropriated from Canaanite religion, as evidenced by the occurrence of the verb in the Ugaritic mythological texts from Ras Shamra and the expression *'l qn 'rṣ* ("El, creator of earth") in the Phoenician inscription of Karatepe. Furthermore, an old poetic fragment found in Solomon's Temple address affirms that "Yahweh has set the sun in the heavens" (1 Kings 8:12; text reconstructed on the basis of the LXX). Also, some scholars hold that in the preexilic period Yahweh's creative work was celebrated at the fall New Year's festival, just as Marduk's victory over Tiamat was celebrated in the liturgy of the Babylonian New Year's festival, and that several psalms reflect that cultic situation (Psalms 24, 47, 93, 95–99). Whether or not a parallel festival was held in Israel, these psalms indicate that in the Jerusalem cult Yahweh was acclaimed as the cosmic king who "established" the earth (that is, ordered it as a human dwelling; Ps. 93:1) and who sustains the world in the face of threats of chaos. Yahweh's greatness as celestial king is summed up in the affirmation that "all the gods of the peoples are idols, but the Lord [Yahweh] made the heavens" (Ps. 96:4-5, NRSV).

Some scholars maintain that even before the period of the monarchy, and indeed at the beginning of Israelite traditions, Yahweh was acclaimed as creator. This view rests heavily on an interpretation of the tetragrammaton, the four consonants of the divine name (YHWH) introduced in Exod. 3:14. The tetragrammaton, it is argued, was originally a causative verbal form (*yahweh,* "he causes to be") meaning "he causes to be what comes into existence" (i.e., creates), and in the patriarchal period was part of a larger liturgical formula in which the ancestral god was praised as the creator of the cosmos, just as in Canaanite circles the high god *'El* was acclaimed as "creator of creatures."[2]

It is striking, however, that in the narrative context of Exodus 3, which gives an etymology of the divine name, Yahweh is presented as the liberating God rather than the creator. Furthermore, in early Israelite poetry, which apparently comes from the premonarchic period, the emphasis falls on divine liberation, even when ancient mythopoeic creation language is used. This is the case in the Song of the Sea (Exod. 15:1-18), which is redolent of the mythopoeic language of the chaos myth and which follows essentially the movement of the mythical drama: the Divine Warrior (v. 3) encounters the powers of chaos, marches triumphantly to the sacred mountain (temple), and there is acclaimed as cosmic king (v. 18). At one point the poet speaks of "the people whom you [Yahweh] have created" (v. 16b, translating the verb *qānâ* as "create"; cf. Gen. 14:19-20, 22).[3] In another ancient poem, the Song of Moses (Deut. 32:1-43), the poet uses this verb and other creation verbs to speak of the creation of a people.[4]

Is not he [Yahweh] your father, who created you,
    who made you and established you? (Deut. 32:6b, NRSV)

2. This is the view of W. F. Albright and his students; see Frank M. Cross's new interpretation in *Canaanite Myth and Hebrew Epic* (Cambridge: Harvard Univ. Press, 1973) 60–75.

3. See Frank M. Cross, "The Song of the Sea and Canaanite Myth," in *Canaanite Myth and Hebrew Epic,* 112–44.

4. Ancient poetic texts are discussed by Dennis J. McCarthy, S.J., "'Creation' Motifs in Ancient Hebrew Poetry," *CBQ* 29 (1967) 393–406; rev. ed. included in *Creation in the Old Testament,* 74–89.

It seems, then, that Israel's earliest traditions did not refer to Yahweh as creator in a cosmic sense but concentrated, rather, on Yahweh's "mighty deeds" of liberation, through which the Holy God became known and formed Israel as a people out of the chaos of historical oblivion and oppression. To be sure, ancient Israelites confessed that the God who is mighty in history could also make the forces of nature serve a redemptive purpose. Yahweh prepared a path for fugitives through the Reed Sea, preserved wanderers in the wilderness by performing signs and wonders, and rescued embattled Israelites at Megiddo by causing the stars to fight on their side and the River Kishon to overflow its banks (Judg. 5:20-21). Nevertheless, from the first, the people of Israel confessed their faith by telling a story—the story of Yahweh's mighty acts of salvation (cf. Deut. 26:5-10). The theme of the creation/liberation of a people is a major motif of Mosaic tradition, whose trajectory one can trace throughout the Old Testament (Pss. 95:6-7; 100:3; Isa. 43:15; 45:11) and into the New.

Gerhard von Rad has argued forcefully that Israel's faith from the very first was primarily concerned with historical redemption and that creation, as an independent doctrine, came into Israelite tradition relatively late through the influence of the wisdom movement.[5] One can find some support for this view in Israel's premonarchic poetry, which, as we have seen, understands creation "soteriologically," as the creation of a people. But this view does not do justice to theological developments in the early monarchy. Creation in the cosmic sense was introduced into the mainstream of Israelite life and thought by Davidic theologians who maintained that Yahweh made a "covenant in perpetuity" [*běrît 'ôlām*] with David (2 Samuel 7; Psalm 89) and chose the Jerusalem Temple as the divine dwelling place (Psalms 78, 132).[6] In this view, king and temple belong to a pattern of symbolization that relates the cosmic order of creation to the mundane order of history. The security, harmony, and peace of society depend upon the cosmic, created order, whose saving benefits are mediated to the social order through the divinely elected king, the "son of God." Accordingly, a hymnic passage in Psalm 89, where the poet elaborates Yahweh's "covenant in perpetuity" with David, praises Yahweh in mythopoeic language as the victor in the battle with chaos (vv. 9-12[10-13]); and the psalmist goes on to say that the Davidic king, as the representative of the deity, will be victorious over the mythical "sea" or "floods" (vv. 24-25[25-26]).

The royal covenant theology, which placed the Davidic kingship in the vertical axis of the cosmic and the mundane, of macrocosm and micro-

---

5. Gerhard von Rad, "The Theological Problem of the Old Testament Doctrine of Creation," in *The Problem of the Hexateuch and Other Essays* (trans. E. W. Trueman Dicken; New York: McGraw-Hill, 1966) 131–43; repr. in *Creation in the Old Testament*, 53–64.

6. See further chap. 5 below.

cosm, is compatible with psalms of the Zion Temple (mentioned previously) that celebrate Yahweh's enthronement as cosmic creator and king.
Other psalms from the period of the monarchy show that reflection on
creation was encouraged by Israel's sages (Psalm 104)[7] and by theologians
and liturgists connected with the Jerusalem Temple (Psalms 8, 33, 136,
148). The first prophet to reckon seriously with the doctrine was Jeremiah,
who declared that divine sovereignty over history is underscored by the
fact that Yahweh is Creator (Jer. 27:5; cf. 32:17), and who perceived in
the constancy of nature a pledge of Yahweh's covenant faithfulness (5:22-
24; 31:35-36). Aside from the Priestly account (Gen. 1:1—2:3), the doctrine of creation finds its deepest expression in the message of Second
Isaiah (Isaiah 40–55) during the exile (see pp. 93–96 below). As evident
from the devotional, apocalyptic, and wisdom literature of the postexilic
period, the doctrine came to be a cardinal tenet of Judaism.

CREATION AND THE BEGINNING OF HISTORY

In the book of Genesis creation does not stand by itself as though it
were a prescientific attempt to explain the origin of the cosmos. Rather, as
indicated by the position of the creation stories at the opening of the Bible,
creation is the prologue to history. It sets the stage for the unfolding of the
divine purpose and inaugurates a historical drama within which Israel and,
in the fullness of time, the church were destined to play a key role. Thus
the creation stands in an inseparable historical relation to the ensuing
narratives that span the generations from Adam to Noah, from Noah to
Abr(ah)am, and from Abraham to Joseph. In the Old Epic tradition (J), the
story of the creation of humanity, together with the stories of primeval
history, is the prologue to the sacred history that unfolds with the call of
Abraham, the deliverance from Egypt, the guidance through the wilderness, and the entrance into the promised land. In this context, creation
provides the background and setting for the vocation of God's people. The
Priestly creation story, too, does not stand in isolation but prepares the way
for a series of historical covenants: the ecological covenant with Noah
(Genesis 9), the land covenant with Abraham (Genesis 17), and the climactic revelation of God under the cultic name Yahweh in the Mosaic
period (Exodus 6). Each of these covenants—the Noachic, the Abrahamic,
and the Mosaic—is understood as a "covenant in perpetuity" (*bĕrît 'ôlām*),
signifying God's unconditional commitment to human beings, as well as
to the earth and to the whole of human creation.[8]

---

7. See Hans-Jürgen Hermisson, "Creation Theology in Wisdom" (trans. Barbara Howard), in
Israelite Wisdom: Theological and Literary Essays in honor of Samuel Terrien (ed. J. G.
Gammie et al.; Missoula, Mont.: Scholars Press, 1978) 43–57; repr. in *Creation in the Old
Testament,* 118–34.
8. I discuss the covenantal context further in chap. 9 below. For fuller discussion, see chap. 8
below.

Just as the creation points forward to the exodus and the making of the covenant with Sinai, so the covenant faith reaches backward and includes the creation. Contrary to the present arrangement of the biblical drama, the theological movement is not from the confession "God is the Creator" to "Yahweh, the God of Israel, is the Redeemer," but in just the opposite direction. In the formulation of the traditions now included in the Pentateuch, the exodus, together with historical events immediately associated with it, had decisive significance for the historical interpreter. This is evident, above all, in the Old Epic tradition (J). From the standpoint of faith provided by exodus and Sinai, "the saving experience" and "the commanding experience,"[9] Israelite narrators undertook the task of interpreting the whole human drama, right from the beginning. The story of Israel's life, which began with the call of Abraham (Gen. 12:1-3), was expanded to include not only the ancestral period (Genesis 12–50) but also the previous world history portrayed in stories dealing with primeval times (Genesis 2–11). Thus a historical line was traced from the faith situation of Israel to the remotest historical beginnings imaginable, with the result that all human history was seen in the light of the revelation given to Israel and was embraced within the saving activity of Yahweh. The Priestly theologians, who have given us the Torah in its final form, have incorporated this enlarged story in the framework of a periodized history that moves from creation to the events that constituted Israel as a worshiping community: the exodus and the Sinai revelation. In a similar manner, the New Testament church, convinced of the decisive character of God's revelation in Jesus Christ, understood the total sweep of historical time and the whole creation in a christological perspective (Eph. 1:9-10; see pp. 244–45 below).

In Israel's understanding, then, creation and history are inseparably related. Creation is the foundation of the covenant; it provides the setting within which Yahweh's saving work takes place. But it is equally true that creation is embraced within the theological meaning of the covenant. Psalmists can therefore regard creation as the first of God's saving deeds (Ps. 74:12-17) and in the recitation of the *Heilsgeschichte* can move without a break from deeds of creation to historical deeds of liberation (Psalm 136).

In view of the inseparable relation between creation and history, it is not surprising to find that Yahweh's historical deeds are regarded as creative acts and, indeed, may be described by the same verbs as are applied to the original creation (*yāṣar,* "form"; *bārā',* "create"; *'āsâ,* "make"); this is true, above all, of Yahweh's creation of Israel (Isa. 43:1, 7, 15, 21; 44:2,

9. These "root experiences" are discussed illuminatingly by Emil Fackenheim, *God's Presence in History: Jewish Affirmations and Philosophical Reflections* (New York: Harper & Row, 1970), esp. 3–34.

21, 24; 45:11) or the servant (49:5). No prophet grasps as profoundly as Second Isaiah the soteriological meaning of creation and the creative significance of redemption. He appeals to the Creator's wisdom and power in order to demonstrate to despairing exiles that Israel's God is sovereign over the whole course of history and therefore can and will redeem the people (Isa. 40:12-31; 43:1-7; 45:9-13; 48:12-13). Furthermore, he declares that Yahweh's imminent coming to redeem the chosen people will result in nothing less than a new act of creation.

This view of creation in relation to a temporal movement displays a distinct break with the religions of antiquity. The gods of the ancient world had a story (mythos) but not a "history." In the perspective of the history of religions, creation is a timeless event—timeless in the sense that it belongs within a cyclical pattern of myth and ritual that must be reenacted each year, as in the case of the Babylonian New Year ritual or the Ras Shamra (Canaanite) mythical drama. So pervasive and appealing was this mythology, especially in the agricultural setting of Canaan, that Israelites were tempted to turn to the mythos of the Canaanite gods and goddesses that assured fertility of the soil (Hos. 2:8[10]) and to "forget" the story that identified Yahweh as their liberator (Jer. 2:4-13). It was no simple task for Israel's interpreters to insist that Yahweh alone is the Power, the fountain of life's meaning and vitality (Jer. 2:13) and the source of all that is. The ancient views of creation had to be demythologized and brought into theological relationship with the story of Yahweh's historical actions. When this was accomplished, as in the Priestly creation story, the foundations of the ancient mythological worldview were shaken. No longer was creation a timeless event—timeless in the sense that it belongs within a cyclical pattern of recurrence ("the myth of the eternal return").[10] Rather, incorporated into Israel's sacred history, creation was a "once-for-all" event that marked the beginning of history.

THE SOVEREIGNTY OF THE CREATOR

The Hebrew Bible does not have the equivalent of the Greek term *kosmos,* which suggests the view of the universe as a rationally constituted and self-sustaining structure of reality. Instead, it speaks of the relationship between the Creator and the creation, a relationship which is essentially that of the covenant. The belief that "heaven and earth" or *kōl,* "everything" (Ps. 8:6[7]; Isa. 44:24), depends on Yahweh, the Creator, is a corollary of Israel's understanding that their whole life depends on Yahweh, their savior and judge, to whom they are bound in covenant relationship.

10. See Mircea Eliade, *Cosmos and History: The Myth of the Eternal Return* (New York: Harper & Row 1959).

The covenant, rather than a rational principle, is the ground of the unity of creation. Hence psalmists exclaim that divine *ḥesed* or covenant loyalty embraces all God's works (see the antiphonal refrains in Psalm 136).

The doctrine of creation, then, is preeminently an affirmation about the sovereignty of God and the absolute dependence of all creatures. To say that Yahweh made the earth is to confess that it belongs to its Maker; Yahweh is its Owner (Pss. 24:1-2; 89:11[12]; 95:5).[11] Nothing in the realm of creation should be glorified, for the creation points beyond itself to the God who is high and lifted up and is therefore worthy of the praise of human beings and all other creatures. Thus the proclamation that Yahweh is Creator is a summons to worship, for the creation testifies to God's wisdom and power (Ps. 104:24; Prov. 3:19-20; Jer. 10:12-13), God's faithfulness (Ps. 136:4-9), and God's incomparable majesty shared with no other (2 Kings 19:15; Neh. 9:6; Isa. 40:25-26). To be sure, the creation does not witness to the Creator so clearly that faith is unnecessary. In the wisdom books of Ecclesiastes and Job, the rational mysteries of the creation witness to divine sovereignty that is beyond human understanding (see esp. Job 38:1-7); even in other contexts, where Yahweh's historical revelation provides the standpoint of faith, the Israelite is aware of the hiddenness of God (Isa. 45:15). Although the language of creation was often mysterious, it was nonetheless sufficiently intelligible to enable those who stood within the covenant to exclaim that the heavens declare the glory of God (Ps. 19:1-4[2–5]). Thus the sovereignty of God, manifest in the works of creation, is the motive for worship and service (Psalm 95; Isa. 40:27-31).

CREATION BY THE WORD

The creation stories of Genesis 1 (Priestly) and 2 (Old Epic) have their differences, but they agree in ascribing creation to the free and spontaneous initiative of God. The Old Epic account vividly portrays the personal relation between God and the creation. This story describes Yahweh as a potter who "forms" (*yāṣar*) a human being from moist soil and then provides an environment suitable for the creature. The strong anthropomorphism of the story, however, does not reduce the Creator to the human level or exalt the creature to a plane of equality with God (cf. Gen. 3:22). Elsewhere the image of the Divine Potter expresses the sovereignty of God over all creatures (Isa. 29:15-16; 45:9-13; Jer. 18:1-6; Rom. 9:20-21).

The sovereignty of God is expressed more forcefully in the Priestly account, which bears the marks of profound theological reflection about creation in the cosmic sense. In this account, God is exalted and transcendent. The Creator's only point of contact with the creation is the uttered

11. On this motif, see chap. 1 above.

command, which punctuates the creative drama with the refrain: "And God said. . . . And it was so." The same thought is echoed by a psalmist:

> Yahweh spoke, and it came to be;
> he commanded, and it stood forth (Ps. 33:9, NRSV; cf. v. 6)

and in other Old Testament passages (Ps. 148:5; cf. Isa. 45:12). Creation by the word came to be the normative expression of the mode of God's creative work (Sir. 42:15; 2 *Apoc. Bar.* 21:4ff.; John 1:1-3; Heb. 11:3; 2 Pet. 3:5-6). It is noteworthy that this view was found also in the theology of ancient Egyptian Memphis, according to which the god Ptah conceived the elements of the universe with his "heart" (mind) and brought them into being with his "tongue" (commanding word).[12]

As Israel learned in its historical experience, the word of God is the sovereign power that shapes people's lives and controls the course of history. Yahweh's word is active and dynamic; it is the means by which the divine will is accomplished. The "word of Yahweh," when put in the mouth of the prophet, makes the prophetic spokesperson sovereign over nations and releases a divine power that both overthrows and rebuilds (Jer. 1:9-10). As the rain and the snow descend from heaven and do not return thither until they have made the earth fertile, so the word that goes forth from Yahweh's mouth does not return empty but accomplishes Yahweh's purpose and effects Yahweh's will (Isa. 55:10-11). God's word is "living and active, sharper than any two-edged sword" (Heb. 4:12, NRSV; cf. Rev. 19:13-15). In these instances, it is clear that the word is not a sound or even an idea. God's word is an act, an event, a sovereign command, which accomplishes a result. The creation story affirms that God's word, mighty in history, is also the very power that brought the creation into being. Since the creative word establishes a personal relationship between the Creator and the creation, the Christian faith affirms with theological consistency that the Logos (Word) became flesh in a person (John 1:1-18).

CREATION *EX NIHILO*

Later theological reflection upon the meaning of creation further emphasized the sovereignty of the Creator with the doctrine that the world was created out of nothing (2 Macc. 7:28; cf. Rom. 4:17; Heb. 11:3). It is doubtful, however, that this teaching occurs explicitly in Genesis 1 or anywhere else in the Old Testament. The statement in the book of Job that God "hangs the earth upon nothing" (Job 26:7) is poetic hyperbole, as the mythopoeic context shows.

---

12. The Egyptian text is translated by John A. Wilson in *ANET*, "The Theology of Memphis," 4–6.

The Genesis creation story opens with a statement that refers to God's transcendence of time and space and seems to point to an absolute beginning (Gen 1:1). But the Hebrew text is ambiguous; grammatically it can be translated as a temporal clause that introduces a main sentence beginning with v. 2 or v. 3, as in some modern translations (e.g., NAB, NEB, NRSV, JPSV), or as a declarative sentence, as in the oldest translation (Septuagint) and other modern translations (e.g., RSV, NIV, REB). A possible parallel with the Babylonian creation story, which begins with a temporal clause (*Enuma elish*, "When on high . . ."), makes it tempting to construe the first three verses as describing a temporal process. Stylistic and contextual considerations, however, favor the view that Gen. 1:1 is an independent sentence that serves as a preface to the entire creation account.[13] On this view, the story actually begins in v. 2 with a portrayal of uncreated chaos as the presupposition and background of God's creative work. The notion of creation out of nothing was undoubtedly too abstract for the Hebraic mind; in any case, the idea of a created chaos would have been strange to a narrative that is governed by the view that creation is the antithesis to chaos (cf. Isa. 45:18).

The main intention of the writer is to emphasize the absolute sovereignty of God. There is no suggestion that God is bound or conditioned by chaos, as in the Babylonian *Enuma elish* myth, which portrays the birth of the gods out of the waters of chaos. Nor does God have the character of a demiurge who works with material that offers some resistance or imposes limitations. On the contrary, God creates with perfect freedom by the commanding word—a view underscored by the use of the verb *bārā'*. In the Old Testament this verb is used exclusively of God's action and expresses the effortless divine creation that surpasses any human analogy such as the potter or the architect (cf. Pss. 51:10[12]; 104:30; Isa. 43:1, 7, 15; 48:7). Since, however, this verb is used in connection with the verb *'āśâ* ("make") in Gen. 1:16-17 and elsewhere is linked with *yāṣar* ("mold"; e.g., Isa. 43:1; 45:18), it was undoubtedly employed to support the view of creation by the Word, rather than creation *ex nihilo*.

THE HARMONY AND GOODNESS OF CREATION

God's creation is characterized by order. This order, however, is not that of Greek *kosmos*, harmonized by reason, but rather a divinely decreed order within which each creature fulfills the Creator's will. The Creator

---

13. See Walther Eichrodt, "In the Beginning: A Contribution to the Interpretation of the First Word of the Bible," in *Israel's Prophetic Heritage*: *Essays in honor of James Muilenburg* (ed. B. W. Anderson and Walter Harrelson; New York: Harper & Row, 1962) 1–10; repr. in *Creation in the Old Testament*, 65–73. The case is presented on stylistic grounds in chap. 3 below.

commands and thereby not only brings a creature into being but also designates its peculiar nature and assigns to it a specific task. For example, the heavenly bodies are not independent deities who control human life, as was supposed in antiquity, but are servants of God whose appointed function is to designate the seasons and to separate the day and the night (Gen. 1:14-19). Earth is not just the fertile "Mother" from whose womb all life proceeds and to which it returns (Job 1:21; Sir. 40:1), but is God's creature who produces vegetation and animals at God's command (Gen. 1:11-12, 14-15). The idea of "nature" as an autonomous sphere governed by natural law or set in motion by a first cause is not found in the Old Testament. The Creator stands in personal relationship to the creation. It is the divine decree (*ḥōq*) that determines order (Job 38:33; Pss. 104:9; 148:6; Jer. 5:24; 31:35-36), and it can even be said that Yahweh has made a covenant with the day and the night (Jer. 33:20). At any moment the Creator could allow the creation to fall back into chaos, for God's continuing power is necessary to uphold and renew the creatures (Ps. 104:29-30). The regularities of nature, as mentioned in the promise to Noah (Gen. 8:22; cf. 9:13-17), are expressions of Yahweh's covenant of faithfulness.

When God looks upon the finished creation, seeing that each creature corresponds to the divine intention and fulfills its assigned function, the verdict is pronounced, "very good" (Gen. 1:31). This is an aesthetic judgment in the sense that in the view of the Cosmic Artist all creatures function perfectly in a marvelous whole that is without fault or blemish. The essential goodness of God's creation is a recurring theme in Israel's praises. Yahweh's name (identity) is majestic throughout all the earth (Ps. 8:1[2]), for those who have eyes to see may behold the Creator's handiwork, and those who have ears to hear may listen to an anthem of praise sung by all creatures (Ps. 19:1-4[2-5]; Rom. 1:20). The creation faith demands a repudiation of all metaphysical dualism, which leads one to suppose that the created world is evil and to seek a pathway of escape into a higher realm of pure Being. Likewise it calls for the surrender of ascetic practices, "for everything created by God is good, and nothing is to be rejected if it is received with thanksgiving" (1 Tim. 4:4, RSV). The positive view of human life on earth, including bodily pleasures, is expressed admirably in Psalm 104, which climaxes with the prayer that God may "rejoice" in the manifold works of creation. This psalmist, whose poem is an exuberant commentary on the "very good" of the creation story, sees only one cloud that mars the beautiful picture: the human "wickedness" mentioned at the very end (Ps. 104:35). A similar observation prompted the Priestly redactors of the Pentateuch to supplement the Priestly creation story with the story of paradise lost (the so-called Fall of humanity; see pp. 73–74, 145–46 below).

HUMANITY'S POSITION OF HONOR

On the one hand, it is striking that Psalm 104, which displays affinities with Genesis 1, puts both humans and animals on a level of equality in God's creation. The poet says that "all of them" (i.e., humans and animals, v. 27) depend on the Creator for their livelihood and are animated by the divine *rûaḥ* (spirit, breath), which renews them day by day in a *creatio continua* (vv. 27-30). On the other hand, the two creation stories affirm, although in different ways, that human beings are elevated to the highest place in God's earthly estate. In the Old Epic (J) story, the human being (*hā'ādām*) is formed from the ground (*hā'ădāmâ*) and must return to the ground at death (2:7; 3:19). But the special status of humanity is symbolized by saying that *'ādām* was created first (contrary to the Priestly account), that a portion of the earth-wilderness was converted into a garden for human beings to tend and enjoy, and that the animals were created with a view toward providing human companionship. The special relation of the human being to God is symbolized by the animation of the human body with the divine breath (2:7), and human superiority over the animals is indicated by the authority to give them names (2:20). Above all, *'ādām* is the creature who lives vis-à-vis God, and whose life is incomplete apart from the woman, the human person who stands in relation to him as a partner (2:18, 21-24; cf. the "male and female" of 1:27, 5:2).[14]

In the Priestly account the creation of humankind occurs at the climax of the creative drama. The plants and the animals stand in only an intermediate relation to God, for they are brought forth by the earth in response to the divine command (Gen. 1:11, 14). But the immediate relation of human beings to God is symbolized by a solemn decision, announced in the heavenly council: "Let us make humanity in our image, after our likeness" (1:26-27; cf. 5:1; 9:6). One should not tone down the anthropomorphism of this statement by attempting to define the "image of God" as something *in* the human body: "spiritual nature," "soul," "rationality," "freedom," "self-transcendence," and so on. The application of the same language to Seth, a son in Adam's image (5:3; cf. v. 1), indicates that human beings, in their total bodily (psychosomatic) existence, are made in the image of the parent, although in Gen. 1:26-27 the immediate reference is probably to the divine beings (angels) who surround God in the celestial realm (cf. Ps. 8:5[6]).

---

14. On the relation between "man" and "woman" in the creation stories, see Phyllis Trible, *God and the Rhetoric of Sexuality* (OBT; Philadelphia: Fortress Press, 1978) 12–13, 72–143. A different hermeneutical slant is provided by Phyllis Bird, "'Male and Female He Created Them': Gen 1:27b in the Context of the Priestly Account of Creation," *HTR* 74 (1981) 129–59.

In Genesis 1, however, the intention is not to define the essence of humanity or the essence of God, but rather to indicate the task of human beings and their relationship to God. As God's living image on earth, human beings—"male and female"—are to act as God's representatives. They are drawn into God's cosmic administration as overseers of God's earthly estate. Hence the thought moves quickly from the "image" to the announcement that God has given human beings a special blessing and has commanded them to exercise dominion over the earth (Gen. 1:28). Likewise in Psalm 8 the thought that human beings have been placed slightly below God (or, reading with the Septuagint, "angels") is quickly followed by the thought that Yahweh has crowned them with royal rank and has put all things under their feet (Ps. 8:6-8[7-9]). Human beings are to exercise sovereignty within God's sovereignty, so that all earthly creatures may be related to God through them and thus join in the creation's symphony of praise to the Creator.

God crowns human beings with glory and honor not only by investing them with rulership in God's earthly empire but also by singling them out for special concern. To the psalmist, the vastness of God's creation prompts the wondering query as to why the Creator chooses to notice and care for human persons, so insignificant and transient in the cosmos (Ps. 8:3-4 [4-5]). Human beings are made to have fellowship with God. They are the only creatures who can answer God, either in defiance or in trust. Although all God's creatures are summoned to praise their Creator, human beings are the only earthlings in whom praise can become articulate. They are made for conversation with God, for a dialogue in an "I and thou" relation; and as Augustine remarked in his *Confessions,* they are restless until they find rest in God. According to Second Isaiah, Israel is Yahweh's "chosen people"—"the people whom I [Yahweh] formed for myself that they might declare my praise" (Isa. 43:21, RSV). Israel's calling is to vocalize the praise that wells up from all peoples and nations.

THE GOOD EARTH

Israel's creation faith endorses a positive this-worldliness, one might even say a healthy materialism. For the natural world is the God-given habitat in which human beings are to find joy in the service of their Maker. Accordingly, the earth and all its resources are put at human disposal, not to exploit and ravish but to explore, to enjoy, and to use within the limits of the wisdom that is based on the "fear [reverence] of Yahweh" (Job 28:28).

As mentioned previously, Israel was tempted to turn to a religious naturalism (the worship of Baal) to satisfy the needs of farmers, who live close to the soil and depend on the earth's seasonal regularities. Prophets who criticized the people for yielding to the allurements of Canaanite religion, however, did not advocate a repudiation of earthly existence and a flight into an otherworldly faith. On the contrary, they were "down to earth" in their preaching. They only summoned the people to recognize that Yahweh, their liberating God, was the source of all earthly benefits. For instance, Jeremiah speaks of the "land" (*'ereṣ*) as "Yahweh's land," "Yahweh's heritage," which the people have polluted with their false way of life (Jer. 2:7). Repentance, that is, turning away from false loyalties (spurious values) and clinging in faith to Yahweh, is the basis for human welfare on "the good earth." In the Mosaic tradition, as represented by Deuteronomy, the people of Israel will be providentially ushered into "a good land, a land with flowing streams, with springs and underground waters welling up in valleys and hills, a land of wheat and barley, of vines and fig trees and pomegranates, a land of olive trees and honey, a land where you may eat bread without scarcity, where you will lack nothing, a land whose stones are iron and from whose hills you may mine copper" (Deut. 8:7-9, NRSV). The one condition, however, is that the people must realize that "the good land," with all its resources, is God's gift—a gift that can be forfeited by false and irresponsible behavior.

Thus the doctrine of creation liberates from the alternatives between which human thought often moves: either the materialistic enjoyment of the natural world for its own sake, or the verdict that the world of change and decay is essentially meaningless. It is significant that prophetic portrayals of God's future are sketched not in unearthly terms but in terms of a transformed earth in which justice and peace will prevail (Mic. 4:1-4; Isa. 2:2-4).

BEGINNING AND END

Just as Israel traced a historical line back to the creation, so Israel looked forward in hope toward the end when the Creator's purpose would finally be realized. The purpose of human history is grounded transcendentally in the will of the Creator who, in the language of Second Isaiah, is "the first and . . . the last" (Isa. 44:6; 48:12). Creation is basically an eschatological doctrine in the sense that it has a future horizon. This is clear in the final Priestly edition of the primeval history in which the movement is from creation to the new beginning after the flood. The opening words of Genesis, "In the beginning God," correspond to the prophetic expectation, "In the end God."

THREATS TO GOD'S CREATION

Although the Creator's work was finished in the beginning (Gen. 2:1), the Bible also speaks of threats to God's creation that must be overcome before the divine purpose is finally realized. The first threat is that of chaos. The Priestly creation story, which is influenced by the mythopoeic thought of the ancient world, portrays a creation out of chaos—the primeval waste and void (*tōhû wābōhû*, Gen. 1:2) and the darkness of the deep or abyss (*tĕhôm*). God's work of creation did not destroy the chaos and darkness but pushed them back, so to speak.[15] Light was separated from the primeval uncreated darkness (vv. 3-5), a firmament separated the upper and lower waters (vv. 6-8), and the waters under the heaven were gathered together in one place so that the dry land might appear (vv. 9-10). According to this mythopoeic view, chaos surrounds the habitable world on every hand. One can best understand this portrayal as coming out of experience rather than speculative, rationalistic inquiry. Ancient people knew existentially that human life is precarious and contingent; it is suspended over the formless abyss and hemmed in by the waters of chaos, which threaten to engulf the world.

Chaos imagery recurs throughout the Old Testament, especially in poetic contexts. A psalmist affirms that the earth belongs to Yahweh, who "has founded it on the seas, and established it on the rivers" (Ps. 24:2, NRSV; cf. 136:6). God has made the firmament strong and assigned boundaries to the primeval sea (Job 38:8-11; Pss. 33:7; 104:7-9; Prov. 8:27-31; Jer. 5:22). Indeed, God watches over the sea (Job 7:12), and if the rebellious waters lift up, God rebukes them and they flee (Pss. 18:15[16]; 77:16[17]; 104:7).

Poets also affirm that God is victorious over the chaos monster, Rahab or Leviathan (Job 9:13; Pss. 74:13-14; 89:9-10[10-11]), and commands the serpent that lurks in the subterranean depths of the sea (Amos 9:3). Chaos imagery figures prominently in apocalyptic literature, as illustrated by a passage from "the little apocalypse of Isaiah" (Isaiah 24–27) that echoes ancient Canaanite (Ugaritic) mythopoeic language: "On that day the Lord with his cruel and great and strong sword will punish Leviathan the fleeing serpent, Leviathan the twisting serpent, and he will kill the dragon that is in the sea" (Isa. 27:1, NRSV). (See chap. 12 below.) In the New Testament a seer declares that in the end time, the sea will be no more (Rev. 21:1)

---

15. The return of the chaos motif prompts Jon Levenson to argue, unconvincingly I believe, that the biblical view is not God's absolute sovereignty (a view he associates with Yehezkel Kaufmann) but God's limited "mastery" over opposition, a mastery that has to be achieved again and again until the eschatological time when "God will become God" indisputably. See his lively and provocative book, *Creation and the Persistence of Evil: The Jewish Drama of Divine Omnipotence* (San Francisco: Harper & Row, 1988).

and there will be no more night (22:5). In the meantime, the Creator's work must continue. For unless God's power upholds the creation, the waters of chaos would sweep in and the earth would return to the precreation watery void, as at the time of the flood (Gen. 7:11; 8:2). In a time of insecurity, when the very foundations of the world tremble and the earth seems about to lapse into the waters of chaos, people of faith confess that God alone is their refuge and strength (Ps. 46:1-3[2-4]).

To Israel's prophets, the work of God is threatened especially by misused or misdirected human freedom (sin). Curiously, the view of a "fallen creation"—not only the "Fall" of humankind but also the "fall" of heavenly beings (Gen. 6:1-4)—had little influence on Old Testament tradition. In Old Epic tradition (J), the story of human banishment from the Garden of Eden (Genesis 3) is intended as a background and preparation for the call of Israel, as personified in Abraham (Gen. 12:1-3). Neither the Priestly creation story nor the creation psalms (Psalms 8, 19, 33, 104) contain the somber note that "every imagination of the thoughts of the human heart was only evil continually" (Gen. 6:5). Although the Priestly version of the flood portrays almost complete divine judgment on the creation, owing to the spread of "violence" (6:11-13), the creation still bears the signature of God, and the divine image is not effaced (cf. 9:6).

But if Old Testament prophets are reluctant to speak of a fallen creation, some speak of Israel's fallen or perverted history, whether the tragedy is traced to the entrance into Canaan (Hosea, Jeremiah) or to the time of the people's beginning in Egypt (Ezekiel). Their diagnosis of Israel's sickness is based not on a general teaching about human sinfulness but on the empirical reality of Israel's persistent blindness and rebellion evident in their false lifestyle. Sin, it was said, is "unnatural," a mysterious fault that characterizes only the human heart (cf. Jer. 17:9). The animal knows its master, but Yahweh's children rebel against the One who nurtured them (Isa. 1:3). The birds follow their homing instincts, but Israel does not know Yahweh's ordinance (Jer 8:7). Even the realm of nature, according to Hosea, has been affected by the corruption of Israel's sin (Hos. 4:3). In a moving poem Jeremiah envisions Yahweh's judgment falling so heavily upon the people that the earth is on the verge of returning to precreation chaos (Jer. 4:23-26; the language in v. 23 echoes Gen. 1:2).

From Jewish Scripture the rabbis derived the view that the human heart is the arena of conflict and decision between two tendencies, the "evil impulse" and the "good impulse" (cf. Sir. 15:14-15). It remained for Christian interpreters to view historical tragedy in the dimension of a fallen creation. The way was prepared, however, especially in the apocalyptic circles of Judaism, by the myth of Satan's rebellion against the Creator and his fall from status within the heavenly council. Viewed in apocalyptic perspective, history is the scene of a cosmic struggle between God and

Satan, the ruler of the present evil age, who seeks to establish a rival kingdom and to seduce human beings into his service. But even this view reflects a historical, rather than a metaphysical, dualism. Satan is not coeternal with God but is a parasite on God's creation. His rule will last only as long as people are deceived by him; in the last day, when God's victory is complete, Satan will be eliminated.

THE NEW CREATION

According to Israel's prophets, once divine judgment has been accomplished, God will make a new beginning, giving human beings a new heart (Ezek. 36:26-28) and bringing them into a new covenant relationship (Jer. 31:31-34; cf. Hos. 2:18-23[20-25]). Not only will humankind enter a new history, but the nonhuman creatures, who are also embraced within God's covenant (Gen. 9:8-17), will be quickened and transformed (Isa. 11:6-9; Hos. 2:18[20]). Thus prophetic eschatology moves toward the vision of the new creation—"the new heaven and the new earth" (Isa. 66:22)—that figured prominently in apocalyptic theology of the postexilic period.

The theme of the new creation dominates the message of Second Isaiah, who grasps profoundly the interrelation of creation and history.[16] At one level of thought, Yahweh's power and wisdom in creating heaven and earth are the ground for the proclamation of divine redemption (Isa. 40:12-31; 42:5-9). At another level, however, confidence in Yahweh, the cosmic creator and king, leads the prophet to announce that the new beginning in Israel's history will be God's new act of creation. In a striking passage, he interprets the old myth about the Creator's triumph over the chaos monster in historical terms (51:9-11). The divine victory over Rahab once occurred at the beginning of Israel's history, when Yahweh created Israel as a people (cf. 43:1). At that time Yahweh dried up the waters of the "great deep" (*těhôm rabbâ*), that is, the Reed Sea, so that the redeemed people could pass over (cf. Ps. 77:16-20[17-21]). In prophetic imagination, this creative/redemptive event was the paradigm of the "new thing" that God was about to do or create (see Isa. 43:18-21): a "new exodus of salvation" that Israel would experience and that would have saving benefits for all nations and peoples. In the prophet's vision, even nature would be marvelously transformed (41:17-20; 43:18-21) as it is taken up into the new beginning in the history of God with Israel and with the creation (a note sounded later by Paul in Rom. 8:19-23).

---

16. Under the stimulus of von Rad's seminal essay ("The Theological Problem of the Old Testament Doctrine of Creation"), numerous essays on creation theology in Second Isaiah have appeared. The central theological issue is posed in P. B. Harner, "Creation Faith in Deutero-Isaiah," *VT* 17 (1967) 298–306.

It is characteristic of eschatology that the visions of the end time are drawn in terms of the pictures of first things. Creation anticipates the consummation; and the consummation is the fulfillment of the beginning. The goal of history will be a return to the beginning, not in the sense of a historical cycle that repeats itself, but in the sense that the original intention of the Creator, frustrated by creaturely rebellion and threatened by the insurgent powers of chaos, will be realized.

CREATION VIEWED CHRISTOLOGICALLY

During the Hellenistic period (after the death of Alexander the Great in 332 B.C.E.) the doctrine of creation was a cardinal tenet of faith that distinguished Judaism from other religions and philosophies. The early Greek translation of Israel's Scriptures known as the Septuagint avoided using the Greek verb *demiourgeō* with respect to God's creative action, owing to its association with the idea of a worker who manufactures or produces things out of previously existing material. The Creator is not the demiurge of gnostic thought. The translators chose instead other verbs, especially *ktizō,* which express the absolute sovereignty of God. The New Testament likewise avoids using *demiourgeō* (although the substantive form occurs in Heb. 11:10) and prefers *ktizō* and its derivatives. The Christian faith is at one with Judaism in affirming that God alone and by the sovereign word created the world and determines its purpose from beginning to end. Frequent reference is made to the original creation (Mark 10:6 par. Matt. 19:4; Mark 13:19 par. Matt. 24:21; Rom. 1:20; 2 Pet. 3:4) or to that which happened "from the foundation of the world" (Matt. 25:34; Luke 11:50; John 17:24; Eph. 1:4; Heb. 4:3; 1 Pet. 1:20; etc.). The apocalyptic vision of the Creator enthroned in glory, while many creatures raise their voices in praise (Revelation 4–5), vividly expresses God's sovereignty over the whole course of history. (See further chap. 14 below.)

CHRIST AND CREATION

Just as in the Old Testament Israel viewed creation in the perspective of its covenant faith, so in the New Testament the church understands creation christologically—in the light of God's action in Jesus Christ, who is the fulfillment of Israel's sacred history and the inaugurator of the new covenant. Since Christ is the center of history, he is also the revelation of God's purpose that undergirds the whole creation. The unity of creation is not disclosed in a rational principle but in God's purpose "which he set forth in Christ as a plan for the fulness of time, to unite all things in him, things in heaven and things on earth" (Eph. 1:9-10, RSV). In Christ all things cohere or "hold together" (Col. 1:17); indeed, he "upholds" the universe by his word of power (Heb. 1:3). He is the bearer of the meaning of history and creation. Therefore, people of faith, convinced of the decisive character of God's action in Jesus Christ, could confess that human salvation was predestined in Christ before the foundation of the world (Matt. 25:34; Eph. 1:4; 1 Pet. 1:20; Rev. 13:8; 17:8).

By making use of the notion of preexistence, Pauline and Johannine circles took an important further step: God created the world through Christ. The Old Testament background for this view is the conception of Wisdom as the first product of God's creative work. Israel's sages not only declared that wisdom is one of the supreme traits of God, but they also regarded "her"[17] as the form of God's creative activity and, indeed, the personal agent of the Creator (Job 28:12-17; Prov. 8:22-31). Thus their thought moved in the direction of hypostatizing Wisdom (Wis. 7:22—8:1). Furthermore, the doctrine of creation by the word (see pp. 45–46 above) was the decisive line of theological thought in the Old Testament. These two views—preexistent, creative Wisdom and creation by the word—converge in the prologue to the Fourth Gospel, which declares that the redeeming Christ is none other than the Logos of creation (John 1:1-18; cf. 1 John 1:1-3; 2:13-14).

By his juxtaposition of the prepositions "from" and "through," Paul makes a similar affirmation. There is one God "*from* whom are all things and for whom we exist," even as there is one Lord, Jesus Christ, "*through* whom are all things and *through* whom we exist" (1 Cor. 8:6, NRSV). A deutero-Pauline writer says of Christ: "in him all things were created, in heaven and on earth," for he is "the image of the invisible God, the first-born of all creation" (Col. 1:15-17, RSV; similar language occurs in Heb. 1:2-3). Everything has its center in Christ, through whom God creates, upholds, and redeems the world.

The doctrine of creation, then, underlines and validates the truth that history, from beginning to end, is under the sovereign purpose of God as revealed in Jesus Christ. The Fourth Gospel begins by echoing the opening words of Genesis, "In the beginning," and speaks about the light shining in the darkness (cf. 2 Cor. 4:6). Even as Christ was in the beginning, so he will triumph at the end (1 Cor. 15:24-28; Revelation 21). Indeed, the very title that Second Isaiah applied to God the book of Revelation ascribes to Christ: he is "the Alpha and the Omega, the first and the last, the beginning and the end" (Rev. 22:13; cf.1:17; 3:14). The whole sweep of history, from creation to the new heaven and the new earth, has its fulcrum in him.

---

17. In Hebrew "wisdom" (*ḥokmâ*) is feminine, and in the book of Proverbs it is personified as a woman who speaks prophetically to human beings (Prov. 1:20-33).

THE NEW CREATION IN CHRIST

The heart of the New Testament gospel is the proclamation that in Christ the kingdom of God has already been inaugurated, the new age anticipated by Old Testament prophets has already been introduced. Echoing the message of Second Isaiah, the New Testament declares that the new creation has already begun. At the same time, however, the new creation is a promise and foretaste of the end time, when there will be a new heaven and a new earth, free from the corruption of evil and death (Rev. 21:1-4), and when all creatures in heaven and earth will join in an anthem of praise to the Creator (Rev. 4:8-11; 5:13). Wherever God's action in Christ is effective for human salvation, God is creatively at work, after the manner of the original creation. Thus Paul, commenting on the transformed life of persons of faith, exclaims that God's redemptive deed is nothing less than a new act of creation: "For it is the God who said [at the dawn of creation, Gen. 1:3], 'Let light shine out of darkness,' who has shone in our hearts to give the light of the knowledge of the glory of God in the face of Christ" (2 Cor. 4:6, RSV). In another context Paul declares that the new life of faith has its source in the grace of God, who creates *ex nihilo* by calling into existence the things that do not exist (Rom. 4:17).

The light of God's new creation, however, breaks forth in the darkness, which is the essence of the "world" (John 1:5, 10; 3:19; 8:12; 12:25-36, 46; 1 John 1:5-6; 2:8-9, 11). In both Pauline and Johannine writings *kosmos* occasionally designates the world as God's creation (e.g., John 17:4; Rom. 1:20; Phil. 2:15), but it usually means the historical sphere—not only the earthly stage of human history but also the context of social relationships in which persons live and move and have their being. In the latter sense, the *kosmos* is a fallen world, for it is characterized by enmity to God and lies under the dominion of evil powers (John 12:31; 16:11; 1 Cor. 1:21; Gal. 4:9; 1 John 5:19; etc.). Moreover, Paul goes so far as to say that the whole created order, affected by human sin, groans under the bondage of corruption, waiting eagerly for the creative and redemptive act that will reveal the children of God (Rom. 8:19-23). But the promise of the coming redemption, not only of humanity in the fullest sense but also of the whole creation, has already been given to those who receive the "first fruits of the Spirit." Through Christ, God has already won the decisive victory over the world and thereby has initiated a new history, a new humanity. To be "in Christ" is to be "a new creature," for "the old has passed away, behold, the new has come" (2 Cor. 5:17; cf. Gal. 6:15). This newness is manifest in a new way of viewing people (2 Cor. 5:16-17) and in a community where old barriers have been broken down and there is unity in Christ (Gal. 3:28; 6:15).

In Jesus Christ, then, God has restored the human pattern intended at the original creation. He is the *'ādām,* of whom Adam was a foreshadowing type (Rom. 5:12-14; cf. 1 Cor. 15:21-22). He is the "likeness of God" (2 Cor. 4:4) and the "image of the invisible God, the first-born of all creation" (Col. 1:15, RSV). This language recalls the "image of God" of Gen. 1:26, just as Heb. 2:5-9 interprets the "man" who is "crowned with glory and honor" (Ps. 8:4-6[5-7]) christologically. He is the beginning of the new humanity into which any person may be born, not through biological parentage but by free decision in response to divine grace. To be sure, the old human nature (*'ādām*) lives on, the flesh wars against the Spirit, the world presents its temptations and frustrations; but the new has come and the old is passing away, for "we all, with unveiled face, beholding the glory of the Lord, are being changed into his likeness from one degree of glory to another" (2 Cor. 3:18, RSV). Through Christ, says a deutero-Pauline writer, persons may put on the "new nature, which is being renewed in knowledge after the image of its creator" (Col. 3:10, RSV; cf. Eph. 4:24). The new person, "created in Christ" (Eph. 2:10, 15), lives in a new relation to God and therefore a new relation to fellow human beings. Human beings, separated by dividing walls of hostility, are reunited by God's reconciling action in Christ (Eph. 2:11-22), and people begin to walk in "newness of life" (Rom. 6:4). The new community, which is "in Christ," is a frontier of the new age, indeed, "a new creation" (Gal. 6:15), in which separating barriers are being broken down; for "there is neither Jew nor Greek, there is neither slave nor free, there is neither male nor female; for you are all one in Christ Jesus" (Gal. 3:28, RSV; cf. Rom. 11:6).

Thus the Christian community, from the standpoint of faith given by God's revelation in Christ, looks both backward and forward. It traces God's purpose to the first creation, saying: "In Christ all things were created"; and it lives toward the future, saying: "God will sum up all things in Christ." The full disclosure of the new creation lies in God's future, when the new age will fully come and there will be "a new heaven and a new earth." Even as the dramatic story of Genesis 1 is not a scientific account of the origin of the universe, so the poetic visions of Revelation are not a speculative projection into the future. The truth of both is perceived by those who participate in the new creation in Christ and who know in faith that the whole span of history, from beginning to end, is embraced within the sovereign purpose of the Creator and Redeemer.[18]

---

18. An extensive bibliography on the subject of the biblical doctrine of creation is provided at the end of *Creation in the Old Testament,* 172–78.

CHAPTER 3

The Priestly
Creation Story:
A Stylistic Study

Discussions of the biblical canon have to take into consideration not only the final literary shape of particular texts or of canonical units (e.g., the Pentateuch) but also the prehistory that preceded the literary conclusion. To use a well-known figure of speech, one must understand the texts in a dimension of depth, not just on a flat surface, "superficially."[1] Yet not all biblical texts provide a clear basis for reconstructing previous literary or tradition-historical *stages* that the interpreter must take into account. Indeed, in some cases one finds the meaning of the text by examining in depth the literary structure of the text itself. A case in point is the Priestly creation story with which the Pentateuch opens. The purpose of this essay is to explore the present literary form of the story, especially the word-event structure that is intrinsic to the narrative.

RELATION OF FORM AND CONTENT

Ever since the publication of Hermann Gunkel's monumental commentary on Genesis, the first edition of which appeared at the turn of the twentieth century,[2] scholars have had to take with increasing seriousness the interrelationship of form and content in biblical literature. Before writ-

---

1. This figure appears in Gerhard von Rad, *Genesis* (trans. John H. Marks; OTL; rev. ed.; Philadelphia: Westminster, 1972) 23; and Brevard S. Childs employs it effectively in *The Book of Exodus: A Critical Theological Commentary* (OTL; Philadelphia: Westminster, 1974).

2. Hermann Gunkel's commentary on Genesis first appeared in *HKAT* (Göttingen: Vandenhoeck & Ruprecht, 1901). The 3d edition appeared in 1910 and the 4th through the 6th (1964) editions were reprints.

ing his commentary, Gunkel had issued his pioneering study, *Schöpfung und Chaos in Urzeit und Endzeit* (1895), a thematic study occasioned by the archaeological discovery of Mesopotamian literary remains at the ancient Babylonian capital of Nineveh. In this work Gunkel shows that the motif of the mythical battle between the creator god and the opposing powers of chaos can be traced through various types of biblical literature, from the opening of the book of Genesis to the Apocalypse of John. But in his Genesis commentary, as Jay Wilcoxen has rightly observed, Gunkel's attention shifted from the *Stoffe* (Gunkel's preferred term for traditional materials) to the *Gattungen* (literary genres) in which traditional matter was formulated and transmitted.[3] Since the literary genres arose out of folk materials and were shaped in the creative oral period, it is the task of the interpreter, according to Gunkel, to go behind the present text and to investigate the original formulation of the material in its *Sitz im Leben* (this discipline has come to be known as form criticism). Furthermore, the interpreter's task is to consider how original formulations underwent an evolution, a *Literaturgeschichte,* which finally resulted in the received text (this discipline came to be known as tradition-historical investigation).

The Priestly creation story provides an excellent example of the inseparable relation of form and content. All commentators, even conservatives like Benno Jacob and Umberto Cassuto, recognize that the story incorporates traditional materials, including the chaos motif. The question is the degree to which traditional materials have been homogenized in the present account, which compresses eight creative acts into six "days of work." Gunkel's thinking about this matter seems to have shifted. In his monograph *Schöpfung und Chaos* he was primarily concerned to show that the creation story rests on an ancient mythical tradition, ultimately Babylonian in origin. In his Genesis commentary, however, he maintained that the Priestly writers were dependent on a *Vorlage* that was reworked "heavily" (*sehr stark*).[4] It was his judgment that the revision was so thoroughgoing that it is no longer possible to recover the content and wording of the original.

Other scholars were not so restrained in their attempts to reconstruct the prehistory of the text. At the beginning of the twentieth century two scholars, Bernhard Stade and Friedrich Schwally, proposed independently that the present creation story is the end result of the blending of two accounts, one dealing with God making the world and the other with creation by

---

3. Jay A. Wilcoxen, "Narrative," in *Old Testament Form Criticism* (ed. John H. Hayes; San Antonio: Trinity Univ. Press, 1974) 58–59.
4. Gunkel, *Genesis* (3d ed.), 119–20. He lists eight "traces of an older *Vorlage,*" in addition to the sequence of creative events.

God's word.[5] Years later Gerhard von Rad attempted to buttress this view with a literary analysis of the Priestly writing in which he posited two identifiable strands (P^A and P^B) and, in the case of Genesis 1, a deed-account (*Tatbericht,* P^A) and a command-account (*Befehlsbericht,* P^B).[6] The attempt to separate out *literary* sources has not been successful. In his *History of Pentateuchal Traditions* Martin Noth rejects this purely literary approach, although he admits that, from the standpoint of the history of traditions, one can discern a tension between *Tatbericht* (deed-account) and *Wortbericht* (word-account).[7]

In more recent years this tradition-historical approach has provided the opportunity for the discussion to take a new turn, along the lines of a supplementary hypothesis. Werner Schmidt maintains that the nucleus of the story is a stratum of tradition that was closely akin to other ancient Near Eastern texts, notably the Babylonian *Enuma elish.* Superimposed on this old level of tradition is a later interpretive expansion that sets forth a more sophisticated theological view. In his judgment, the present text is the end result of a tradition-historical development, in the course of which the old *Tatbericht,* with its emphasis on creation by making, was reinterpreted to stress creation by fiat, thereby giving the final story the tone of a *Wortbericht.*[8] P. A. H. de Boer carries this tradition-historical analysis one stage further, finding *three* tradition-strata in the story: (1) a myth portraying God as a divine "handicraftsman," like the divine potter in prophetical sayings; (2) a myth portraying God as the divine king who made heaven and earth (as in some psalms), and (3) various supplements by late Priestly writers who sought to systematize received traditions.[9]

It is not my intention to deny the use of traditional materials in the creation story. The question is whether the text provides evidence of a

5. Bernhard Stade, *Biblische Theologie des Alten Testaments* (2 vols.; Tübingen: Mohr, 1905–11) 1.349; Friedrich Schwally, "Die biblischen Schöpfungsberichte," *ARW* 9 (1906) 159–75.

6. Gerhard von Rad, *Die Priesterschrift im Hexateuch* (BWANT 65; Stuttgart: Kohlhammer, 1934) 11–18, 167–71; see his synoptic outline, 190–91. In his *Genesis,* he is more cautious about reconstructing "the long road in the history of tradition which lies behind the present form of this account of creation," but he still speaks (p. 64) about earlier and later versions (creation by act and creation by word).

7. Martin Noth, *A History of Pentateuchal Traditions* (trans. Bernhard W. Anderson; Englewood Cliffs, N.J.: Prentice-Hall, 1972) 10–12, 235. For a trenchant criticism of von Rad's theory of the duality of literary sources in the Priestly writing, see Paul Humbert, "Die literarische Zweiheit des Priester-Codex in der Genesis," *ZAW* 58 (1940–41) 30–57, esp. 30–35 on the creation story.

8. Werner H. Schmidt, *Die Schöpfungsgeschichte der Priesterschrift* (WMANT 17; Neukirchen-Vluyn: Neukirchener Verlag, 1964). See pp. 160–63 for his reconstruction of "the oldest stage of the tradition."

9. P. A. H. de Boer, *Fatherhood and Motherhood in Israelite and Judean Piety* (Leiden: Brill, 1974) 47–48, 49–51. He maintains that at the earliest level of tradition, God and Goddess were coparticipants in the creation of humankind (Gen. 1:26).

tradition-historical evolution whose stages are still evident and that the interpreter must consider to some degree; or whether the story is a meticulously wrought composition in which form and content are indissolubly united. In my opinion, the latter is the case. In this essay I am returning, though in a restricted sense, to Gunkel's view that the composers of this story, while drawing on traditional motifs, have so completely reworked the materials by casting them into a new literary form that it is impossible to recover an earlier *Vorlage*. My thesis is that a stylistic study of the shape of the text itself, rather than explorations into its presumed prehistory, will throw light on various theological matters, such as the translation of the opening sentence (1:1), the alternating descriptions of God as Maker and Creator, and the preeminent role of human beings on the earth.

ELEMENTS OF THE OVERALL LITERARY DESIGN

Careful study of the Hebrew text of the creation story discloses many rhetorical features that I cannot examine within the limitations of this essay: examples of verbal assonance, chiastic arrangement, the strategic positioning and collocation of words, among others. Here I will focus on the overall form of the story, which displays throughout a striking literary symmetry and integrity.

THE FORMULAIC PATTERN

The first thing that strikes one is that the story as a whole is structured in a sequence of literary "panels" or paragraphs, each of which is governed by a divine command and its execution.[10] Creation takes place not by word-events but by word-fulfillment events. For some reason, Sean McEvenue, in his study of Priestly narrative style, does not deal with this phenomenon in the Priestly creation story; but he has provided ample evidence that the command-execution sequence, which is characteristic of narrative art generally, was a distinctive feature of Priestly style, notably in the laws of Sinai (Exodus 25–31) that Moses faithfully executes (Exodus 35–40).[11] The connection between word and deed is emphasized by repeating verbally the content of the command, though with some variations. For instance, the flood story uses the command formula, "then God said to Noah" (*wayyō'mer 'ĕlōhîm lĕnōaḥ,* 6:13), and the corresponding obedience formula, "And Noah did according to everything that God com-

---

10. See especially the excellent commentary by Claus Westermann, *Genesis* (trans. John J. Scullion; Continental Commentary; 3 vols.; Minneapolis: Augsburg, 1984–86) 1.80–93. Westermann analyzes the component formal elements of "the structure of the command."

11. Sean E. McEvenue, *The Narrative Style of the Priestly Writer* (AnBib 50; Rome: Biblical Institute, 1971).

manded him, so he did" (*wayya'aś nōaḥ kĕkōl 'ăšer ṣiwwâ 'ōtô 'ĕlōhîm kēn 'āśâ,* 6:22). The stylistic connection between command and execution, or word and fulfillment, is found in both the Old Epic flood tradition and its Priestly recension, and in both cases repetition is characteristic of narrative style.

In the creation story God is the one who both announces and fulfills God's word. With this qualification, which puts the story in a different category from those dealing with the obedience of Noah or Moses, each of the panels displays a command-execution sequence. Reduced to a minimum, the formulaic elements of the pattern are: (1) a declarative formula, "then God said" (*wayyō'mer 'ĕlōhîm*); (2) a command that, with the possible exception of the heavenly council implied in 1:26, was addressed to no one, since no other being was present to participate in the creation; (3) execution of the command, usually introduced by the formula "and so it happened" (*wayyĕhî kēn*);[12] and finally (4) a formula of divine approbation that indicates the perfect correspondence between the command and its execution.[13]

This pattern is not followed inflexibly. The *wayyĕhî kēn* formula is conspicuously absent in the first panel, perhaps because light was conceived to be an instantaneous flash, like lightning, out of uncreated darkness; moreover, the formula is lacking between vv. 26 and 27, where one would expect it, and occurs instead in v. 31, probably because of the expansion of the story to make room for a special divine blessing upon human beings (v. 28) and a formal grant of food (vv. 29-30).[14] Furthermore, at three points the pattern is expanded with the motif of naming (vv. 5, 8, 10). Verse 22 has a blessing upon marine and flying creatures that in its linguistic formulation is akin to the blessing given to human beings (1:28). These and other deviations,[15] however, do not disturb the fundamental D-C-E-A literary pattern: Declarative Formula, Command, Execution, Approbation.

When one takes these stylistic features seriously, important consequences for exegesis follow. First, from a stylistic viewpoint one has no reason to suppose that the declarative formula (*wayyō'mer 'ĕlōhîm*) of

12. Following LXX, one should probably transpose this formula from the end of v. 7 to the end of v. 6, corresponding to the sequence in vv. 9, 11, 15, 24. Also in v. 20, following LXX, one should probably restore the formula.

13. The formula of approbation probably belongs at the end of v. 8, as in LXX, following the creation of the celestial vault. In every other case God responds to an act of creation with a word of approval.

14. See Humbert, *ZAW* 58 (1940–41) 31–32.

15. In the first panel, the divine approbation comes immediately after the creation of light, not after the separation of light and darkness, lest it be suggested that God also approved the darkness of chaos.

v. 3a is the apodosis of a temporal clause, whose protasis begins with v. 1. Some translators, arguing that grammatically v. 1 may be either an independent sentence or a dependent temporal clause, attempt to resolve the problem by appealing to other texts, biblical or extrabiblical. But when one views the text in terms of its own internal structure, there is clear reason to believe that the declarative formula in v. 3a functions in the same manner as it does elsewhere in the creation story: as a discrete introduction to a following creative word-act.

Second, from a stylistic point of view the command-execution structure is intrinsic to the narrative, apparently from the time of its literary formulation. The repetition in the execution provides no basis for positing duplications that, in turn, justify attempts to reconstruct an *Urtext* or an *Urstadium der Tradition*.[16] It is noteworthy that Werner Schmidt, while admitting that the *Urtext* can no longer be recovered with certainty, finds traces of the supposedly early *Tatbericht* precisely at those points where the divine command is executed (vv. 4b, 7, 9 [LXX], 12a, 16-17a, 21, 25). Inconsistently, he makes an exception in the case of the creation of humanity (vv. 26-27a), at which point the reconstructed early level of tradition contained both a cohortative command ("Let us make . . .") and its execution ("And God created . . .").[17]

This tradition-historical analysis, in my judgment, finds the feeblest support from an appeal to the difference between the verbs of making (*'āśâ*) and creating (*bārā'*). Significantly, the episode of the creation of humanity begins with the command "let us make" (*na'ăśeh*), and the execution of the command is reported by saying, "So, God created . . ." (*wayyibrā'*). It is arbitrary to change the second verb to "made" (*machte*), as does Schmidt, for the sake of a hypothesis. The prophet Second Isaiah, an approximate contemporary of the so-called Priestly writer, used these verbs interchangeably, even within the compass of a single sentence (43:7).[18] Further, speaking out of Israel's cultic tradition, a psalmist could exclaim:

---

16. Westermann, who is sensitive to the depth dimension of the text but is even more impressed with the stylistic features of the present text, observes: "And so it only confuses the issue when one wants to divide Gen 1 into a 'command-account' and an 'action-account'; the former never existed as such, and the latter account cannot be reconstructed" (*Genesis*, 1.86).

17. Schmidt, *Schöpfungsgeschichte*, 161; see also 127–49. Von Rad's literary analysis (*Priesterschrift*, 11–18, 167–71) also cuts into the command-execution sequence.

18. For the table of creation verbs used by Second Isaiah, see my *Creation versus Chaos: The Reinterpretation of Mythical Symbolism in the Bible* (New York: Association, 1967; repr. Philadelphia: Fortress Press, 1987) 124–26.

By the word of Yahweh the heavens were made [*na'ăśû*],
   and by the breath of his mouth all their array!

. . . .

For he spoke and it happened,
   he commanded and it occurred! (Ps. 33:6, 9, au. trans.)

The tension between "creating" and "making," between creative word and creative deed, in the creation story has been grossly exaggerated. In any case, the narrative style of the story, with its essential connection between command and execution, provides no basis for supposing that the text is the end product of a literary or tradition-historical evolution in which *Tatbericht* and *Wortbericht* were finally united. Theologically, the statement that God is the Maker and that God is the Creator are not different at all.

THE TWOFOLD MOVEMENT

Turn now to another major stylistic feature of the creation story. The creative drama falls into two parts, each of which comes to its own climax. The first section (vv. 3-13), the first triad of days, consists of four creative word-deeds, with two at the climax; correspondingly, the second section (vv. 14-31), the second triad of days, consists of four creative word-deeds, with two at the climax. In the past, commentators have been troubled by this scheme, which compresses eight acts of creation into the confines of a six-day workweek and which introduces a theological tension between God's effortless, instantaneous creation and the extension of creation over a period of time, at the end of which God "ceased" from all God's work (cf. Exod. 31:15 [P]: "on the seventh day he rested, and was refreshed"). What some regard as problematic, however, may not have troubled the composer of the text. It is noteworthy that some scholars (e.g., Schmidt) believe that the calendar scheme belongs to the latest phase of the history of the tradition; but von Rad, who also attempted to separate out an early *Tatbericht* and a later *Befehlsbericht,* came to the conclusion that the motif of God's "resting" (*šābat*) from God's "work" (*mělā'kâ*) belongs to the oldest version. "We reckon it to be an important result that the seven-day scheme, though it finally conforms to the material in small degree, nevertheless does not represent literarily a late reworking but is firmly anchored in the oldest ascertainable form of Genesis 1."[19] At this point one faces again the issue of the interrelationship of form and content, which one should consider anew from the standpoint of stylistic study.

So much attention has been given to the possible prehistory of the creation story that one thing has not received sufficient attention: the story

---

19. Von Rad, *Priesterschrift,* 17.

in its present form is structured in parallel sections[20] so as to portray a twofold movement from heaven to earth, thereby elucidating the theme stated in the superscription to the whole: "In the beginning God created the heaven and the earth." The narrator's focus on the earth is indicated at the outset in v. 2, which serves as the immediate preface to the creative drama proper. The prefatory portrayal of chaos opens with an express interest in *the earth,* which stands in an emphatic position: "Now, the earth was once a chaotic waste . . ." (*wĕhā' āreṣ hāyĕtâ tōhû wābōhû*). Accordingly, in the two triads of days there is a double movement from the cosmic realm to the earth—from heaven, to waters, to earth; and the terrestrial focus is evident at the climax point of each section (that is, the third and sixth days), where in each case two creative events pertain to the earth. (See figure 2.)

Let us see how this double movement occurs. The presuppositions for the unfolding drama of creation are given in the portrayal of primeval chaos in the prefatory v. 2. The chaotic waste (*tōhû wābōhû,* a hendiadys), which constitutes the background of God's creative activity, has two characteristics: primeval, uncreated darkness, and watery depth over which an awesome wind was sweeping.[21] Darkness (*ḥōšek*) and water (*mayîm*) are the two chaos dimensions that figure in the ensuing drama.

In the first panel (first day), which opens with the declarative formula "Then God said," the Creator caused light to burst forth in the uncreated darkness. This *Urlicht,* for which there is no anticipation in the prefatory portrayal of chaos, was not permitted to become twilight, a suffused mixture of light and darkness; for God separated created light and uncreated darkness into their proper spheres, naming the one Day and the other Night. In the second panel (second day) the narrator turns to the other dimension of primeval chaos, the watery abyss. Executing the divine command, God made a celestial vault to separate the upper waters from the lower waters. God named the vault Heaven (*šāmayîm*), although nothing is said about the cosmic realm, for instance, the number of heavens or the location of the Creator's heavenly palace in or above the cosmic ocean (cf. Ps. 8:1[2]). In the third panel (first part of the third day) the narrator's vision descends to the lower waters, the remnant of primeval watery chaos. At God's executive command, the waters were accumulated into a bounded

---

20. Scholars have long emphasized the twofold division and have perceived correlations between the two series: first and fourth days (light/luminaries); second and fifth days (firmament separating the waters/birds and water creatures); third and sixth days (dry land plus vegetation/land animals plus man). "Dieser Parallelismus springt in die Augen," observed Franz Delitzsch; and he insisted that the correspondence remains even if one supposes that there was an older eight-act account without the division into days. See his *Genesis* (Leipzig: Dörffling und Franke, 1887) 45–46.

21. Compare this "wind of Elohim" with "the wind of Yahweh" mentioned in Isa. 40:7, the hot wind from the desert that is likewise not creative but signalizes death and chaos.

Figure 2: THE MOVEMENT OF THE CREATION STORY

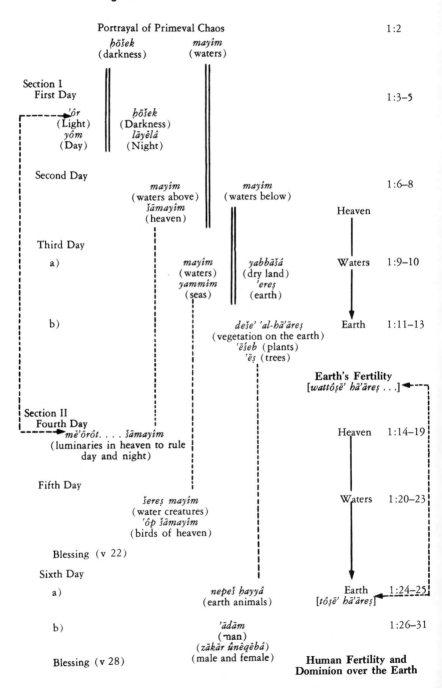

location (a third act of separation) and the submerged "dry land" (*yabbāšâ*) became visible.[22] The accumulated waters were named Seas (*yammîm*) and the *yabbāšâ* was named Earth (*'ereṣ*). Nothing further is said about the lower waters at this point: this matter is picked up again in the second section, vv. 20-23. In the fourth panel (second part of the third day), which is paired with the third panel, the narrator turns specifically to the *yabbāšâ* ("dry land") named Earth, which at God's command produced vegetation. The narrator emphasizes the greening of the earth by using an assonant verb and noun (*tadšē'*/*dēše'*) and stresses the earth's fecundity by using the maternal verb *wattôṣē'* ("and the earth brought forth"), a verb that is recapitulated at the climactic point of the second part of the story, as we shall see. Thus the paired third and fourth panels, which deal with the earth and its fertility, constitute the climax in the unfolding drama of creation.

The second part of the story (vv. 14-31) follows essentially the same movement: heaven—waters—earth. The fifth panel (fourth day) begins by recapitulating, though in a modified sense, the motif of cosmic light that was introduced at the first (v. 3). At the same time, attention turns to heaven, specifically, the celestial vault (*rāqîa' haššāmayim*) mentioned previously in vv. 6-8. Executing the divine command, God made the luminaries (*mě' ōrôt*) and placed them in the celestial expanse to perform functions that are given in chiastic reversal of the command itself: to shed light on the earth, to govern day and night (i.e., to mark times), and "to separate" (*lěhabdîl*) the light and darkness from an earthly standpoint (in contrast to the separation referred to in v. 4). In the sixth panel (fifth day) the drama moves from the *šāmayim* ("heaven") to the *mayîm* ("waters") that previously had been accumulated and named *yammîm* ("seas," "lakes"). Fulfilling God's own word, God created swarms of marine creatures, including monsters of the deep. Interestingly, the flying creatures, although they soar over the earth and beneath the celestial vault, are in some sense associated with the waters. Indeed, some construe v. 20 to mean that the waters were commanded to "bring forth" not only fish but birds as well,[23] although it is doubtful that the Masoretic text implies this. The first appearance of *nepeš ḥayyâ* (biological life in contrast to organic life) is accompanied by a special blessing (v. 22).

Finally, in the paired seventh and eighth panels (sixth day) the story returns once again to the earth. Just as the two sections of the story are

---

22. LXX preserves the verbal repetition of the command, which is appropriate in the context of execution, thus presupposing Hebrew *wayyiqqāwû hammayim mittaḥat haššāmayim 'el-miqwêhem wattērā' hayyabbāšâ,* in addition to MT.

23. See LXX: *Exagagetō ta hydata herpeta psychōn zōsōn kai peteina petomena epi tēs gēs.* JPSV translates MT: "Let the waters bring forth swarms of living creatures, and birds that fly above the earth across the expanse of the sky."

bracketed together at their beginnings with the motif of heavenly light, so at their respective climax points a link is made by repeating the maternal verb *tôṣē'* (cf. 1:12). God commanded the earth (v. 24) to "bring forth" (*tôṣē' hā'āreṣ*) living beings (*nepeš ḥayyâ*); and the execution sequence, which repeats the content of the command, states that God "made" them (v. 25). The eighth and concluding panel deals with the preeminent *nepeš ḥayyâ* ("living being"), humanity, consisting of "male and female" (*zākār ûněqēbâ*). The close affinity of this earth creature with the land animals is indicated not only by the pairing of these two creative acts, as in the former pair dealing with the earth (third day), but also by the subsequent announcement that human beings share the same table with the animals (vv. 29-30). At its second climax, however, the story shows that a human being is more than an earth animal. Created in the image of God, humanity is related to the sphere of God's cosmic administration by virtue of a decree announced in the heavenly council and hence is God's representative on earth. No blessing is given to the animals. The blessing is reserved for human beings, who are empowered to be fertile, multiply, and exercise dominion over the earth.[24]

FURTHER STYLISTIC CONSIDERATIONS

So far I have considered the main body of the creation story. I have argued that the story discloses an overall literary design, based on a double movement, in two triads of days, from heaven, to waters, to earth. At both of the climactic points the earth is the focus of concern. The twin panels at the climax of the first section emphasize the earth's fertility, which is released at God's command. The twin panels at the climax of the second part once again emphasize the earth, but above all God's supreme creature, *'ādām*, to whom is granted fertility and dominion over the earth.

RELATION OF BEGINNING TO END

The unity of the story is further strengthened by the *inclusio* that relates the end of the story to its beginning. Echoing the superscription of 1:1, the epilogue (2:1-3) opens with an epitomizing statement that "the heaven and the earth in their whole array were completed." The text seems heavy, especially in 2:2, and therefore some literary critics have suspected doublets, indicating different sources.

God completed on the seventh day his work that he made.
He ceased on the seventh day from all the work that he made.

24. See further chap. 7 below.

Here, however, the narrators emphasize the seventh day by means of complementary positive and negative statements. Picking up the previous verb (*wayyĕkullû*) at the end of 2:1, though modulating it from the passive to the active (*wayyĕkal*), they state positively that God brought his work to completion; and, with rhetorical balance, they state negatively that God ceased from the work that God made. This balancing of the positive and negative, as Paul Humbert has observed, is continued in the next line, which speaks about the blessing of the seventh day and also about its removal from the profane sphere, that is, its sanctification.[25] Thus positive and negative statements complement each other, and the epilogue is rounded off with a motive clause, introduced by the particle *kî* ("for"):

> God blessed the seventh day and declared it holy;
> for [*kî*] on it God ceased from all the work that he creatively made.

The final words, *'ăšer bārā' 'ĕlōhîm la'ăśôt* (lit.: "which God created to make"), are difficult to render smoothly into English. The reader of the Hebrew, however, will sense that the clause echoes the *bārā' 'ĕlōhîm* ("God created") of the superscription (1:1) and at the same time recalls the usage of both verbs, *bārā'* and *'āśâ*, in the main body of the story.[26] Thus the conclusion, forming an *inclusio* with the opening statement, rounds off and completes the whole. Cassuto's attempt to defend the integrity of the creation story on the basis of numerical harmony (e.g., the mystical signif- icance of the number seven: thirty-five references to *'ĕlōhîm* = 7 x 5; twenty-one occurrences of *'ereṣ* = 7 x 3; etc.) is clearly a tour de force; yet in dealing with the concluding verse of the creation story he has displayed a sound sensitivity to literary style:

> Just as the prologue announces at the outset the main subject-matter of the account that follows, so the epilogue looks back and epitomizes within the limits of one short sentence the content of the preceding narrative, reawakening in the heart of the reader, by means of this synthesis inherent in its words, the sentiments that were aroused within him in the course of his reading.[27]

It is striking that Gerhard von Rad, though advocating a different view of the tradition history of the creation story, moves toward a similar conclu-

---

25. Humbert, *ZAW* 58 (1940–41) 34.

26. *'āśâ* is used in vv. 7, 16, 25, 26, 31; *bārā'* in vv. 21, 27. No sharp distinction can be made between the usage of these verbs. Notice that the epilogue (2:2) even stresses the verb *'āśâ* by using it twice in one sentence.

27. Umberto Cassuto, *Genesis* (trans. Israel Abrahams; 2 vols.; Jerusalem: Magnes, Hebrew University, 1961–64) 1.70. This stylistic feature is also stressed by Benno Jacob in his *Das erste Buch der Tora: Genesis* (Berlin: Schocken, 1934) 68.

sion. The opening verse of Genesis 1, he says, is "the summary statement of everything that is unfolded step by step in the following verses."[28]

THEOLOGICAL IMPLICATIONS

One final matter deserves consideration. It is often said that the Priestly creation story extends from Gen. 1:1 through 2:4a. This declaration assumes that the *tôlĕdôt* formula in 2:4a ("These are the generations of the heaven and the earth when they were created" [*bĕhibbārĕ'ām*]) belongs essentially to the creation story, either as its misplaced introduction or, as most recent interpreters believe, as its summary conclusion. This view, however, is not consonant with the usage of the *tôlĕdôt* formula elsewhere in the Priestly work. It is noteworthy that the Priestly writers/editors use the formula five times to organize their presentation of the primeval history and five times in the patriarchal history, and in every instance, as Frank Cross has shown, it is a superscription to what follows.[29] The rubric in 2:4a is no exception to the general rule. The formula is a superscription to the following paradise story—a story appropriated from the Old Epic tradition to supplement and enrich the Priestly work that leads through the succession of the generations of Noah and eventually to the patriarchal history. It is not accurate to say that the creation story extends from 1:1 through 2:4a. The proper conclusion is found in 2:3, an *inclusio* that corresponds with 1:1.

This observation of the structure of the Priestly work (the final form of the Tetrateuch or Pentateuch) has important theological implications. Properly speaking, the creation story, according to the Priestly scheme, is not really part of the primeval history (*Urgeschichte*), which begins with the portrayal of human history in the genealogies and narratives from Gen. 2:4a on. Rather, the creation story is the preface to the primeval history. It sets the stage and provides the theological and anthropological presuppositions for the ensuing story (world history, patriarchal history, folk history), which, in its received edition, comes from the hand of the Priestly writers/editors. In the Priestly presentation, then, creation is not the beginning of history. It is protohistorical, for it lies in the realm of mystery that belongs properly and exclusively to God, as Job was reminded (Job 38:4-7). Thus the pentateuchal story of redemption, in which Israel has a special role, is grounded in the prior affirmation of faith that God is the Creator. This theological accent is also found in the prophecy of Second Isaiah, an approximate contemporary of the Priestly writers, who announced to Israel

28. Von Rad, *Genesis,* 49.
29. Frank M. Cross, "The Priestly Work," in *Canaanite Myth and Hebrew Epic* (Cambridge: Harvard Univ. Press, 1973) 293–325, esp. 301–5.

that hope for the redemption of Israel and of the nations of the world is grounded in faith in God as creator (e.g., Isa. 40:12-31).

In summary, a stylistic study of the creation story yields more satisfying results than the widely accepted hypothesis that the present shape of the text is the end result of literary or tradition-historical stages in which *Tatbericht* and *Wortbericht* were conflated and harmonized. It is clear that the composers of the story have made use of the traditional material; but form and content are so inseparably united that attempts to reconstruct a prehistory of the text, and to derive theological judgments from that presumed evolution, are not fruitful. When viewed stylistically, the story is a unified and symmetrical whole, whose meaning is disclosed in the internal structure of the narrative itself, with its word-event pattern. Furthermore, the theological meaning of the story is also disclosed by considering its *function* in the larger narrative whole that we have received from the hands of the Priestly writers.

CHAPTER 4

The Flood Story
in Context:
From Analysis
to Synthesis

The vitality of biblical scholarship is shown by a disposition to test and challenge working hypotheses, even those that are supported by a broad consensus. Today new signals call for advance, like the rustling of leaves in the tops of the balsam trees, to cite a biblical figure of speech (2 Sam 5:24).[1] The purpose of this essay is to reexamine some old-fashioned views that have constituted the critical orthodoxy of the twentieth century and to look toward the new era of biblical study that is dawning. I will focus on the book of Genesis, which has been a storm center of biblical criticism in the modern period. In order to make the task somewhat manageable, however, I shall bracket out the patriarchal history and consider only the primeval history (Gen. 1:1—11:26). But even this is too much to deal with; so, within the primeval history, I shall concentrate on the flood story. Everyone will admit that there are more than enough problems to handle within this pericope!

METHODOLOGICAL APPROACHES TO GENESIS

Before coming to the flood story, consider briefly the current methodological crisis. As one looks back over the history of pentateuchal criticism in the twentieth century, it is clear that the mainstream of biblical scholarship, as represented by the Society of Biblical Literature, has been

---

1. Examples, inter alia, of the new ferment are Hans Heinrich Schmid, *Der sogenannte Jawist: Beobachtungen und Fragen zur Pentateuchforschung* (Zurich: Theologischer Verlag, 1976); and Rolf Rendtorff, *Das überlieferungsgeschichtliche Problem des Pentateuch* (BZAW 147; Berlin and New York: de Gruyter, 1977).

concerned with the genetic development of the biblical materials. Otto Eissfeldt's little book, *Die Genesis der Genesis,* is symptomatic of the major interest of past generations.[2] In this period the interpretive task has been both analytic and diachronic: analytic in the sense that one dissects the received text into its component parts, and diachronic in the sense that one seeks to understand the genesis of the text from its earliest origin to its final formulation. Thus the source critic begins by analyzing the text into its component "documents" on the basis of criteria applicable to literary texts. As Eissfeldt points out, however, these "narrative threads" have had a prehistory. Accordingly, it is the task of the form critic, following the lead of Hermann Gunkel, to venture behind the literary sources into the previous period of oral tradition and to recover the *Urform* of a particular text and its setting in life. Finally, the task of the historian of traditions is to realize Gunkel's goal of presenting a *Literaturgeschichte,* a reconstruction of the whole genetic development from the early phase of oral tradition through the stages of various literary formulations to the end result of the Pentateuch that we have received.

It is not my intention to denigrate this period of scholarship, for it has contributed to our understanding of the depth dimension of the texts. To borrow a figure of speech used by Gerhard von Rad in his Genesis commentary and employed effectively by Brevard Childs in his commentary on Exodus, one must not read the final text on a flat surface, "superficially," but in a dimension of depth,[3] that is, with sensitivity to the voices of the past—the whole history of traditions—that resound in the final polyphonic presentation. Nevertheless, one ought to be aware of some of the assumptions that have governed this genetic interpretation. First, the early period of tradition, which one seeks to recover, is the creative stage of tradition. This was clearly Gunkel's conviction, apparently influenced by romanticism;[4] and it survives in a modified form in von Rad's emphasis on the primacy of the Yahwist's epic, which, being based on early creedal formulations, provided the determinative ("canonical") tradition that was accepted basically in the final Priestly formulation of the traditions. Second, the earliest stages of the transmission of traditions are reconstructed with help from the literary models employed in source or documentary criticism. Tensions in the text, as evidenced by literary style, vocabulary, inconsistencies, and duplications, are transferred from the literary stage to

---

2. Otto Eissfeldt, *Die Genesis der Genesis* (Tübingen: Mohr [Siebeck], 1958); an English translation appears in the article "Genesis," *IDB* 2.366–80.

3. Gerhard von Rad, *Genesis* (trans. John H. Marks; OTL; rev. ed.; Philadelphia: Westminster, 1972) 28; Brevard S. Childs, *The Book of Exodus* (OTL; Philadelphia: Westminster, 1974).

4. See my introductory essay to Martin Noth, *A History of Pentateuchal Traditions* (trans. Bernhard W. Anderson; Englewood Cliffs, N.J.: Prentice-Hall, 1972) xviii–xx.

an earlier, preliterary stage. Using these accepted literary criteria, one attempts to reconstruct the prehistory of the written text, that is, "Scripture." Third, scholars have assumed that the way to understand the combination of strata in the final text is to explore their origin and development. As Eissfeldt's essay on "the genesis of Genesis" indicates, excursions into the prehistory of the text are motivated by a concern for historicity; criticism enables one to make judgments about the historical value of narratives for the time about which they claim to speak or about their place in religious history.[5] This perspective seems to imply that the scriptural text points to a meaning that lies, to some degree, outside the text: in the history of the ancient world or in the ideas or customs reflected in various circles during the history of traditions.

If I am not mistaken, a new generation of biblical scholars has arisen that wants to move beyond this kind of analysis into some sort of synthesis, beyond a method that is rigidly diachronic to one that gives appropriate weight to the synchronic dimension of the text. Without attempting to survey the whole scholarly scene, I will mention several scholarly impulses that are potentially significant for the study of Genesis.

First, stylistic or rhetorical criticism was given new impetus by James Muilenburg—my esteemed teacher—in his presidential address to the Society of Biblical Literature on "Form Criticism and Beyond."[6] Muilenberg certainly did not intend to throw overboard the substantial contributions of past scholarship, including Julius Wellhausen, in spite of increasing reservations about Wellhausen's method of historical criticism and that of Gunkel, from whom he learned most. In a statement that summarizes his career Muilenberg concludes: "'We affirm the necessity of form criticism'—and that demands appropriate exploration of the prehistory of the text; 'but we also lay claim to the legitimacy of what we have called rhetorical criticism'—and that requires attention to the text itself: its own integrity, its dramatic structure, and its stylistic features."[7]

This type of "rhetorical" criticism is applied by J. P. Fokkelman in dealing with various specimens of narrative art in Genesis;[8] and his study, in turn, is influenced by the so-called new literary criticism advocated, for instance, by René Wellek and Austin Warren, who call into question scholarly preoccupation with questions of authorship, social context, and prehistory of the text and insist that the proper task of the literary critic is the

---

5. Otto Eissfeldt, "Genesis," *IDB* 2.378–80.

6. Published in *JBL* 88 (1969) 1–18. See further my essay, "The New Frontier of Rhetorical Criticism," in *Rhetorical Criticism: Essays in Honor of James Muilenburg* (ed. Jared J. Jackson and Martin Kessler; PTMS 1; Pittsburgh: Pickwick, 1974) ix–xviii.

7. See my essay, "The New Frontier of Rhetorical Criticism," xviii.

8. J. P. Fokkelman, *Narrative Art in Genesis: Specimens of Stylistic and Structural Analysis* (Amsterdam: Van Gorcum, 1975).

study of the work itself.[9] Fokkelman uses a vivid figure of speech to describe this view:

> The birth of a text resembles that of man: the umbilical cord which connected the text with its time and the man or men who produced it, is severed once its existence has become a fact; the text is going to lead a life of its own, for whenever a reader grants it an adequate reading it will come alive and become operative and it usually survives its maker. Whereas the creation of a text is finite, finished after hours, years or centuries, its re-creation is infinite. It is a task for each new age, each new generation, each new reader, never to be considered complete.[10]

Frankly, I must admit to misgivings about some exercises in rhetorical criticism that seem to be purely formal, almost mathematical, and lack a dimension of depth that adds richness to the text. Moreover, some biblical theologians wonder whether this new form of literalism, which disavows interest in historical questions, leads to a docetic view of revelation, if indeed revelation is considered a meaningful term at all. Despite these reservations, one is compelled to agree that the proper starting point methodologically is with the text as given, not with the reconstruction of the prehistory of the text, which, as Fokkelman observes, is usually "an unattainable ideal." Something more is involved, however, than the epistemological problem that the prehistory of the texts is unknowable in any certain sense. What is at stake is the question, to which Hans Frei has directed attention, whether the narrative can be split apart from its meaning (a hermeneutical presupposition inherited from the 18th century) or whether "the story is the meaning," as he puts it.[11] The beginning and end of exegesis is the text itself—not something beyond it. Given this textual basis, excursions beyond the text are appropriate and often illuminating, but, as Amos Wilder has pointed out, one should guard against the "historicist habit of mind" that "may still operate unconsciously to handicap a free encounter with a writing in its final form."[12]

Second, recent studies in oral tradition should make one more cautious about basing a study of the depth dimension of the text on the literary presuppositions that, in the past, have been applied by both source criticism and form criticism (i.e., differences of style and vocabulary, seams

---

9. René Wellek and Austin Warren, *Theory of Literature* (3d ed.; London: Harcourt, Brace & World, 1963).

10. Fokkelman, *Narrative Art in Genesis,* 3–4.

11. Hans Frei, *The Eclipse of Biblical Narrative: A Study in Eighteenth and Nineteenth Century Hermeneutics* (New Haven and London: Yale Univ. Press, 1974).

12. Amos N. Wilder, "Norman Perrin, *What Is Redaction Criticism?*" in *Christology and a Modern Pilgrimage: A Discussion with Norman Perrin* (ed. Hans Dieter Betz; Missoula, Mont.: SBL, 1971) 143.

and inconsistencies, duplications and repetitions). Field studies in oral tradition, to which scholars like R. C. Culley and Burke Long have drawn attention,[13] challenge the view, near and dear to source and form critics, that it is possible to recover *Urtradition* and even an *Urtext* behind the final, written formulation of the Pentateuch as we have received it.

This problem struck me as I was reviewing the work of Martin Noth and Claus Westermann. Careful reading of Noth's study of pentateuchal traditions[14] will disclose that, although he adhered to the literary model of source criticism and could even outdo Wellhausen in refined source analysis, he was somewhat sensitive to the fluid, dynamic character of the transmission of the traditions, based on major themes and their elaboration. This central thrust of Noth's work has not escaped the attention of Westermann, a consistent form critic who has carried Gunkel's work to a logical and brilliant conclusion. Westermann observes that Gunkel "set into relief the importance of the pre-literary history of the individual narrative"—a narrative that had its own life (*Eigenleben*) and that was governed by "laws different from those of a written text." But, he insists that Noth fails to stress the smallest literary units and their respective forms; instead, he concentrates on the major themes of the Israelite tradition that were elaborated and filled out in the course of their transmission.[15]

Almost everyone will admit—even conservative scholars like Umberto Cassuto and Benno Jacob—that ancient traditions have been utilized in the final formulation of the Pentateuch. The debatable question is twofold: (1) whether these traditions were cast into a *fixed* form, and (2) whether we are in a position to recover the *Urform* or *Vorlage*. In the past, scholars have proceeded on the assumption that, as Albert Lord put it in the context of a study of Homeric texts, poets "*did* something to a fixed text or a fixed group of texts," as though they composed "with pen in hand."[16] This *scribal* view of composition does not do justice to the dynamic of oral performance, which involves the role of the narrator, the response of a live audience, and improvisation on traditional materials in various and changing settings. Some of the phenomena that in the past have prompted source- or form-critical analysis, such as repetitions or inconsistencies, may well be the stigmata of oral transmission. Burke Long wisely points out that, in view of the limited knowledge of the sociology of ancient

13. See Burke O. Long, "Recent Field Studies in Oral Literature and Their Bearing on Old Testament Criticism," *VT* 26 (1976) 187–98; he carries forward the discussion of R. C. Culley, "An Approach to the Problem of Oral Tradition," *VT* 13 (1963) 113–25.

14. Noth, *A History of Pentateuchal Traditions*.

15. Claus Westermann, *Genesis* (trans. John J. Scullion; Continental Commentary; 3 vols.; Minneapolis: Augsburg, 1984–86) 1.577. See further my reviews of the German original: *JBL* 91 (1972) 243–45; and *JBL* 96 (1976) 291–94.

16. Albert B. Lord, *The Singer of Tales* (Cambridge: Harvard Univ. Press, 1960) 11; cf. 57.

Israel and the nature of oral composition, one should be cautious about attempting to reconstruct the original wording or *Vorlage* of a text that is available only in its final, written form.[17] I would add a further caveat: since efforts to recover preliterary stages lead us away from the givenness of the text itself into the realm of hypothesis, it is not valid to regard the reconstructed *Urform* as normative for interpretation or as having some superiority to Scripture itself. Whatever excursions into the prehistory of the text are possible or necessary, the beginning and end of interpretation is "a free encounter with a writing in its final form" (Wilder).

A third scholarly movement I mention with some hesitance, for I do not claim to understand it fully or sympathetically, and therefore I shall treat it with an undeserved brevity. Structuralism is an invitation to explore the depth dimension of biblical texts in a new way: not by analytically juxta-posing various levels of tradition and tracing a genetic development to the final composition, but by exploring the subsurface unity, coherence, and even dramatic structure at "deep levels" of language that generate the text as it is heard or read. In the view of one of the advocates of this method, Hugh White, it is structural exegesis that lies beyond form criticism and beyond redaction criticism; for one cannot adequately account for the "artistic power" of the narrative art in the received text by understanding the text as a function of an ancient *Sitz im Leben,* whether social or cultic, nor can "the large contours of the narrative" be simply the product of "a more or less insensitive redactor of relatively fixed traditional materials." In his judgment, "the enormous role played by the narrator of ancient tales in the formation of the structure and texture of the form of literature" (as emphasized by Lord, Culley, Long, et al.) calls for a method that enables one to penetrate and to articulate the deep linguistic and dramatic structure that is implicit in the narrative.[18] Whatever more should be said about structuralism, at least this deserves attention: in contrast to analytic methods of the past, this method attempts to grasp wholes or totalities (*l'attitude totalisante*).

PAST ANALYSIS OF THE FLOOD STORY

Thus various impulses have moved scholarship away from an excessive preoccupation with the genetic development of the text to exegesis that takes with greater seriousness the style and structure of the received texts and that considers how these texts function in their narrative contexts. In a previous essay on the creation story,[19] I tried to show that form and con-

---

17. Long, *VT* 26 (1976) 194-98.

18. Hugh C. White, "Structural Analysis of Old Testament Narrative," unpublished manu-script (Sept. 1975) 5.

19. See chap. 3 above.

tent are so inseparably related that attempts to separate out traditions (*Tatbericht* and *Wortbericht*) are not successful. That endeavor was facilitated by the general recognition that the story in its present form is homogeneous (P). Now, however, I turn to a pericope, the flood story, about which there is just as great scholarly agreement, only in this case it is agreed that the text is composite (a combination of J and P).

In past analysis of the flood story, scholars have pointed to various evidences for the disunity of the story in its present form. (1) Some passages prefer the divine name Yahweh, others Elohim (e.g., 6:13 and 7:1). (2) There are irregularities and inconsistencies: (a) some passages speak about a downpour (*gešem*) lasting forty days and forty nights (7:4, 12, 17a), others of a cosmic deluge (*mabbûl*) whose waters maintained their crest for 150 days (7:11, 24); (b) some passages distinguish between clean and unclean animals—seven pairs of the former and a pair of the latter (7:2-3), while others speak only of the pairing of every kind of animal (6:19-20). (3) There are instances of parallel or duplicate passages; for example, the command to enter the ark (6:18b-20) seems to be paralleled in 7:1-3, and the execution of the command (7:5, 7-9) is paralleled in 7:13-16a. (4) Peculiarities of style and vocabulary suggest that the story is not of one piece (see the standard commentaries). In his commentary on Genesis, Gunkel declared that the analysis of the story into separate sources, J and P, is "a masterpiece of modern criticism." According to him, the redactor had at hand two full and distinct versions of the flood story, quite similar in structure and sequence. "The redactor," he averred, "attempted to preserve both accounts as much as possible" and allowed no "kernel" *(Körnlein)* to be lost, especially from the Priestly version that this editor highly esteemed.[20]

Since Gunkel's time, there has been a broad consensus regarding this scribal view of the composition of the flood story. Commentators have agreed that the first step is to separate analytically the two component parts and to comment on each independently, although—like Gunkel—giving only short shrift to the artistic work presented in the whole, that is, the accomplishment of the editor or "redactor." For example, in the introduction to his commentary von Rad draws attention to Franz Rosenzweig's observation that the underrated siglum "R" (redactor) should be understood to mean *Rabbenu,* "our master," because it is from these hands that we have received the scriptural tradition as a finished product. In this context, however, von Rad jumps immediately to the question of what it means in the Christian community to receive the Old Testament "from the hands of Jesus Christ," *Rabbenu.*[21] True, von Rad stresses the overall

20. Hermann Gunkel, *Genesis* (HKAT; 3d ed.; Göttingen: Vandenhoeck & Ruprecht, 1910) 137. See his brief treatment of the redactor, 139–40.
21. Von Rad, *Genesis,* 42–43.

thematic unity of the Hexateuch in which the themes of the early Israelite credo are elaborated; but in exegetical practice he does not reflect on the final shape of the pentateuchal (hexateuchal) tradition. Hence, in his exegesis of the flood story he comments separately on the isolated J and P versions and even resorts to textual rearrangement to restore the putative original texts.

It is noteworthy that E. A. Speiser, a Jewish scholar who accepts the view that "the received biblical account of the Flood is beyond reasonable doubt a composite narrative, reflecting more than one separate source," admits to misgivings about "reshuffling the text" in violation of "a tradition that antedates the LXX translation of twenty-two centuries ago."[22] Without following up on the possible implications of this caveat, however, he settles for translating the received text with slash marks to indicate J and P sources. But Speiser's initial caveat is important. At least since the time of the LXX translation the flood story has functioned in its present form in Judaism and Christianity, rather than in separable traditions lying behind the text. Indeed, it is in this form that the story continues to make its impact upon the reader today.

Although operating within the scholarly consensus of the twentieth century, these scholars seem to raise questions about the relative priority of a genetic versus a synthetic, a diachronic versus a synchronic, approach to the task of exegesis. In his massive commentary on the *Urgeschichte*, Westermann also addresses himself to this issue:

> When commentators exegete the flood narratives of J and P separately, as they generally do, there is danger that justice will not be done to the individual narrative form as it has come down to us. One cannot avoid the fact that R's composite narrative has something important of its own to say, and that the scope of its effect [*Wirkungsgeschichte*] belongs neither to J nor to P but to R.[23]

In exegetical practice Westermann juxtaposes J and P and at times relocates verses for the sake of emphasizing the separate identity of the two sources. This reflects his view that the unity of the flood story lies primarily in a prehistory of tradition that is refracted separately in the two sources. At the conclusion of his commentary, however, he devotes a couple of paragraphs to the work of the redactor, whose intention, he maintains, was to preserve the *Mehrstimmigkeit* of the tradition—a musical figure suggesting a polyphonic performance in which each voice sings its own part according to fixed texts. "R created out of these [i.e., J and P] a new, coherent and self-contained narrative" in which the separate voices of J, P,

---

22. E. A. Speiser, *Genesis* (AB; 2d ed.; Garden City, N.Y.: Doubleday, 1964) 54.
23. Westermann, *Genesis,* 1.431.

and R are heard; and this was possible because all three shared the same "basic attitude to reality and event."[24]

Westermann's commentary is a laudable witness to the need to go beyond analysis of separate sources to interpretive synthesis, to grasping the text as a whole. Even in this endeavor, however, he falls into the genetic fallacy of the past in that he posits a unity outside and before the text that, he maintains, one may recover by a phenomenological exposition of the religious consciousness expressed in ancient myths. The creativity of R is evidenced in this editor's ability to combine texts, each of which gives its own variation on the basic mythical datum. The question is whether this view is adequate to account for the final narrative, which, to use Westermann's adjectives, is "new," "coherent," and "self-contained." Similar claims for the final composition have been made by others, for instance, Eduard Nielsen, a representative of the Scandinavian circle. "Our present text," Nielsen observes (speaking of the flood story), "is a work of art, composed of different traditions, it is true, but in such a way that a unified work has been the result."[25] If we are dealing with "a work of art," however, is not the final whole greater than—or at least different from— the sum of its parts? This, it seems to me, is the basic issue. Without denying the legitimacy of excursions into the prehistory of the text in their proper place, the question is whether one can understand and appreciate the present narrative art by a genetic study of its origin and development.

Finally, the symbol R constitutes a special problem.[26] R is a shadowy figure, to whom virtually nothing is attributed except the synthesis of discrete traditions, J and P. Gunkel said precious little about this mystery person in his commentary and, as indicated above, Westermann devotes very brief space to R in the lengthy conclusion to his commentary on the *Urgeschichte*. R is merely a synthetic agent, statements about whom are inferences from the fact that traditions have been reworked or reshaped so as to produce a new totality. My own study of the primeval history has corroborated the judicious proposal of Frank Cross that P and R should be merged into one. While accepting the broad results of source criticism, Cross observes that "the Flood story has been completely rewritten by P. . . . The interweaving of the sources is not the work of a redactor juxtaposing blocks of materials, but that of a tradent reworking and supplementing a traditional story."[27]

24. Ibid., 600.

25. Eduard Nielsen, *Oral Tradition* (SBT 1/11; London: SCM, 1954) 102. For his criticism of source analysis of the flood story, see pp. 93–103.

26. This has already been observed by Samuel Sandmel in "The Haggada Within Scripture," in *Old Testament Issues* (ed. S. Sandmel; New York: Harper & Row, 1968) 94–118, esp. 97–98; repr. from *JBL* 80 (1961) 105–22.

27. Frank M. Cross, "The Priestly Work," in *Canaanite Myth and Hebrew Epic* (Cambridge: Harvard Univ. Press, 1973) 303. See also Sandmel, "The Haggada Within Scripture," 106.

This tantalizingly brief reference to the flood story contains implications that may lead beyond the rather artificial source analysis of the past. This story is not a mere combination of discrete texts (J juxtaposed to P and conflated by R), according to the usual understanding; rather, it is a story from the Priestly circle into which one or more "tradents" (carriers of tradition) have incorporated Old Epic material. The Priestly version is a reworking and recasting of the story, not just a preservation of past tradition in their polyphonic character *(Mehrstimmigkeit)*. The re-presentation of the flood story in this elaborated and expanded form is a work of art in its own right and deserves to be considered in the form in which it is given. We must admit our ignorance about the circumstances of the composition. Was the story the scribal result of retelling in situations of performance? Was it the result of purely literary activity in the time of the exile? There is much that we do not know. But the important point is that, whatever the history of transmission or whatever the immediate occasion of final composition, the Priestly tradents shaped the story to produce a dramatic effect as a totality.

DRAMATIC MOVEMENT OF THE FLOOD STORY

I turn now to the flood story itself and the structural and stylistic features that make it a dramatic unity in its present form.

In an important monograph on the Priestly work, Sean McEvenue shows that Priestly narrative style, far from being pedantic and unartistic, displays rhetorical and structural features that are characteristic of narrative art generally, such as a sequence of panels in which formulaic patterns are repeated. (He uses the homely example of the story of "The Little Red Hen."[28]) With specific regard to the flood story, he maintains that in the P version the narrative builds up dramatically to the turning point reached in 8:1a: "However, God remembered Noah and all the wild and tame animals that were with him in the ark." The narrative, as he puts it, "swells toward the climax" and, after the turning point is reached, moves "toward repose."[29] His stylistic study, one should note, is based exclusively on the juxtaposition of J and P components of the story. He maintains that P was "writing from a Yahwist narrative, which he either knew by heart or had in front of him"; and he aims to understand the divergences of P from J— divergences that are all the more striking since "P has stuck so closely to

28. Sean E. McEvenue, *The Narrative Style of the Priestly Writer* (AnBib 50; Rome: Biblical Institute, 1971) 1–21. See further Joseph Blenkinsopp, "The Structure of P," *CBQ* 38 (1976) 275–92.

29. McEvenue, *Narrative Style,* 36.

his source."[30] McEvenue, however, does not take the step that I am advocating and that is implicit in his own view that P reworked J tradition, namely, to consider the narrative as a totality in which the Priestly tradents have absorbed into a new composition elements of Old Epic tradition.

Since the story in its final form has been shaped by the Priestly tradents, McEvenue's observation about the dramatic movement of the P narrative applies also to the story as a whole—as people read it today. Indeed, it is not surprising that Umberto Cassuto, who rejects source analysis,[31] makes a similar observation. According to Cassuto, the story is organized into a series of "paragraphs" that move in crescendo toward a climax as the rising waters of chaos lift up the ark on the crest and then, after the turning point in 8:1 ("God remembered Noah"), falls away in decrescendo as the waters of chaos ebb and there is the beginning of a new creation. Of the twelve paragraphs that constitute the story, according to his division, he writes:

> The first group depicts for us, step by step, the acts of Divine justice that bring destruction upon the earth, which had become filled with violence; and the scenes that pass before us grow increasingly gloomier until in the darkness of death portrayed in the sixth paragraph there remains only one tiny, faint point of light, to wit, the ark, which floats on the fearful waters that have covered everything, and which guards between its walls the hope of future life. The second group shows us consecutively the various stages of the Divine compassion that renews life upon earth. The light that waned until it became a minute point in the midst of a dark world, begins to grow bigger and brighter till it illumines again the entire scene before us, and shows us a calm and peaceful world, crowned with the rainbow that irradiates the cloud with its colours—a sign and pledge of life and peace for the coming generations.[32]

Readers who submit to the text of the story in its present form find themselves caught up in this rising and falling movement, corresponding to the ebb and flow of the waters of chaos. At the climax, God's remembrance of Noah and the remnant anticipates the conclusion, where God promises to remember the "everlasting covenant" that signals the beginning of a new humanity and, indeed, a new creation, paralleling the original creation portrayed in Genesis 1. In short, the flood narrative in its present form is composed of a sequence of episodic units, each of which has an essential function in the dramatic movement of the whole. The story as a totality deserves attention.

---

30. Ibid., 27. McEvenue adopts as a working basis Karl Elliger's delimitation of P set forth in Elliger's "Sinn und Ursprung der priesterlichen Geschichtserzählung," *ZTK* 49 (1952) 121–42, esp. 121–22.

31. See Umberto Cassuto, *The Documentary Hypothesis* (trans. Israel Abrahams; Jerusalem: Magnes, Hebrew University, 1961).

32. Cassuto, *Commentary on Genesis* (trans. Israel Abrahams; 2 vols.; Jerusalem: Magnes, Hebrew University 1961–64) 2.30–31.

To begin with, notice the immediate context in which the story is placed, namely, the genealogical outline followed by the Priestly tradents. Between 6:1 and 9:27 is a long block of narrative material dealing with Noah's lifetime that has been inserted into the heart of Noah's genealogy as presented in the *tôlĕdôt* document (5:1). In this document the genealogies follow a fixed lineal, rather than ramified, pattern: (a) N lived x years, (b) and he fathered S; (c) after the birth of S, N lived y years; (d) he fathered sons and daughters; (e) the lifetime of N was z years; and (f) then he died. Now, the first two elements of Noah's genealogy (a and b) are found in 5:32, right at the end of a series of excerpts from the *tôlĕdôt* document, namely, (a) Noah lived five hundred years, and (b) he fathered Shem, Ham, and Japheth. The conclusion of the genealogy comes in 9:28-29, although the pattern is modified to refer to the flood, the principal event in Noah's lifetime: (c) After the flood Noah lived 350 years; (d) . . . ; (e) the lifetime of Noah was 950 years; and (f) then he died. Whether the Noachic entry in the *tôlĕdôt* document once contained a brief reference to the flood, on the analogy of some editions of the Sumerian King List,[33] is uncertain. In any case, the narrative material extending from the episodes that deal with the promiscuity of the celestial beings (6:1-4) and the "sorrow of Yahweh" (6:5-8) to the postdiluvian story of Noah's intoxication and the condemnation of Canaan (9:20-27) is encased within the genealogical frame. According to this sequence, the initial epic material constitutes the prologue to the flood, or as Speiser phrases it, "Prelude to Disaster," and the subsequent material, dealing with Noah's postdiluvian situation, is an epilogue.

The Priestly drama proper begins with the transitional passage concerning the *ṣaddîq,* Noah and his three sons, which is formulated in the style of the *tôlĕdôt* document (6:9-10). At the end of the Priestly story is another transitional passage (9:18-19) that both recapitulates previous elements and prepares for the sequel by saying that the sons of Noah who went forth from the ark were Shem, Ham, and Japheth, and that from them the whole earth was repopulated.[34] In between these boundaries the drama of the

---

33. See the translation by A. Leo Oppenheim, *ANET,* 265–66.

34. These verses are usually assigned to J, mainly because P has already mentioned Noah's sons by name (6:10; 7:13) and a third mention seems too repetitious. Also, the "scattering" verb (*nāpĕṣâ*) is found in other passages that must be assigned to J. Westermann (*Genesis,* 1.486) quotes with approval Gunkel's dictum: "The expression has its setting *[Sitz]* in the story of the building of the tower." But these arguments are questionable. The argument based on repetition is not strong when dealing with Priestly material; and there is no reason why the Priestly tradent could not have used the "scattering" verb, one that is prominent in his approximate contemporary, Ezekiel. Furthermore, the participial expression "those who went forth *[hayyôṣĕ'îm]* from the ark" (9:18) corresponds to the same formulation in the preceding Priestly material (9:10: *yôṣĕ'ê hattēbâ*). In any case, the passage now has a transitional function in the overall narrative.

flood unfolds in a succession of episodic units, each of which has a definite function in relation to the whole. I follow the sequence as it is given, at the expense of paying closer attention to details.

1. The keynote is struck in 6:11-12: violence and corruption in the earth—first announced as an objective fact (v. 11) and then reiterated in terms of God's perception (v. 12). These verses display noteworthy stylistic features, such as the emphasis achieved through repetition, the play upon the verbal root *šāḥat* in three variations ("become corrupt," "spoil," "ruin"), and the climactic use of the particle *kî* ("for") to provide explanation (v. 12b). The discordant note struck at the beginning is resolved at the end with the restoration of harmony and peace in God's creation (9:1-17).

2. The main action of the drama begins in 6:13-22, introduced by the declarative formula "Then God said." God's first address, in good Priestly narrative style, is structured according to a twofold announcement-command sequence: announcement of God's resolution to destroy (6:13), followed by the command to build the ark (vv. 14-16); repeated announcement of the imminence of the *mabbûl* waters (vv. 17-18), followed by a command that deals mainly with laying away supplies of food for those to be saved (vv. 19-21). This passage concludes with the execution formula: "Noah did this. Just as Elohim commanded him, so he acted" (6:22).

3. The divine command to load the ark with its passengers is the subject of the next unit in 7:1-10, usually ascribed to J (except for the chronological notation in v. 6). Strikingly, the second divine address is introduced by the declarative formula "then *Yahweh* said." Also, the execution of the command is indicated in the formula "Noah did just as Yahweh commanded him" (7:5), though the unit concludes (7:9): "just as Elohim commanded him." It is clear in my judgment that in this passage the Priestly tradents have drawn upon and reworked Old Epic tradition whose peculiarities are evident in various matters of content (for instance, seven pairs of clean animals and a pair that is not clean, 7:2-3; but cf. 7:8-9), and in turns of speech (e.g., "a male and his mate" rather than "male and female," 7:2; but cf. 7:9).[35] But the question is whether these phenomena, which we perceive as inconsistencies, actually disturb the structure and movement of the narrative in its final form.[36] I do not see that this is the case. On the contrary, this unit, which is also formulated in a command-

---

35. See the commentaries for a treatment of words and phrases characteristic of J and P. It is noteworthy that the execution passage (7:7-9) states that the animals, clean and unclean, went into the ark by pairs, "two and two." The Priestly tradent, who reworked the Old Epic tradition, may have been concerned at this point with the sexual pairing of the animals, not the total number of clean and unclean.

36. George Coats asks the same question in his study of the Joseph Story, *From Canaan to Egypt: Structural and Theological Context for the Joseph Story* (CBQMS 4; Washington, D.C.: Catholic Biblical Association, 1976) 57.

execution sequence, advances the motion of the previous unit by showing that the disaster is at hand, only seven days away, and therefore it is time to get on board the ark. In spite of modern views based on alternation in the usage of divine names in the book of Genesis, the Priestly tradents seem to have had no compunction about using both names, Yahweh and Elohim, in their reworking of the pre-Mosaic traditions.[37]

4. The two divine addresses are followed by a unit found in 7:11-16 that source critics have credited to the Priestly tradition, except for the statement about the forty-day downpour (*gešem*) in 7:12 and the brief anthropomorphic touch in 7:16b, "Yahweh closed him inside." This unit clearly involves repetition, for it resumes and summarizes the earlier narrative, beginning with the point reached in 7:10 of the previous episode ("At the end of seven days the waters of the flood were upon the earth") and harking back to the command regarding the saving of animals and humans, anticipated in 6:18b-21 and definitely mandated and executed in 7:1-10. The new element in the dramatic movement of the story is the announcement of the manner in which "the waters of the flood" came upon the earth (vv. 11-12). The Priestly tradents clearly sought to rework the received tradition of a violent forty-day rainstorm into their conception of the *mabbûl* as a cosmic catastrophe that threatened the earth with a return to primeval chaos. The chief function of this unit, however, is to indicate the inception of disaster, and this provides the opportunity to rehearse once again the number of those whom God commanded to be saved in 7:13-16a, a passage that harks back to the priestly command passage in 6:18b-21 by way of resumption and inclusion.

The recapitulation of the divine command is indicated once again by the obedience formula: "just as Elohim had commanded him" (7:16a). This is followed by the celebrated sentence, "Then Yahweh closed him inside." This sentence is usually regarded as a fragment of the J epic because of the usage of the name Yahweh and the anthropomorphism implicit in God's action, which some scholars allege is out of keeping with Priestly tradition. But this brief sentence—a snippet of only three Hebrew words (*wayyisgōr YHWH ba'ǎdô*) in a predominantly P context—calls into question the analytical procedure of the past. How does this notice function in the received text? Coming after the summarizing recapitulation of the divine command to enter the ark and its execution, these words serve as a final punctuation of the unit and at the same time anticipate what follows: God's "remembrance" of those who were sealed in the ark.

---

37. Arguments based on the alternation of divine names in Genesis, which appeal to Exod. 6:2-3 for support, perhaps need to be reexamined. It is noteworthy that the Priestly tradent clearly uses the divine name Yahweh in Gen. 17:1 ("Yahweh appeared to Abram, and said to him, 'I am El Shaddai'"); and he even uses the compound "Yahweh Elohim" in the paradise story (e.g., 3:1, 13).

Thus one can argue that anthropomorphism is stressed in the Priestly recension (cf. Exod. 2:24-25). 5. The storm is now raging, as indicated in the next unit, 7:17-24. This unit is framed within two chronological statements, the first (7:17) stating that the *mabbûl* innundated the earth for forty days (apparently the Priestly tradents' reinterpretation of the epic tradition [7:4] to mean the time required for the ark to be buoyed on the waters), and the last (7:24) giving the total duration of the cresting waters, that is, 40 + 110 = 150 days. The swelling of the waters is vividly portrayed by the repeated use of the words "the waters prevailed" to create an ascending effect.

> *wayyigbĕrû hammāyim* (v. 18)
> *wĕhammāyim gābĕrû* (v. 19)
> *gābĕrû hammāyim* (v. 20)

Source critics find traces of Old Epic tradition (J) in vv. 22-23, largely because these verses seem to repeat the content of v. 21, "All flesh died that moved upon the earth." But in the reworking of the tradition, the repetition serves to heighten the dramatic contrast between the perishing of "every human" (v. 21) and the climactic statement, "Only Noah was left [the verb suggests the 'remnant'], and those that were with him in the ark" (7:23b).[38] Thus the narrative swells to a climax, with the ark and its precious remnant tossed on the waters of chaos. "We see water everywhere," Cassuto comments, "as though the world had reverted to its primeval state at the dawn of Creation, when the waters of the deep submerged everything."[39]

6. The next unit, 8:1-5, brings us to the turning point of the story with the dramatic announcement of God's remembrance of Noah and the remnant with him in the ark. The statement "God caused a wind to blow over the earth," which recalls the "wind from God" (*rûaḥ 'ĕlōhîm*) of 1:2, introduces by way of contrast the theme of the new creation, which becomes explicit in 9:1-17, where the *imago Dei* reappears. Source critics attribute this passage to P, with the exception of the notice about the restraining of the downpour (*gešem*) from the sky (8:2b). This traditional element, however, should not be separated out, for the Priestly tradents, as already mentioned, have absorbed the forty-day rainstorm into their view of a cosmic deluge and into their chronology. The effect of the text at this point is to show dramatically that when all seems to be lost, from a human point of view, God's faithfulness makes possible a new beginning.

7. The decrescendo from the climax is effectively carried out in the text unit, 8:6-14. The first part, the vignette about the release of the birds (8:6-

---

38. See Martin Kessler, "Rhetorical Criticism of Genesis 7," in *Rhetorical Criticism*, 1–17.
39. Cassuto, *Genesis*, 2.97.

12), is derived from Old Epic tradition (J). This material, however, should not be detached from its present context, for it now has a definite narrative function, namely, to portray the gradual ebbing of the waters from their crest and the emergence of dry land, as at the time of creation (cf. 1:9-12). The dramatic action is retarded and extended over a span of time so that the hearer or reader may sense in Noah's experiment with the birds (including his tender treatment of the dove, vv. 8-9) the wonder of what was taking place. The unit concludes by dating the emergence of dry land, and therefore the possibility of the earth's renewed fertility, in relation to the New Year, which was also the 601st anniversary of Noah's birth. This wonderful event is indicated in two ways (as in 6:11-12): one in terms of Noah's perception (8:13b) and the other as an objective fact (8:14)— sentences that source critics attribute to J and P, respectively.

8. After the drama of the rising and the falling of the waters, the story returns to a scheme of divine addresses, as at the beginning. Notice that the address in 8:15-19, which is attributed to Priestly tradition, is also structured in a command-execution sequence. In this case, the theme is God's command to leave the ark (vv. 16-17), accompanied by a special word that the animals should swarm, be fertile, and increase on the earth, and the fulfillment of that command (vv. 18-19).

9. Next comes a unit, 8:20-22, dealing with Noah's sacrifice and Yahweh's resolution never again to engage in wholesale destruction but, rather, to maintain the regularities and rhythms on which earthly existence depends. It is true that this episodic unit, derived from Old Epic tradition, harks back to the passage about the "sorrow of Yahweh" (6:5-8) and forms an inclusion with it.[40] The episode, however, has an important function in its present narrative context. On the one hand, it provides the appropriate sequel to disembarking from the ark, namely, a human act of praise; on the other hand, the divine response to the sacrifice (i.e., Yahweh's resolution) serves as a transition to the final Priestly discourse that elaborates God's pledge in the theological perspective intended to govern the whole story.

10. The final unit, 9:1-17, is also cast in the form of a divine address, though this one is articulated in three parts, each marked by the declarative formula "Then God said" or variations of it (9:1, 8, 12). In the fourth address the narrators round off the story by re-sounding tones that were heard earlier. God's promise to establish his covenant with Noah (6:18a) is fulfilled in the "everlasting covenant" (*bĕrît 'ôlām*)—a covenant that is made, however, not just with Noah but with "every living creature of all flesh that is upon the earth" (9:8-11). God's remembrance of Noah and the remnant in the ark (8:1a) is consummated in God's pledge to "remember" his covenant, whose visible sign is the rainbow (9:12-17). Above all, the

40. See McEvenue, *Narrative Style,* 28.

initial discordant note—violence in God's creation (6:11-12)—is resolved into the harmony of a new creation, as shown by the renewal of the blessing given at the original creation (9:1: "Be fertile, multiply, and fill the earth"), by a restatement of the role of human beings, who are made in the image of God (9:6), and by the Creator's pledge, based unconditionally on divine faithfulness, that the earth will not be threatened by a return to precreation chaos.

THE OVERALL DESIGN OF THE FLOOD STORY

Thus the present flood story, in which the Priestly tradents have incorporated Old Epic tradition into their narrative, discloses an overall design, a dramatic movement in which each episodic unit has an essential function. McEvenue attempted to demonstrate that the story displays a chiastic structure—or, as he prefers to put it, "a rough palistrophe."[41] He would have had more success in tracing a symmetrical design had he not restricted his attention to the analysis of P, regarded as a discrete document, and had he concentrated instead on the total Priestly revision of the tradition. It is indeed striking that the story in its final form flows in a sequence of units toward a turning point and then follows the same sequence in reverse, as the following outline indicates:

Transitional introduction (6:9-10)
   1. Violence in God's creation (6:11-12)
     2. First divine address: resolution to destroy (6:13-22)
       3. Second divine address: command to enter the ark (7:1-10)
         4. Beginning of the flood (7:11-16)
           5. The rising flood waters (7:17-24)
           GOD'S REMEMBRANCE OF NOAH
           6. The receding flood waters (8:1-5)
         7. The drying of the earth (8:6-14)
       8. Third divine address: command to leave the ark (8:15-19)
     9. God's resolution to preserve order (8:20-22)
   10. Fourth divine address: covenant blessing and peace (9:1-17)
Transitional conclusion (9:18-19)

The first part of the story represents a movement toward chaos, with the hero Noah and the remnant with him as survivors of the catastrophe. The second part represents a movement toward the new creation, with Noah

41. Ibid., 31.

and his sons as the representatives of the new humankind who were to inherit the earth.

As I see it, one need not try to harmonize the flood story by denying the irregularities and inconsistencies that source analysis has sought to understand in its own way and according to its presuppositions. The question is whether one is to be bound exclusively or even primarily by this analytical method. Source analysis requires one to *begin* by analyzing and juxtaposing "sources" or "levels of tradition." The assumption is that by charting the genesis of the text one can best understand the text itself, which is regarded as a conflation of discrete, identifiable traditions, loosely joined together by a redactor. An alternative method, however, is to begin by examining the structural unity of the story received from the Priestly tradents, actually *Rabbenu* (to recall once again the remark of Rosenzweig). In this case, the first priority would be to understand the text in its received form and to consider what George Coats has termed its "functional unity";[42] and after that one would turn—as the second priority—to an investigation of the prehistory of the text, hoping to find further light in the richness and dynamic of the received text. In regard to the flood story, this set of priorities is dictated by at least two considerations. First, the Priestly tradents have absorbed the Old Epic tradition into a new presentation, though under circumstances that are not as yet clear; second, the result of this reinterpretation of the tradition is not a literary patchwork but a story whose overall design and dramatic movement make it a work of art, one that even yet stirs and involves the hearer or reader.

It is not enough, however, to consider the dramatic unity of the story by itself, in isolation. To understand the story theologically, it is equally important to consider how this story functions in its present context in the book of Genesis and specifically within the *tôlĕdôt* scheme used by the Priestly tradents to organize the primeval history. When the Priestly revision of the story is regarded as a separate pericope, the *ḥāmās* ("violence," "lawlessness") that prompted God's resolve to bring the flood hangs in the air (6:11, 13), and the prohibition against murder in 9:6 is unmotivated. "P's summary statement referring to violence and corruption," Frank Cross observes, "must presume a knowledge of concrete and colorful narratives of the corruption of the creation. Otherwise, it has neither literary nor theological force."[43] By appropriating the Old Epic tradition, the Priestly tradents have provided a vivid portrayal of the disorder rooted primarily in creaturely freedom, as illustrated in the stories of primeval rebellion in the

42. Coats, *From Canaan to Egypt*, 7–8.
43. Cross, *Canaanite Myth and Hebrew Epic*, 306.

garden, fratricide in the first family, Lamech's measureless revenge, and the marriage of celestial beings with human daughters.[44] Thus the *Urgeschichte* in its final form displays an overall design: a dramatic movement from the original harmony of creation, through the violent disruption of that order and the near return to chaos, and finally to a new creation under the rainbow sign of the everlasting covenant.

---

44. See Paul D. Hanson, "Rebellion in Heaven, Azazel, and Euhemeristic Heroes in 1 Enoch 6–11," *JBL* 96 (1977) 195–233, who points out that in Old Epic tradition (J) the mythic fragment in 6:1-4 serves to illustrate the degeneration of humankind and specifically to highlight two related themes: "the divinely ordained separation of heaven and earth as two distinct realms, and the enforcement of distinct limits upon the human race" (p. 214). The Priestly tradents clearly saw in this enigmatic episode the final evidence of "violence" and "corruption" in God's creation.

CHAPTER 5

Mythopoeic and Theological
Dimensions of
Biblical Creation Faith

The exposition of biblical creation theology in the twentieth century has been profoundly affected by two dramatic publication events that occurred in the mid-nineteenth century, indeed within a few years of each other. The first event was the publication in 1859 of Charles R. Darwin's great work, *The Origin of Species*. The reverberations of this event have continued well into the twentieth century, as evident from the lawsuit (1982) over an Arkansas law permitting the teaching of "creationism" in public schools.[1] The second event was the discovery in 1853 of the library of Ashurbanipal, the last great king of the Assyrian empire, at the site of ancient Nineveh (Kuyunjik, near Mosul, Iraq). The impact of this early venture in archaeology was like a delayed time bomb. It was not until some twenty years later that George Smith, a young Assyriologist employed as an assistant in the British Museum, came to realize that the library contained documents that relate to the biblical primeval history, including a creation story that he published in 1876 under the title *The Chaldean Account of Genesis*. This report fired an archaeological shot heard around the world, owing to the enterprising journalism of *The Daily Telegraph*.[2] The reverberations of this event have also been felt during the twentieth century, thanks especially to the monumental book on creation

---

1. See the various essays in *Is God a Creationist? Religious Arguments against Creation-Science* (ed. Roland M. Frye; New York: Charles Scribner's Sons, 1983).

2. The story is told, for instance, in Reginald C. Thompson, *A Century of Exploration at Nineveh* (London: Lusac, 1929) 46–51.

and chaos by Hermann Gunkel, published in 1895 under the title *Schöpfung und Chaos in Urzeit und Endzeit*.[3]

Before these events the account of creation, as formulated classically in the Genesis creation story (1:1—2:3), was generally accepted as both "gospel truth" and sober fact. The challenge to the traditional belief came from two sides: from the modern scientific worldview and from the history of religions. One may regard the history of biblical creation theology in the twentieth century as a response to this pincer movement, whether in defensiveness, accommodation, or retrenchment.

After decades of discussion the controversy is far from settled. The distinguished American theologian Langdon Gilkey, who composed a major work on creation theology[4] and who was drawn into the Arkansas lawsuit as an "expert witness," has helped to clarify that the fundamental issue is the relation between scientific truth and religious truth and their respective modes of apprehension. Reflecting on the Arkansas court case, he observes that there is not only a powerful religious fundamentalism entrenched in parts of the United States but also "there is another kind of fundamentalism manifested by scientists—including some on both sides of the issue argued in Little Rock."[5]

Perhaps the time has come when the issues may be seen in a clarifying light. Today many scientists are aware of the boundaries of natural science and are not inclined to hold that the scientific method is the only approach to the truth. Moreover, the history of religions has opened up mythopoeic dimensions of Scripture that enhance our theological understanding. As already observed, it was Gunkel who, after the sensational publicity had subsided, pursued the biblical implications of the archaeological discovery at the site of ancient Nineveh. His seminal book on creation and chaos carried a subtitle that characterized the study as a "history-of-religions investigation," extending from Genesis 1 to Revelation 12. He believed that the Babylonian creation account, with its characteristic theme of the *Chaoskampf*, the battle between the creator god and the powers of chaos, was the source of the mythopoeic imagery found in Scripture.

When Gunkel looked at the Babylonian materials, he perceived only the tip of an iceberg. Since his time, the discovery of other materials, such

---

3. Hermann Gunkel, *Schöpfung und Chaos in Urzeit und Endzeit* (Göttingen: Vandenhoeck & Ruprecht, 1895); abridged translation by Charles A. Muenchow in *Creation in the Old Testament* (ed. Bernhard W. Anderson; IRT 6; Philadelphia: Fortress Press, 1984) 1–24. I picked up some of the theological reverberations in my book, *Creation versus Chaos: The Reinterpretation of Mythical Symbolism in the Bible* (New York: Association, 1967; repr. Philadelphia: Fortress Press, 1987).

4. Langdon Gilkey, *Maker of Heaven and Earth* (Garden City, N.Y.: Doubleday, 1959).

5. Langdon Gilkey, "Creationism: The Roots of the Conflict," *Christianity & Crisis* 42 (1982) 108–15, quotation, 108; repr. in *Is God a Creationist?* 56–67.

as the Ugaritic mythological literature in the 1920s, has widened our horizons. No longer can one view the Bible solely from a Babylonian perspective, for the *Chaoskampf* is a more ubiquitous motif, indeed one that is not only ancient Near Eastern in the broad sense but also touches the depths of a mythical apprehension of reality found in "archaic" societies, as Mircea Eliade and others have shown.[6] Nevertheless, Gunkel's book has proved to be a major breakthrough in theological understanding. For by inviting people to read biblical texts in the light of the mythopoeic language of the ancient world, it has introduced a linguistic revolution in our understanding of how biblical language—even cosmological language—functions in various circles of tradition and in particular biblical contexts.

The myth of the *Chaoskampf* is cosmological in the sense that it portrays the origin and ordering of the world in which people live and move and have their being. Yet the "truth" that is apprehended and expressed in mythopoeic language is of a different order than the speculative thought that has dominated Western civilization. This point was made in an important book that appeared in 1946 under the title *The Intellectual Adventure of Ancient Man:*

> Myth is a form of poetry which transcends poetry in that it proclaims a truth; a form of reasoning which transcends reasoning in that it wants to bring about the truth it proclaims; a form of action, of ritual behavior, which does not find its fulfilment in act but must proclaim and elaborate a poetic form of truth.[7]

Insofar as biblical creation texts have been cast in, or influenced by, mythopoeic language, as Gunkel rightly demonstrated, the interpreter must take two matters seriously. First, one must give due regard to the poetic character of biblical language, and that demands a refusal to let traditional doctrinal or philosophical considerations dictate the way questions are raised. Second, one must consider the way the biblical language functions in its given literary contexts or circles of tradition, and that requires refusing to "use" the Bible by appealing to isolated texts in support of positions arrived at on other grounds. When these two things—poetic form and literary function—guide interpretation, one can see that biblical creation faith has various theological dimensions, though not all need be present at one time or in one text. The task of the biblical theologian is to differentiate these theological dimensions, to notice how one or another facet

---

6. See, for instance, Mircea Eliade, *Cosmos and History: The Myth of the Eternal Return* (New York: Harper & Row, 1959); also Raffaele Pettazoni, "Myths of Beginnings and Creation Myths," *Proceedings of the Seventh Congress for the History of Religions* (1951) 67–78.

7. H. and H. A. Frankfort et al., *The Intellectual Adventure of Ancient Man* (Chicago: University of Chicago Press, 1946) 8; repr. as *Before Philosophy* (Baltimore: Penguin, 1973) 16.

receives special attention in a particular circle or stream of tradition, and finally to perceive how they are all interrelated in the final canonical Scriptures.

MOSAIC TRADITION: THE CREATION OF A PEOPLE

I begin, insofar as possible, with the earliest, and undoubtedly the fundamental, stage of Israelite tradition: the period before the monarchy. In past decades scholars carried on a lively debate over the question as to whether Yahweh was originally a creator deity.[8] The debate was touched off in 1924 when W. F. Albright, picking up suggestions made earlier by Paul Haupt, proposed that the divine name "Yahweh" was originally a causative verb form meaning "he causes to be," and that the formula in Exod. 3:14 means "he causes to be what comes into existence." Albright maintained that the divine name, whether invoked in the Mosaic period or in the period of the ancestors of Israel, was part of a liturgical formula (such as *yahweh 'ăšer yihweh* or *yahweh sĕbā' ôt*), in which the ancestral god was praised as creator of the cosmos. Frank M. Cross has advanced this discussion, arguing forcefully, on the basis of epigraphic evidence and mythological parallels, that in the earliest tradition Israel's God was "described as *ḏū yahwī saba' ōt*, 'He who creates the (heavenly) armies.'" The title of Israel's God, "the divine warrior and creator," Cross maintains, was "thus not greatly different from 'El's epithets 'Father of the gods,' 'creator of creatures.'"[9]

This is a strong counterargument to those who maintain, under the influence of Gerhard von Rad, that the faith of Israel was originally restricted to Yahweh's historical acts of liberation and that creation in a cosmic sense was peripheral if not absent altogether at first. The argument of Albright and his followers, however, though bringing a burst of light from extrabiblical sources, suffers under the limitation of the etymology of the tetragrammaton. It is worth noting that the context of the cryptic etymological passage Exod. 3:14-15, a singular occurence in the Old Testament, does not deal with cosmic issues at all; there Yahweh is intro-

8. See J. P. Hyatt, "Was Yahweh Originally a Creator Deity?" *JBL* 86 (1967) 369–77.

9. Albright's position is discussed in connection with Frank M. Cross's interpretation in *Canaanite Myth and Hebrew Epic* (Cambridge: Harvard Univ. Press, 1973) 60–75; quotation from 70. On the question of identification of Yahweh with the Semitic deity *'El*, see, inter alia, Frank M. Cross, "Yahweh and the God of the Patriarchs," *HTR* (1962) 250–59; idem, "*'ēl*," *TDOT* 1.242–61; Norman Habel, "Yahweh, Maker of Heaven and Earth," *JBL* 91 (1972) 321–37; Patrick D. Miller, "El, the Creator of Earth," *BASOR* 239 (1980) 43–46.

duced as the liberating God rather than as the creator.[10] Thus one may find a bit firmer ground methodologically by following the lead of Dennis McCarthy and concentrating on references to Yahweh's "creative" actions in early poetic texts.[11] In these texts one may see how Yahweh (whatever the etymology) is identified.

Of all the examples of early Israelite poetry, the Song of the Sea (Exod. 15:1-18) clearly claims the primary attention of those who seek to explore Israel's earliest creation faith. The research of Frank M. Cross and David Noel Freedman has convincingly demonstrated that this poem comes from the premonarchic period of the tribal confederacy and that, in poetic style and in literary structure, it exhibits a striking affinity with Canaanite (Ugaritic) literature. The movement of the poem corresponds to the mythical drama: the Divine Warrior faces adversaries (the power of chaos), moves triumphantly to the sacred mountain (temple), and there is acclaimed as divine king over the cosmos.[12]

This poem clearly employs the cosmological language of the ancient creation myth, the *Chaoskampf*. To be sure, Sea (*yām*) is not the adversary of the Divine Warrior but is only "a passive instrument in Yahweh's control" in the combat against Pharaoh's hosts.[13] Yet the language, as Umberto Cassuto has pointed out, is redolent of the ancient chaos myth, hinting that the victory was regarded "not only as a mighty act of the Lord against Pharaoh and his host, but also as an act of might against the sea, which was compelled to submit to His will." The language was understood in this way, Cassuto observes, in inner-biblical interpretation and in rabbinical exegesis.[14]

The question, however, is how this cosmological language actually functions in its poetic context. There is no suggestion here of creation in a cosmic sense; rather, the emphasis falls on the coming to be of a people. At one point the poet praises Yahweh, who "faithfully led the people whom you redeemed" (Exod. 15:13a; the verb is *gā'al*). The poet proceeds to relate that the Divine Warrior inspired panic in the peoples in 15:16b: "While your people passed over, Yahweh, the people whom you

10. In "Creation and Liberation" (*USQR* 33/2 [1978] 79–99, repr. in *Creation in the Old Testament*, 135–51), George M. Landes emphasizes this point, while defending Albright's etymology.

11. Dennis J. McCarthy, S.J., "'Creation' Motifs in Ancient Hebrew Poetry," *CBQ* 29 (1967) 393–406; repr. in *Creation in the Old Testament*, 74–89.

12. See Frank M. Cross, "The Song of the Sea and Canaanite Myth," in *Canaanite Myth and Hebrew Epic*, 112–44.

13. Ibid., 131.

14. Umberto Cassuto, *A Commentary on the Book of Exodus* (trans. Israel Abrahams; Jerusalem: Magnes, Hebrew University, 1967) 177–78.

have created." Here I follow the translation of Cross, who construes the verb *qānâ* to mean "create" (cf. Gen. 14:19-20, 22), as in Ugaritic texts where this verb displays "sexual overtones" of procreation.[15] Another ancient poem, the covenant lawsuit known as "the Song of Moses" (Deut. 32:1-43), uses the same verb, along with other creation verbs, to refer to the creation of the people in 32:6b (cf. Ps. 74:2): "Is not Yahweh your Father, who created you, who made you and established you?"

These early poems belong to the Mosaic covenant tradition, whose trajectory one can trace throughout the Old Testament and beyond. In this circle of tradition, represented for instance by the prophet Hosea, the people are reminded of the mystery of their existence, their creation out of chaos, so to speak. Once they were "no people" (cf. 1 Pet. 2:10); but they were formed to be a people through the action of Yahweh, their "Maker" (Hos. 8:14). They depend on Yahweh for their very existence, so much so that betrayal of their covenant loyalty is under the curse of *lô' 'ammî* ("not my people," Hos. 1:9). This view of creation is echoed in some of the psalms, as in the Old Hundredth.

> Recognize that Yahweh is God!
>   He made us, and to him we belong.
> His people we are, and the sheep of his pasture. (Ps. 100:3; cf. 95:6-7;
>   au. trans.)

The view receives its consummate expression in the poems of Second Isaiah. There Yahweh is extolled as "the Creator of Israel" (Isa. 43:15; cf. 43:1a), the one "who made you, who formed you from the womb" (44:2a), "the Holy One of Israel, and its Maker" (45:11). Overwhelmed by the wonder of Israel's existence and survival as a people, this poet often turns to the ancestral traditions that stress the divine blessing of creation and fertility, evident preeminently in procreation by Abraham and Sarah.

> Look to the rock from which you were cut,
>   to the quarry from which you were mined.
> Look to Abraham, your father,
>   and to Sarah who gave birth to you. (Isa. 51:1b-2a; au. trans.)

It is the exodus tradition that especially fires the prophet's imagination, prompting a poetic identification of the passage through the Sea of Reeds with the Divine Warrior's triumph over the powers of chaos (Isa. 51:9-11). In this respect, the prophet stands in a tradition that accords with Israel's earliest poetry, wherein cosmological language functions to portray the

---

15. See McCarthy, *CBQ* 29 (1967) 393–406; repr. in *Creation in the Old Testament*, 74–89.

creation (or re-creation) of a people. Creation and redemption belong together, as the obverse and reverse of the same theological coin.

In one context, however, Second Isaiah uses images of the potter fashioning clay, and of parents giving birth to a child, to refer to the creation of Israel (Isa. 45:9-13). This imagery expands the horizon to the creation of humanity. Yahweh, "the Holy One of Israel, and its Maker," has disposition over the people ("my children," "the work of my hands") precisely because "I made the earth, and created humankind upon it" (45:11–12a, NRSV). The creation of humanity (*'ādām*) in the broadest sense is, of course, the subject of the Genesis creation account (Gen. 1:26-27) and especially of the paradise story (Gen. 2:4b—3:24), where again the image of the potter occurs (2:7). Even the latter story, however, highlights the social dimension of creation, as Phyllis Trible has shown in her exquisite and incisive treatment of "A Love Story Gone Awry."[16] To be sure, human beings are bound to the soil, from which they are taken and to which they return (as scientific naturalism reminds us). But the narrator also portrays the transcendence that arises from the social nature of human beings: "Ein Mensch ist kein Mensch" ("A single human being is not human at all"), as the German proverb goes. In this story, whose full meaning is given by its function within the primeval history (see chap. 8 below), creation is the coming to be of *'ādām*—human being that is made for community in which life is given in relation to God and in relation to the other, the partner.

ROYAL COVENANT TRADITION:
CREATION AND ORDER

I turn now to a second dimension of Israel's creation faith: the divine creation and maintenance of order. While the first dimension, the creation of a people, belongs primarily in the Mosaic covenant tradition, this second dimension, which stresses the correspondence between the cosmic order and the social order, is peculiarly at home in the royal covenant tradition. Viewed in this theological perspective, the relationship between God and the social world is not grounded fundamentally in the events of the Mosaic age, though these are not excluded, but primarily in the election of the Davidic king and the choice of Zion as the divine dwelling place. This is the theme of Psalm 78.

In 1936 Gerhard von Rad penned "The Theological Problem of the Old Testament Doctrine of Creation," in which he set forth the thesis that the faith of Israel is "based on the notion of election [of a people] and there-

16. In *God and the Rhetoric of Sexuality* (OBT; Philadelphia: Fortress Press, 1978) 72–143.

fore primarily concerned with [historical] redemption."[17] In this seminal essay von Rad admitted that the doctrine of creation is indeed early: it "was known in Canaan in extremely early times, and played a large part in the cultus in the pre-Israelite period through mythical representations of the struggle against primaeval chaos." Israel was able to absorb these mythical elements; "but because of the exclusive commitment of Israel's faith to historical salvation, the doctrine of creation was never able to attain to independent existence in its own right." The independence of creation from soteriology, in his view, came into Israelite creation faith through the influence of wisdom—"a highly rationalized mode of speculation concerning the divine economy in this world which we may regard as being of Egyptian origin."[18]

The sharp separation of creation from soteriology, of cosmology from history—a separation that von Rad later came to qualify[19]—may find some support in Israel's premonarchic poetry such as the Song of the Sea, in which, as we have seen, creation is a soteriological event: the creation of a people. Von Rad's view, however, completely ignores the new theology espoused by Davidic theologians, a theology that coexisted with, and interacted with, the Mosaic covenant tradition during the period of the monarchy. The main axis of Davidic (royal) covenant theology was vertical (cosmic) rather than horizontal (historical). According to this circle of tradition, the security, health, and peace of society depend on the cosmic, created order, whose saving benefits are mediated through the Davidic monarch. Creation in the sense of the maintenance of cosmic and social order was "the broad horizon" that Israel shared with peoples of the ancient Near East, as H. H. Schmid has shown in a forceful rejoinder to von Rad.[20] In my judgment, however, this cosmic view of creation was probably introduced into the mainstream of Israelite faith by interpreters who stood in the royal covenant tradition. Hence the view was not alien to Israelite faith, or a late contribution of the wisdom school, but belonged essentially to worship in the Temple of Zion.[21]

17. Translated in *The Problem of the Hexateuch and Other Essays* (trans. E. W. Trueman Dicken; New York: McGraw-Hill, 1966) 131–43; quotation from 131; repr. in *Creation in the Old Testament*, 53–64; quotation from 53.

18. Von Rad, *Problem of the Hexateuch*, 142–43. Von Rad's view is expounded by Davie Napier, "On Creation-Faith in the Old Testament," *Int* 10 (1956) 21–42.

19. See von Rad's 1964 essay, "Some Aspects of the Old Testament World-View," in *Problem of the Hexateuch*, 144–65. He wrote that "we are nowadays in serious danger of looking at the theological problems of the Old Testament far too much from the one-sided standpoint of an historically conditioned theology" and ignoring "the greater part of what the Old Testament has to say about what we call Nature" (p. 144).

20. H. H. Schmid, "Schöpfung, Gerechtigkeit und Heil," *ZTK* 70 (1973) 1–19; abridged translation by Bernhard W. Anderson and Dan G. Johnson, "Creation, Righteousness, and Salvation," in *Creation in the Old Testament*, 102–17.

21. I made this suggestion some years ago in my *Creation versus Chaos*, 43–77, esp. 60–68.

One of the chief witnesses to this theological perspective is Psalm 89, a combined hymn and lament based on the premise of Yahweh's promises of grace to David (2 Samuel 7). In the past some interpreters have supposed that the hymnic interlude dealing with Yahweh's power as creator (Ps. 89:5-18[6-19]) was a later addition to the psalm. But when the psalm is considered as a unity, it is evident that the cosmic dimension of creation corresponds to the mundane sphere and hence provides the basis for the stability of the Davidic throne and the order of society.[22] In the hymnic passage Yahweh is praised as the Incomparable One in the heavenly council—the Divine Warrior who "rules the raging of the sea" and is triumphant in the *Chaoskampf*.

> You rule the raging of the sea;
>> when its waves rise, you still them.
> You crushed Rahab like a carcass;
>> you scattered your enemies with your mighty arm.
> The heavens are yours, the earth also is yours;
>> the world and all that is in it—
>> you have founded them. (Ps. 89:9-12, NRSV)

In this instance, the mythopoeic language does not portray the creation of a people, as in the Song of the Sea; indeed, the psalm is silent about the exodus tradition, the so-called saving history (*Heilsgeschichte*). The language functions, rather, to place the Davidic kingdom in a vertical, cosmic dimension. The poet announces that "righteousness and justice are the foundation of [Yahweh's] celestial throne." The Davidic rule, therefore, is related to cosmic righteousness, just as the Egyptian throne is founded on the cosmic principle of *Maat* (truth, order, justice).[23] Moreover, just as Yahweh, the Divine Warrior, is victorious over the powers of chaos, so the earthly king, the representative of the Deity, will be victorious over the mythical "floods."

> My faithfulness and loyalty will be with him,
>> and in my name his horn will be exalted.
> I will set his hand against the sea,
>> and his right hand against the floods. (Ps. 89:24-25[25-26])

A later phase of this royal covenant tradition occurs in Psalm 74, a community lament that appeals to God (Yahweh) for help in a time of

---

22. See Richard J. Clifford, "Psalm 89: A Lament over the Davidic Ruler's Continued Failure," *HTR* 73 (1980) 35–47; also his paper presented to the Catholic Biblical Association (1983), "Creation in the Old Testament," 10–11.

23. See Schmid, "Creation, Righteousness, and Salvation," in *Creation in the Old Testament*, 105.

historical chaos, probably after the fall of Jerusalem and the exile of the people. Here the poet uses the parallel creation/redemption verbs (*qānâ* and *gā'al*)—to refer not to the exodus but to the founding of Zion:

> Remember your community that you created in ancient times,
> > the tribe of your inheritance that you redeemed,
> > Mount Zion wherein you tabernacled. (Ps. 74:2)

The lament contains a hymnic interlude that extols Yahweh's power as creator:

> Yet you God [Yahweh] are my King from ancient times,
> > who accomplishes salvation in the center of the earth.
> You divided Sea by your might,
> > you shattered the heads of the dragons on the waters.
> You crushed the heads of Leviathan,
> > giving him as food for desert creatures (Ps. 74:12-14)

Here the mythopoeic language functions cosmologically, for the poet goes on to speak of the creation of springs and brooks, the alternation of day and night, the establishment of the heavenly bodies, the fixing of the boundaries of the earth, and the creation of the seasons (vv. 15-17). The center, or omphalos, of the earth (v. 12) refers to Mount Zion (v. 2b), where the Divine King is sacramentally present ("tabernacles"). God's creative activity, which suppliants hope to reexperience in chaotic times, is the working of salvation in Zion—that is, the restoration of the order and stability that correspond to the cosmic creation. In this cosmic perspective, Israel's creation theology, like other ancient Near Eastern views, was liberation theology. To quote George Landes, it was "a freeing of the ordered cosmos from the ever-present menace of primordial chaos, so that especially human social and political structures might be prevented from disintegration, the bonds of cohesion, cooperation, and stability maintained and strengthened, and continuity, social unity, and solidarity ensured."[24]

The theme of divine kingship that appears in Psalm 74 in a creation context is emphasized in a number of psalms that celebrate Yahweh's enthronement as king of the cosmos. These psalms (47, 91, 93–99) are oriented primarily in the vertical axis of the relation between the celestial and the mundane realms. Accordingly, mythopoeic creation language functions to show that the order and stability of Zion are established and maintained by the cosmic King, who is victorious over all powers of chaos that threaten the divine rule. In Psalm 93, for instance, the cultic exclamation that "Yahweh is King" prompts the announcement that the world is

---

24. Landes, USQR 33/2 (1978) 79; repr. in *Creation in the Old Testament*, 136.

"established"; and this statement is parallel to the affirmation that Yahweh's throne, both macrocosmically (in the heavenly palace) and microcosmically (in the Temple of Zion) is founded or established from of old. The "establishing of the earth," as Theodore H. Ludwig has shown, is language that was peculiarly at home in the Jerusalem cult and has to do especially with "the ordering of the world" as a human dwelling.[25] It is appropriate, then, that psalms of Yahweh's kingship employ the "sea" or "floods." "Creation of the Baal type,"[26] to use Loren Fisher's expression, is reflected for instance in Psalm 93:

> The floods lift up, O Yahweh,
>> the floods lift up their roaring,
>> the floods lift up their pounding.
> Above the thunders of many waters,
>> mightier than the breakers of the sea,
>> Yahweh on high is majestic. (Ps. 93:3-4; cf. 29:10)

Creation and redemption are intimately related in these psalms of the Jerusalem cult, as in the early poems of the Mosaic tradition. Indeed, as Ben Ollenburger remarks in his perceptive study of Zion theology, "the notion of Yahweh's kingship was closely associated with his function as creator and defender of Israel. These two functions were, in fact, two modes of the same activity."[27]

I must add, however, that these psalms display a definite cosmological interest in the sense that they see the cosmic order in relation to the social world, that is, they see "the heavens and the earth" as corresponding spheres. Even when poets speak of the "foundation" of the world, the linguistic horizon at times seems to recede beyond the maintenance of order and implies the origination of the cosmos. In Psalm 96, a hymn celebrating Yahweh's enthronement as celestial king, a poet exclaims:

> Yahweh is to be revered above all gods!
> Indeed, all the gods of the peoples are idols,
>> but Yahweh made the heavens. (Ps. 96:4-5)

---

25. Theodore M. Ludwig, "The Tradition of Establishing the Earth in Deutero-Isaiah," *JBL* 92 (1973) 345–57.

26. Loren R. Fisher, "Creation in Ugarit and in the Old Testament," *VT* 15 (1965) 313–24; idem, "From Chaos to Cosmos," *Encounter* 26 (1965) 313–24. Arvid Kapelrud questions whether Canaanite theology really deals with creation in the proper sense in "The Relationship between El and Baal in the Ras Shamra Texts," *The Bible World: Essays in Honor of Cyrus H. Gordon* (ed. G. Rendsburg et al.; New York: KTAV, 1981) 79–85.

27. Bennie C. Ollenburger, *Zion, the City of the Great King: A Theological Investigation of Zion Symbolism in the Tradition of the Jerusalem Cult* (JSOTSup 41; Sheffield: JSOT, 1987) 54–58; quotation from 58.

Here, as in another hymn to Yahweh's enthronement (Ps. 95:3-5), the issue is not just that the world is established on firm foundations but is that of "making" the cosmos: the heavens above and the habitable earth with its waters, dry land, and mountains. In contrast to the "gods of the peoples," which are phenomena of the world and hence "idols," Yahweh is the one who transcends the world and everything in it and is acclaimed as creator in a cosmic sense.

WISDOM TRADITION: PSALM 104 AND THE EQUALITY OF CREATION

The discussion of creation in the royal or Zion tradition brings one close to the Genesis creation story. Before turning to that classical account, however, consider Psalm 104, one of the most important and exquisite creation texts in the Old Testament. Psalm 104 has numerous affinities to Genesis 1, such as linguistic parallels and similarity in the sequence of events of creation. In a seminal essay Paul Humbert argued that both texts originally served as librettos for a festival in the Jerusalem Temple.[28]

Psalm 104 is cast in the literary form of the hymn. It begins with an invocation addressed to the poet's *nepeš* or self (v. 1a). There follows a long ascription of praise to Yahweh (much of it in participial "who" clauses characteristic of hymnic ascriptions of praise) in seven strophes that parallel essentially the sequence of creative events in the Genesis story (vv. 1b-30). Finally, it concludes with a refrain (vv. 31-35) that echoes the initial invocation, thereby rounding off the whole. It is important to notice what is lacking in this text. It does not refer to the creation of a people; indeed it does not even mention Israel. Moreover, it does not refer to the social order or to the king, who mediates the blessings of the cosmic order. At the conclusion of the psalm the poet does exclaim about the glorious majesty of the Creator before whom the earth trembles (vv. 31-32) and prays that those elements ("sinners," "the wicked") that are incongruous with the created order may be eradicated (v. 34). This "eschatological" note, if it be such, is predicated on the tension between the cosmic order and the mundane order. In general, however, the psalmist's interest is cosmological and lacks the dimension of history or even *Heilsgeschichte* found in the Mosaic tradition.[29] It is noteworthy that this psalm, in contrast to the Genesis

---

28. Paul Humbert, "La relation de Genèse 1 et du Psaume 104 avec la liturgie du Nouvel-An israélite," in *Opuscules d'un hébraïsant* (Neuchâtel: Université de Neuchâtel, 1958) 60–83.

29. It is difficult to see how some scholars maintain that the psalmist's interest is primarily historical: "the coming to be of a people, not just humanity in general but Israel who invokes the name of Yahweh" (Clifford, "Creation," 14–15); or that here "the realm of nature is subsumed to the economy of history" (Samuel Terrien, "Creation, Cultus, and Faith in the Psalter," *Theological Education* 2/4 [1966] 117–23; quotation, 123).

creation story (and Psalm 8), puts all creatures, including human beings, on a plane of equality in the wonderful order of God's creation (see Ps. 104:27-30). Here one does not find the "dualism" of humanity and nature or the Creator's grant of human dominion over the nonhuman creation— views that, in the judgment of Lynn White, Jr., lie at the root of the current ecological crisis.[30]

Another major difference between Psalm 104 and the Genesis creation story deserves attention: the psalmist freely uses the mythopoeic language of the *Chaoskampf*. In describing how Yahweh "set Earth on its founda- tions" so that "it would be immovable forever," the poet says that Yahweh overspread the earth with *těhôm* ("deep, abyss"; vv. 5-6). The waters, however, were not passive before Yahweh as in the Song of the Sea. They offered resistance; therefore Yahweh "rebuked" them, and they "took to flight" at the thunderous command of the Creator, who assigned limits not to be transgressed (vv. 7-9). Here the mythopoeic language functions not to portray the creation of a people or a well-ordered society but to depict the order of creation. Every creature is assigned its proper place and time, and all function harmoniously in the wondrous whole: the springs that gush forth in the valleys, the birds that sing in the branches of the trees, the cattle that pasture in the meadows and the wild goats that cling to the mountain crags, the moon and the sun that mark the times and the seasons, human beings who go forth to their labor. From a human perspec- tive this is meaningful, intelligible order; hence in v. 24 the poet breaks out in praise to the divine wisdom that is manifest in the cosmos:

> How manifold are your works, Yahweh!
>   In wisdom you have made all of them.
> The earth is full of your creatures.

In this psalm creation faith stands by itself, without being related to redemption. This does not mean, as von Rad concludes, that one cannot regard the psalm as "wholly original to Yahwistic belief."[31] Rather, here is an authentic expression of Israelite faith at a relatively early period in the monarchy. One may well suppose that it was the sages of Israel, perhaps under the sponsorship of the royal court, who mediated to the Israelite cult influences from the surrounding culture. That would account for the affin- ities with the Egyptian Hymn to the Aten, and the overtones of the Canaan- ite myth of the battle of the Divine Warrior against Sea or the chaos

---

30. Lynn White, Jr., "The Historical Roots of Our Ecological Crisis," *Science* 155 (1967) 1203–7; repr. in *The Environmental Handbook* (ed. Garrett De Bell; New York: Ballantine, 1970) 12–26; idem, *Science* 156 (1967) 737–38. For a theological response, see chap. 7 below.

31. Von Rad, *Problem of the Hexateuch,* 140; repr. in *Creation in the Old Testament,* 60–61.

monster Leviathan, who, however, is demythologized into a zoological curiosity, indeed, Yahweh's plaything (v. 26; cf. Job 40–41).

The hymnic praise of Psalm 104 includes theological dimensions characteristic of wisdom. Wisdom is concerned not just with the "ordered functions" of the world but, as Hans-Jürgen Hermisson has shown, also with "the foundation of the orders of the world," and these concerns prompt reflection on Yahweh's creative activity in the past as well as the continuation of that activity in the present.[32] Whereas hymns in the Zion tradition (e.g., Psalm 93) tend to speak of Yahweh's creative action as being repeated in the present, as the Divine King overcomes the powers of chaos, in Psalm 104 statements like "Yahweh has founded the earth" (v. 4) or "Yahweh has made the moon" (v. 19) refer to "basic data of the past: the environment of the earth, like the changing of festival times and the times of the day, has been created by Yahweh once, and once and for all."[33] The mythopoeic language expresses a cosmological interest, not just in the order of creation but in origination. Moreover, the poetic language also indicates the contingency of the cosmos or, in theological language, the radical dependence of all creatures upon the Creator. The powers of chaos are, to speak mythopoeically, pushed back and assigned their boundaries. The implication is that if the Creator's power were suspended chaos would return. The cosmos is not an autonomous whole, governed by its own laws, but depends completely on the God who transcends it. Moment by moment it is held in being by the sovereign will of the Creator. Even the regularities of "nature" are not iron-bound laws but are expressions of the Creator's faithfulness and trustworthiness (cf. Gen. 8:22).

This view of creaturely dependence is expressed magnificently at the very climax of Psalm 104. The Hebrew verbs (so-called imperfects) in the climactic strophe refer to action that is incomplete, continuing, frequentative; and this meaning can be rendered into English only in the present tense:

> All of them [animals and humans] look to you,
>   to give them their food in its season.
> When you give to them, they gather up;
>   when you open your hand, they are satisfied to the full.
> When you hide your face, they are disturbed,
>   when you take away their breath, they expire
>   and return to their dust.

32. H.-J. Hermisson, "Observations on the Creation Theology in Wisdom" (trans. Barbara Howard), in *Israelite Wisdom: Theological and Literary Essays in Honor of Samuel Terrien* (ed. J. Gammie et al.; Missoula, Mont.: Scholars Press, 1978) 43–57; repr. in *Creation in the Old Testament,* 118–34. See also Schmid, "Creation, Righteousness, and Salvation," in ibid., 102–17.

33. Hermisson, "Observations," 49; repr. in *Creation in the Old Testament,* 125.

When you send forth your spirit, they are [re-]created,
and you renew the surface of the soil. (Ps. 104:27-30)

Here the creation verb *bārā'* refers to *creatio continua*. Creation is not just an event that occurred in the beginning, at the foundation of the earth, but is God's continuing activity of sustaining creatures and holding everything in being.

PRIESTLY TRADITION: CREATION AS ORIGINATION

So far we have seen that creation theology has a special accent in particular streams of tradition that one can trace through the Old Testament—and beyond. The Mosaic tradition uses mythopoeic creation language to speak of the creation of a people who are given identity and vocation. In the royal covenant tradition, the language functions to show that the mundane social order is stable and wholesome by virtue of its relationship to the created order of the cosmos. In Israelite wisdom, initially sponsored by the royal court, the language expresses cosmological interest in God's past and present creative activity. These traditions, with their special theological accents, were not isolated from one another; rather, they interacted and were interrelated, as one can see from the psalms used in worship.

I turn now to another major theological tradition: the Priestly circle that gave us the Torah in final form. In Priestly perspective creation initiates a dramatic sequence of divine covenants: the Noachic (Gen. 9:8-17), the Abrahamic (Gen. 17:1-21), and the Sinaitic (Exod. 31:12-17), all of which are put under the rubric of "covenant in perpetuity" (*běrît 'ôlām*), a covenant that is binding and lasting precisely because it is based on God's unconditional commitment.

Two considerations must govern interpretation of the Genesis creation story (1:1—2:3). First, one must study it as a discrete literary composition with its own structure, style, and dynamic. It is a pericope that one can excise from its present context without damaging its internal coherence and integrity. Second, one must interpret this literary unit contextually, that is, in terms of its function in the primeval history—and indeed, the entire Torah—that the Priestly writers have given to us. The story may have been used once in a cultic setting, possibly as a festival libretto (Humbert); but it now functions within a scriptural context, and particularly within the primeval history that moves from creation to flood (Genesis 1–9).[34]

---

34. For further discussion of the literary structure and dynamic of this pericope, see chap. 3 above. The function of this literary unit in the final context of the primeval history is discussed in chap. 8 below.

The Priestly creation story of Genesis displays some of the cosmological dimensions that we have seen in other contexts, especially in Psalm 104. First, God's creation is a cosmic order, which is without blemish and is harmonious in all its parts. The verdict of the divine Artist, upon perceiving the completed whole, was "very good" (Gen 1:31). This judgment, however, is not ethical but aesthetic. "The creation in itself is then neither good nor evil," observes J. Alberto Soggin, "it is only functional, responding to what God wanted it to be."[35] In Priestly perspective the ethical problem is not emphasized until the time of Noah, when God perceived that the earth was filled with "violence" (6:11-12, the Priestly introduction to the flood story). This creation theology, with its bold monotheism, led inevitably to the question of theodicy, evident in the various expostulations with God found in the Old Testament, beginning with Abraham (18:22-23) and including such figures as Moses, Jeremiah, Habakkuk, and Job.

Second, the Genesis story portrays the radical dependence of the cosmic order upon the transcendent Creator. As Gunkel observed in his monumental study, this story has traces of the mythopoeic language of creation, even though it has no *Chaoskampf*. God created out of chaos (not *ex nihilo*), as shown by the prefatory verse that portrays the earth as once being a chaotic waste: stygian darkness, turbulent waters, utter disorder. In the mythopoeic portrayal, chaos is not destroyed but only placed within bounds—if God so determines, these bounds may be removed, allowing the earth to return to chaos. According to the Priestly view of primeval history, this almost happened during the great flood, when "all the fountains of the great deep burst forth, and the windows of the heavens were opened" (7:11, NRSV). No language could portray more powerfully the contingent character of the creation. The cosmos is not eternal and self-perpetuating, as Greek philosophers maintained; it is sustained in being by the Creator. Were God to relax this upholding power, everything would lapse into chaos.

In various ways the Genesis creation story touches contemporary concerns. The *imago Dei* introduces the issue of the relation between man and woman in God's creation; they are accorded equal status.[36] Moreover, the elevation of '*ādām,* consisting of "male and female," to a position of

---

35. J. Alberto Soggin, "God the Creator in the First Chapter of Genesis," in *Old Testament and Oriental Studies* (BibOr 29; Rome: Biblical Institute Press, 1975) 120–29; quotation, 126.

36. On Gen. 1:26-28, see chap. 7 below; and Phyllis Trible, *God and the Rhetoric of Sexuality* (OBT; Philadelphia: Fortress Press, 1978) 12–23. For a challenge to the view that the Priestly story sets forth the equality of the sexes, see Phyllis Bird, "'Male and Female He Created Them': Gen 1:27b in the Context of the Priestly Account of Creation," *HTR* 74 (1981) 129–59. See further chap. 8 below.

dominion over the Creator's earthly estate raises ecological issues such as the relation between animals and humans and the use, or exploitation, of earth's resources.[37] Further, the biblical doctrine of creation has implications for liberation theologies of the Third World.[38]

Another fascinating issue is the relation of the creation story to the new vistas of science, especially in view of the apparent dominance of the so-called big-bang theory of the origin of the universe. In a flamboyant essay, Robert Jastrow, himself an agnostic, dared to suggest that developments in modern astrophysics bring us close to the Genesis view of the origin of the universe in a cosmic flash.[39]

It is undoubtedly true that the mythopoeic language of the Bible leads one finally to the mystery of the origination of the cosmos—the mystery that Job (38:4-7) was asked to contemplate. The voice out of the whirlwind asks, "Where were you when I laid the foundations of the earth? Tell me, if you have understanding" (38:4, NRSV). In recent years this matter has been difficult for theologians, owing in part to the lack of adequate metaphysical categories. In a presidential address to the American Theological Society in 1971, George Hendry spoke about "The Eclipse of Creation" and chided theologians, especially biblical theologians, for reducing creation to redemption or creaturely dependence and for failing to deal with the biblical witness to creation as origination.[40] At least since von Rad's 1936 essay dealing with the problem of creation faith in the Old Testament, theologians have retreated from cosmology. This is true of both Karl Barth and Rudolf Bultmann, two biblical theologians who stand at opposite ends of the theological spectrum.[41] Claus Westermann states flatly that "the stories of the origins are concerned with the subsistence of the world and of mankind, not with the intellectual question of the origin."[42] Westermann proceeds from a phenomenological understanding of myth, which he sets forth in his essay "Biblical Reflection on Creator-Creation."[43]

Admittedly, the mythopoeic language of the Bible often expresses the existential apprehension of a world threatened by chaos, of human life in

---

37. See Karlfried Froehlich, "The Ecology of Creation," *TToday* 27 (1971) 263–76; also chap. 8 below.

38. See Landes, *USQR* 33/2 (1978) 79–99; repr. in *Creation in the Old Testament,* 135–51.

39. Robert Jastrow, *God and the Astronomers* (New York: Warner, 1980) 105–6.

40. George S. Hendry, "The Eclipse of Creation," *TToday* 28 (1972) 406–25.

41. The views of Barth, Bultmann, and other theologians are discussed and evaluated in Norman Young, *Creator, Creation and Faith* (Philadelphia: Westminster, 1976), 83–102, 128–44.

42. Claus Westermann, *Creation* (trans. John J. Scullion; Philadelphia: Fortress Press, 1974) 120. See Westermann's essay in his introduction to *Creation,* 1–15; repr. in *Creation in the Old Testament,* 90–101.

43. Westermann, *Creation,* 1–15; repr. in *Creation in the Old Testament,* 90–101.

its limitation, of radical dependence on divine power(s) and the cosmic order of reality. The theological question, however, is whether the creation story of Genesis 1 is only a mythical portrayal of what always is and what is timelessly true or whether, in addition, it speaks in its own way of origination. This problem will never be solved by concentrating on the syntax of the initial sentence of the Genesis creation story. Grammatically, some translators argue that "in the beginning" (*běrē'šît*) introduces a circumstantial clause that precedes v. 3, "Then God said, 'Let there be light'" (as in NEB, NAB, and NRSV). Others maintain that the first Hebrew word of the Bible introduces an absolute statement that is prefatory to the story as a whole (as in RSV, JB, NIV, REB).[44] But the creation verbs that are used, *bārā'* ("created") and *'āśâ* ("made"), indicate something more than "the subsistence of the world and humankind": they connote origination. Further, if the *tôlĕdôt* ("generations") formula in 2:4a actually introduces what follows, as it does in the other occurrences in primeval history and ancestral history, then the creation story is placed redactionally before the genealogical sequence and hence is prehistorical and even pretemporal.[45] Add to this evidence the testimony of the Septuagint, which translates the first verse as an independent statement (*en archē epoiēsen ho theos ton ouranon kai tēn gēn*), and one reaches the plausible conclusion with Walther Eichrodt that the first Hebrew word of the Bible refers to an absolute beginning.[46] It was therefore appropriate for the Priestly redactors to begin the Torah story with creation, the liturgical sequence found also in Psalm 136.

It is another question altogether, however, whether this language, which is set in a mythopoeic context and which serves a doxological purpose, is related to the scientific view of the origination of the world in a flash of light, like a cosmic hydrogen explosion, at a sharply defined instant some sixteen billion years ago. Mythopoeic language cannot be converted into scientific language any more than poetry can be reduced to prose. It is hard to see how creationists can divest the creation story of its God-centered language and can propose teaching it, theologically denuded, as an alternative to a scientific hypothesis. Mythopoeic language provides a different approach to reality via the faculty of poetic intuition or imagina-

---

44. See, e.g., W. R. Lane, "The Initiation of Creation," *VT* 13 (1963) 63–73; Bruce Waltke, "The Creation Account in Genesis 1:1-3," a five-part essay in *BSac* 132/525, 526, 527, 528 (1975) 25–36, 136–44, 216–28, 327–42, ibid., 133/529 (1976) 28–41.

45. A conclusion of chap. 3 above; see pp. 54–55.

46. Walther Eichrodt, "In the Beginning: A Contribution to the Interpretation of the First Word of the Bible," in *Israel's Prophetic Heritage: Essays in Honor of James Muilenburg* (ed. Bernhard W. Anderson and Walter Harrelson; New York: Harper & Row, 1962) 1–10; repr. in *Creation in the Old Testament*, 65–73.

tion. While this approach may coexist, and even be compatible, with the scientific method with its methodological limitations, it is questionable whether the two languages say the same things. The scientist is concerned with description and control, and is neutral about meaning, while the theologian is concerned with ultimate meaning and purpose. The scientist speaks of contingency (chance), whereas the theologian perceives that the earth and everything in it belong to God and depend on God constantly. The scientist may speak of a first cause in a chain of events, but the theologian declares that God, who transcends the whole cause-effect scheme, created the cosmos in freedom. (See further chap. 8 below.)

In any case the creation story, which now functions within the scriptural context of the Priestly Torah and especially the Priestly version of the primeval history, introduces a dramatic movement toward the near return of the earth to precreation chaos (the *tōhû wābōhû* of Gen. 1:2), owing to violence. Violence is illustrated by incorporating into the Priestly history selected episodes of the Old Epic (J) version of the primeval history: rebellion in the garden, fratricide in the first family, Lamech's measureless revenge, and the strange story of the breaching of the separation of heaven and earth by the heavenly beings who seized and had intercourse with beautiful human maidens (Genesis 2–3; 4; 6:1-4). Whether the problem of violence, which raises the whole question of theodicy, is dealt with satisfactorily in this narrative is doubtful. At the climax of primeval history, however, the story speaks of a new beginning in God's purpose—indeed, of a new creation, as evident from the recurrence of motifs of the Genesis creation story, such as the wind that dries the waters so that the dry land appears and the greening of the earth with vegetation again. Thus creation has a future—one might even say, an eschatological—horizon. In the comprehensive sense, creation deals with origination, maintenance, and consummation.[47]

PROPHETIC TRADITION: SECOND ISAIAH
AND NEW CREATION

These are precisely the theological dimensions found in the poetry of Second Isaiah, whose proclamation draws upon all Israelite traditions and fuses them in matchless synthesis. According to this anonymous prophet, Yahweh is "the God who made all things" (Isa. 44:26), who established the earth so that chaos does not prevail (45:18), who formed Israel as a worshiping community (43:21), and who even now is beginning to create something new in human history never heard of before (48:6-7). The question, much debated in recent decades, is how these dimensions of

47. See further chap. 9 below.

creation theology are integrated in the prophet's message. Gerhard von Rad, followed by a number of scholars, maintains that these lyrical poems are the supreme witness to how Israel's creation faith "is brought into harmony with soteriology." In his view, creation has only an ancillary function in the prophetic proclamation: to provide support for faith in Yahweh's saving activity.[48]

One can readily agree that the poet appeals to Yahweh's wisdom and power as creator in order to awaken a disheartened people to believe that they, and all peoples, have a future in the divine purpose. The question is, however, whether creation is a "subsidiary theme" or whether, as P. B. Harner proposes, it plays "a major role" in the prophet's thinking.[49] This issue deserves reexamination if creation in a cosmological sense was integral to Israel's faith in earlier Israelite traditions.

A starting point for study is the prophet's proclamation that Yahweh is incomparable—the unique God beside whom there is no other (45:5), the one who is the first and the last (48:12). The question "Who is like you, O Yahweh, in the heavenly council?" which was raised in Israel's hymns (Exod. 15:11; Ps. 89:6-8[7-9]), is treated in two ways by the prophet. First, the poet Second Isaiah appeals to Yahweh's saving purpose in history, though with the special nuance that no other god has been able to announce a plan in advance and execute it (e.g., Isa. 48:14-16). This argument draws deeply upon the story of Israel's life, the "former things," though the prophet insists that "the new exodus of salvation" will completely outshine anything experienced in the past.[50] At one point the prophet portrays the redemption of Israel at the Reed Sea in the mythopoeic language of the old creation myth. In an apostrophe to the mighty arm of the Divine Warrior the poet exclaims:

> Awake, awake, put on strength,
>   O arm of the Lord!
> Awake, as in days of old,
>   the generations of long ago!
> Was it not you who cut Rahab in pieces,
>   who pierced the dragon?
> Was it not you who dried up the sea,
>   the waters of the great deep;
> who made the depths of the sea a way
>   for the redeemed to cross over? (Isa. 51:9-10, NRSV)

---

48. Von Rad, "The Theological Problem," 134–37; repr. in *Creation in the Old Testament,* 56–59. For scholars influenced by von Rad, see the bibliography in that volume under Werner Foerster, Rolf Rendtorff, John Reumann, and Carroll Stuhlmueller.

49. P. B. Harner, "Creation Faith in Deutero-Isaiah," *VT* 17 (1967) 298–306.

50. For further discussion of the argument from prophecy see my essay, "Exodus Typology in Second Isaiah," in *Israel's Prophetic Heritage,* 177–95.

The creation of Israel, according to the prophet, was a historical witness to what Yahweh is on the verge of doing in the present. Also in a context that recalls the event of the Reed Sea is this oracle:

> Do not remember the former things,
>   or consider the things of old.
> I am about to do a new thing;
>   now it springs forth, do you not perceive it? (Isa. 43:18-19, NRSV)

The second argument for the incomparability of Yahweh is based on the announcement that Yahweh alone is the Creator who brought the cosmos into being and who maintains the cosmic order.

> To whom then will you compare me,
>   or who is my equal? says the Holy One.
> Lift up your eyes on high and see:
>   Who created these?
> He who brings out their host and numbers them,
>   calling them all by name;
> because he is great in strength,
>   mighty in power,
>   not one is missing. (Isa. 40:25-26, NRSV)

Admittedly, this appeal to Yahweh as cosmic creator is intended to provide support for faith that Yahweh has not ignored Israel's "justice" (40:27-31). It is striking, however, that in passages like this (see also 42:5-9, 12-13, 18; 48:12-13) Yahweh's uniqueness is based on cosmic creation, without mention of the exodus tradition.[51]

These two arguments, that Yahweh is the Creator of the ends of the earth (40:28) and that Yahweh has prophetically announced his saving historical purpose, converge to support the proclamation that Yahweh is the only God, the Creator and the Savior, to whom all peoples should turn.

> Turn to me and be saved,
>   all the ends of the earth!
> For I am God, and there is no other. (Isa. 45:22, NRSV)

Because human history—not only the history of Israel but of all peoples— is given meaning and direction by the transcendent God, the Holy One, there is hope for the future. Yahweh is the one:

---

51. Harner, who makes this point, observes that in these passages "creation faith is so closely interrelated with the idea of the uniqueness of Yahweh that it is indeed uncertain which is represented as the basis of the other" (*VT* 17[1967] 302).

who created the heavens
(he is God!),
who formed the earth and made it
(he established it;
he did not create it a chaos [*tōhû*],
he formed it to be inhabited!) (Isa. 45:18, NRSV)

This God does not say to people, "Seek me in chaos" (45:19).

Here we find a complete synthesis of the theological dimensions of Israel's creation faith. The God whom Israel worships and to whom it bears witness is the Creator who originated the cosmos, who maintains order in the face of threats of chaos, and who created—and now re-creates—a people out of the chaos of bondage. In a time of historical tragedy, this people was called to bear witness to the "new thing" that God creates in history and to anticipate prophetically a new creation. The theme of the new creation was further developed in Third Isaiah (e.g., Isa. 65:17-25), in later apocalyptic literature, and in the New Testament, where creation theology was transposed into a new key.

CHAPTER 6

Theology and Science:
Cosmic Dimensions of
the Creation Account
in Genesis*

In the late 1970s and early 1980s three books focused attention sharply on the biblical doctrine of creation, and specifically the Genesis creation account. The first carries the curious title *Is God a Creationist?*[1] As indicated by the subtitle, *The Religious Case against Creation-Science*, this book was evoked by the recent controversy over the teaching of the origin of the universe in public schools. Advocates of "creation science," that is, a strictly literal interpretation of the Genesis creation account, maintained in a losing court case that this view deserves equal time with a scientific account, especially the doctrine of evolution. In this book, the case against creationism is argued by Jewish, Protestant, and Roman Catholic leaders (including Pope John Paul II). The argument rests on the premise that God has two books—one the Bible, which deals with God's relation to human beings, and the other the book of nature, which displays God's works of creation. It is a mistake to confuse these two books by supposing that each gives the same kind of knowledge, although they belong side by side in the library.

The second volume is entitled *Cry of the Environment: Rebuilding the Christian Creation Tradition.*[2] The contributors to this volume, a project

* The Carl Michalson Memorial Lecture, 1985. It first appeared in the *Drew Gateway* 56 (1986) 1–13.

1. Roland M. Frye, ed., *Is God a Creationist? The Religious Case against Creation Science* (New York: Charles Scribner's Sons, 1983).

2. Philip Joranson and Ken Butigan, eds., *Cry of the Environment: Rebuilding the Christian Creation Tradition* (Santa Fe, N.M.: Bear, 1984).

of the Center for Ethics and Social Policy, in Berkeley, California, agree that Christian tradition has been so preoccupied with human salvation, that is, the relation between God and human beings, that it has failed to give adequate attention to the natural world. The essayists, however, are primarily concerned about refurbishing the doctrine of creation, so that both nature and history, the human and the nonhuman creation, are given proper theological consideration.

The third book, *God and the Astronomers*, is by Robert Jastrow, the NASA astrophysicist who has a flair for writing about science.[3] The essay describes the debate between the "steady-state" theory, which holds that the universe had no beginning and will have no ending, hence is eternal, and the "big-bang" theory, which holds that the universe was created in a fiery explosion at a sharply defined instant some sixteen billion years ago. Jastrow, a self-professed agnostic, maintains that the big-bang theory, which now commands the field, is close to the story of creation found at the beginning of the Bible, a story that opens by portraying the origin of the universe in a cosmic flash of light. He concludes with an oft-quoted paragraph that has brought laughter to many:

> At this moment it seems as though science will never be able to raise the curtain on the mystery of creation. For the scientist who has lived by his faith in the power of reason, the story ends like a bad dream. He has scaled the mountains of ignorance; he is about to conquer the highest peak; as he pulls himself over the final rock, he is greeted by a band of theologians who have been sitting there for centuries.[4]

What these three books have in common, despite their divergent approaches, is the attempt to understand the cosmic dimension of the biblical creation faith. Not too long ago, theologians and biblical interpreters were in swift retreat from "cosmology," the study of the universe as a whole and of the interrelation of its parts. The Bible, it was said, deals with anthropology, not cosmology. What cosmology it has belongs to the naive "three-storied view of the universe"—heaven, earth and underworld—that Israel shared with other ancient peoples. Hence the task of the interpreter is to demythologize the worldview of the Bible, to translate its cosmological language into terms that modern persons can appreciate existentially. Carl Michalson, to whom my work here is dedicated, was one of the most scintillating stars in this hermeneutical constellation, which is generally identified with the name of Rudolf Bultmann.

In seeking to come to terms with the exciting new vistas of science,

3. Robert Jastrow, *God and the Astronomers* (New York: Norton, 1978).
4. Ibid., 105.

Michalson and others came to realize that the Bible is not a book of nature but a book that addresses the inescapable issues of what it means to be a human being in a world of mystery, uncertainty, and threat. The Bible deals not with the processes and interconnections of the *how* but with the purpose and design of the *who*. Moreover, the Bible is not written in the kind of language in which words represent the precise sense of factual propositions (Wittgenstein). Biblical literalism, as Conrad Hyers observes in a stunning essay, is a form of "constricting the cosmic dance." Quoting the statement of the early ethnologist R. R. Marett that "religion is not so much thought out as danced out," he goes on to say, "But even when thought out, religion is focused in the verbal equivalent of the dance: myth, symbol, and metaphor. To insist on assigning to it a literal, one-dimensional meaning is to shrink and stifle and distort the significance."[5]

All of this is true as far as it goes, as many have agreed. But the danger of a retreat from the dimension of the cosmological into the dimension of the anthropological, the existential, or the aesthetic is that the realm of the nonhuman—what we call nature—may come to be regarded as theologically out of bounds. This in turn may foster a sharp dichotomy between religion and science, resulting in an abdication of responsibility for the environment in which we live and move and have our being. Theologians today find themselves in a time of startling new horizons of science—in astronomy, physics, biology, medicine, and more—and that calls for a theology with cosmological interests.

In this new situation I would like to take a new step—maybe a "giant step" comparable to that human step on the moon—and consider the *cosmic* implications of the Genesis creation story. I am intrigued by Jastrow's suggestion that scientists have ventured into an area theologians have occupied for centuries. I am not altogether satisfied, however, with his illustration. For one thing, many theologians in recent years have left the mountain in order to concentrate on more pressing issues of liberation down in the valley. Moreover, one wonders about the encounter itself. Can these two, the agnostic scientist and the believing theologian, who speak different languages and espouse different modes of knowing, actually shake hands on meeting and talk together, realizing that they share—if not common meanings—common interest at least? Modestly realizing that as a biblical theologian I am going out beyond my depth, I turn again to the Genesis creation story and, specifically, to consider three matters of common interest: the mystery of origination, the mystery of cosmic order, and the mystery of the emergence of life.

---

5. Conrad Hyers, "Biblical Literalism: Constricting the Cosmic Dance," in *Is God a Creationist?* 97.

THE MYSTERY OF ORIGINATION

The Genesis creation story opens in a cosmic perspective with words that unfold before the reader the far horizon of the ultimate beginning of all things: "In the beginning God created the heaven and the earth" (Gen. 1:1). This lapidary sentence, according to the traditional translation, carries one imaginatively into that time known only to God, before there were any witnesses to the mystery of creation, before there were any instruments to measure or calculate. Nothing survives as evidence for human examination, and even the boldest scientists can fall back only on imaginative inference. It is the beginning, therefore, that exceeds human comprehension and that can be spoken about only in poetic or mythopoeic language. This is the mystery that finally overwhelmed Job after all his expostulations with God and his attempts to penetrate the secret of the cosmos. The voice out of the whirlwind ignored his questioning and, instead, put the question to him:

Where were you when I laid the foundation of the earth?
    Tell me, if you have understanding.
Who determined its measurements—surely you know!
    Or who stretched the line upon it?
On what were its bases sunk,
    or who laid its cornerstone,
when the morning stars sang together
    and all the heavenly beings shouted for joy? (Job 38:4-7, NRSV)

Admittedly, there is some grammatical uncertainty about the first word of the Bible (*bĕrē'šît,* lit.: "in beginning"). Some translators argue that this word does not refer to an absolute beginning but initiates a circumstantial clause that leads up to Gen. 1:3: "In the beginning of God's creating the heavens and the earth . . . then God said, 'Let there be light.'" So, for instance, the JPSV: "When God began to create heaven and earth—the earth being unformed and void, with darkness over the surface of the deep and a wind from God sweeping over the water—God said, 'Let there be light,' and there was light" (so also NRSV and NAB). This interpretation goes back especially to the medieval scholar Rashi (Rabbi Shlomo son of Yitzhaq), who said that the "plain sense" of this passage is not to teach the order of creation (that is, that heaven and earth are first in the sequence) but rather to say that in the creative process the first significant divine event was the creation of light.

Translation is, of course, an act of interpretation. The Italians have a proverb to the effect that "translators are betrayers" ("traduttori sono traditori"), and perhaps scholarly interpretations of the first verses of Genesis illustrate this hermeneutical boldness. Addressing this issue in his paper

"The Eclipse of Creation,"[6] George Hendry chided theologians, especially biblical theologians (myself included), for reducing creation to a relationship between God and creation (creaturely dependence) or a dimension of history (salvation) and for failing to deal with the biblical witness to creation as origination. For example, Gerhard von Rad insisted that in Israel's faith creation was ancillary to "election,"—the story of God's involvement with Israel.[7] Claus Westermann went so far as to say that "the stories of origins are concerned with the subsistence of the world and of mankind, not with the intellectual question of the origin."[8] It may be that it is time for biblical theologians, like Job, to "repent in dust and ashes" in the face of the cosmological mysteries of creation.

Even if one follows Rashi and construes the first two verses of Genesis as a circumstantial clause leading up to the main sentence in Gen. 1:3, the creation of light is to be understood as a cosmological event. But there are compelling reasons to follow translations (e.g., REB, JB, NIV) that take the first Hebrew word of the Bible (*běrē'šît;* Greek: *en archē*) to refer to an absolute beginning. For one thing, the creation verbs *bārā'* ("created") and *'āśâ* ("made") indicate something more than the "subsistence of the world and mankind": they connote origination. Furthermore, if the formula "these are the generations of" actually introduces the story of the Garden of Eden (Gen. 2:4a), as redaction criticism would show, then the creation story in Genesis 1 is placed before the genealogical sequences of the book of Genesis and deals with what is prehistorical and even suprahistorical.[9] Add to this evidence the testimony of the Greek translation of the Old Testament (Septuagint), which renders the first verse as an independent sentence, and one reaches the plausible conclusion that the first word of the Hebrew Bible refers to an absolute beginning of the cosmos.

It is not accidental, then, that the Bible opens with the story of creation or that this story opens with a sentence that deals with the very beginning. The biblical story starts at the beginning, as does any good story, but this is the beginning for which there was no other beginning, no other story.

In short, the biblical creation story deals with a cosmic matter—*the origination of all things*—and it is in this sense that theologians have understood creation down through the centuries. Creation means that the cosmos is finite: it had a beginning and it will have an end. This belief

6. George S. Hendry, "The Eclipse of Creation," *TToday* 28 (1972) 406–25.

7. Gerhard von Rad, "The Theological Problem of the Old Testament Doctrine of Creation," in *The Problem of the Hexateuch and Other Essays* (trans. E. W. Trueman Dicken; New York: McGraw-Hill, 1966) 131–43; repr. in *Creation in the Old Testament* (ed. Bernhard W. Anderson; IRT 6; Philadelphia: Fortress Press, 1984) 53–64.

8. Claus Westermann, *Creation* (trans. John J. Scullion; Philadelphia: Fortress Press, 1974) 120.

9. See chap. 3 above.

seems to agree, at least superficially, with the scientific view that the universe came into being in a cosmic flash, like the flash of a cosmic hydrogen explosion, at a sharply defined instant some sixteen billion years ago. That explosion, says the poet Robinson Jeffers, exceeds the powers of human expression:

> . . . All that exists
> Roars into flame, the tortured fragments rush away from each
>   other into all the sky, new universes
> Jewel the black breast of night; and far off
>   the outer nebulae
>   like charging spearmen again
> Invade emptiness.[10]

That is the way the biblical story begins: with a cosmic flash of light. "God said, 'Let there be light,' and light came." Furthermore, in the biblical story this primeval light (*Urlicht*) is not associated with the light from the sun and the stars, heavenly bodies that came later in the drama of creation (Gen. 1:14-15). It seems that the scientists and the theologians share a common cosmological interest, though they see things from different angles and with different modes of knowing.

Here we face a problem in the philosophy of language. Scientific language aims for mathematical exactitude and objectivity even though its symbolism presses reason into the realm of imagination. It is based on human observation, experimentation, and control, and is—above all—neutral about questions of meaning. That language has enabled us to bend nature to human control, to achieve marvels in the field of medicine, to revolutionize transportation and communication, and to launch explorations into space. But the biblical story is written in a different kind of language—language that provides a different approach to reality via the faculty of poetic intuition and artistic imagination. This language, akin to expressions in art, poetry, and music, functions metaphorically to reveal the God who is beyond the human world yet involved in it. Biblical language does not aim for accuracy of description but uses language inaccurately, as does a poet, to allude to God, who is beyond description and explanation.

These two languages should not be confused. On the one hand, religious (mythopoeic) language cannot be converted into scientific language any more than poetry can be reduced to prose. On the other hand, scientific language, which methodologically is godless, can hardly be equated with religious language that deals with who the Creator is and what the Cre-

10. Quoted by Owen Gingrich in "Let There be Light: Modern Cosmogony and Biblical Creation," in *Is God a Creationist?* 121.

ator's design is. Nevertheless, these languages intersect at points of common cosmological interest. When the scientist and the theologian meet, therefore, neither should claim to be "king of the mountain." They should be able to enter into a dialogue as friends who stand humbly before the mysteries of creation.

THE MYSTERY OF ORDER

Consider now a second dimension of the biblical creation story: cosmic order. It is not just that the cosmos originated in the creative will of God, but that God is the one who gives order to the vast cosmic whole in which everything from the least particle to the largest star has its proper place and function.

If, according to the judgment of critical scholarship, the Genesis creation account comes from the hand of Priestly theologians, one can understand the concern for order that is manifest in the structure of the story itself. The story displays an aesthetic order. It begins with an announcement of God's creation in the beginning (1:1), and the story is rounded off at the end with the announcement that the Creator's purpose was accomplished (2:1-3). Each creative act is stated in a formulaic style that emphasizes order: the Creator (the Executive) speaks, and the command is executed. Moreover, in between the opening and the closing of the literary unit, the creation drama unfolds in two major movements, each of which occupies three "days," with two acts of creation on each of the triads of days. In each of these two major sections, the reader's attention is directed from heaven to earth: in the first instance, to the greening of the earth with vegetation, and in the second to the population of the green earth with creatures that live and move and breathe. (See further chap. 3 above.)

It is possible to study this story only as a work of literary art and to observe its stylistic symmetry and ordered wholeness. What strikes me theologically, however, is the narrator's emphasis on cosmic order, which was a matter not only of observation but of theological wonder.

This is true also in the case of Psalm 104, which follows essentially the same sequences as the Genesis creation story. This psalm displays the motif of wisdom: "In wisdom God made all the creatures" (Ps. 104:24). The sages of the ancient world produced lists of observed phenomena and cataloged them in categories based on observation. The Genesis creation story reflects wisdom thinking to the degree that it displays a studied reflection on things observed in the earth and the universe. To mention only one small detail: "the earth brought forth vegetation: [1] plants yielding seed according to their *kind [mîn]*, and [2] trees bearing fruit in which is their own seed, each according to its kind" (Gen. 1:12). This one sentence discloses a great deal of botanical information: not only the distinction between plants and trees but also the recognition that these reproduce according to their own species or *mîn*. This empirical observation, found here and elsewhere in the Genesis creation story, is surely akin to the scientific approach, even though science has refined its methods of observation and the categories of classification.

The narrator's sense of cosmic order, however, is manifest above all in the view of the whole in which each of the creatures has its proper place and function. Nothing is out of place, nothing is unnecessary, nothing is without meaning. Rather, the narrator invites us to be amazed that we— observers from an earthly vantage point of the vast creation—are, as Samuel Taylor Coleridge once put it, "parts and proportions of one wondrous whole." This poetic sense of the mystery and wonder of the cosmos that finds expression in the Genesis creation story is an invitation to praise the Creator.

In this doxological perspective, God's creation is a wonderful cosmic order, without blemish and harmonious in all its parts. The verdict of the Divine Artist, upon perceiving the whole, was *ṭôb mĕ'ōd,* "very good" (1:31). This judgment, however, was not ethical but aesthetic, in the sense that everything belongs where it should be and functions according to the divine design. Maybe this is something like the judgment we make of our new car: "beautiful," in the sense that it functions perfectly according to the purpose for which it was designed.

This sense of marvelous order is surely akin to the modern scientific worldview, but something else about this cosmic order may be consonant with the scientist's perception. This marvelous order is "contingent"—it is constantly threatened by disorder or "chaos."[11] The power of the Creator is evident not only in origination but also in maintaining and sustaining the order of creation.

In the Genesis creation story the contingency of the cosmos is expressed in poetic language derived ultimately from the ancient myth of the conflict of the creator god with the powers of chaos. One of the best examples of this ancient myth is the Babylonian creation epic *Enuma elish,* which describes how the creator god Marduk defeated the powers of chaos, represented by a monster (dragon), and split the carcass in two; part of the carcass becomes the watery realm above the firmament and the other the abyss upon which the earth rests. Faint allusions to this ancient myth occur in the biblical story, which begins with a portrayal of chaos: a watery abyss, inky black in darkness, and a wind sweeping over the waters. In the preface, as in the rest of the story, creation is seen in relation to

---

11. The Newtonian view of the universe, with its neat and orderly system, has given way to a mathematical physics that must take account of randomness, unpredictability, and chance. See James Gleick, *Chaos: Making a New Science* (New York: Viking, 1987).

chaos. By the command of God, light is separated from the primeval darkness, a firmament is placed in the midst of the waters to separate the waters above from the waters below, and the waters under the heaven are gathered into one place so that the dry land appears. In this view the watery chaos is not destroyed; rather, the primeval sea surrounds the habitable earth on every hand. Were it not for the Creator's power, by which the firmament was created and the sea assigned its boundaries, the earth would be engulfed by the flowing together of the waters and would return to primeval chaos—as almost happened in the story of the flood (Genesis 6–9).

No language could express more forcefully the contingency of the creation. Contrary to the ancient Greek way of thinking, the cosmos is not a self-existent, self-operating realm without beginning and end. The cosmos is finite: in scientific perspective, it began with a "big bang" and it will end with "a big burnout." In agreement with this view, the biblical language of faith assumes the contingency of the earth, as in the covenantal pledge at the end of the great flood, according to Old Epic tradition:

So long as the earth endures,
Seedtime and harvest,
Cold and heat,
Summer and winter,
Day and night
Shall not cease. (Gen. 8:22, JPSV)

Meanwhile, the Creator holds the world in being, so to speak, in the face of the potentialities of chaos.

Ecologists have taught us how delicate is the "web of life."[12] All living beings from bacteria to human beings "fit into a pattern of life and depend upon each other and the world around them for existence." We also know how our human lifestyle can upset this delicate balance and threaten to release the powers of chaos.

Indeed, the original creation was only part of the Creator's activity: there is also a continuing creation, in which the Creator not only sustains the order of the cosmos but, more than that, does the "new thing" that surprises all expectations (see Isa. 42:9; 43:18-19).

One of the most eloquent statements about *creatio continua* is found at the climax of Psalm 104, where the poet uses verbs that express action that is incomplete and frequentative—a meaning that can be translated into English idiom only by using the present tense. The psalmist's prayer to the Creator expresses the confidence that creation is not just an event that

---

12. See John H. Storer, *The Web of Life* (New York: New American Library, 1972).

occurred in the beginning but God's continuing activity of sustaining creatures and holding everything in being.

> All of them [animals and humans] look to you
>   to give them their food in its season.
> When you give to them, they gather up;
>   when you open your hand, they are satisfied to the full.
> When you hide your face, they are disturbed,
>   when you take away their breath, they expire
>   and return to their dust.
> When you send forth your spirit, they are [re-]created,
>   and you renew the surface of the soil. (Ps. 104:27-30)

THE MYSTERY OF THE EMERGENCE OF LIFE

The theologian shares with the scientist one more interest—and this one has become highly controversial in the twentieth century—the emergence of life on this planet.

I have observed that the creation drama is divided into two main movements: the first reaching its climax in the greening of the earth with vegetation, plants and trees according to their various kinds, and the second reaching its climax with the creation of life, especially human life. All of this is conceived as a dramatic totality. We must guard against imposing upon the story philosophical views derived from our Western tradition, such as the philosophical separation between nature and history, mind and matter, and the cosmic and the existential.

Biblical theologians have noticed that nature provides God's "peculiar language" for praising the Creator. For in the Bible nature is regarded not as a sphere of mechanical operations as in the Newtonian worldview but as a sphere that is somehow "alive" and that therefore joins with human beings in praise of the Creator. In 1946, in a projected work on Old Testament theology (which was never fully realized), H. Wheeler Robinson called attention to this divine aspect of nature. "Nature is alive through and through, and therefore the more capable of sympathy with man, and of response to the rule of its Creator and Upholder, on whom it directly depends."[13]

This view of the responsiveness of "nature" to the Creator has been picked up with poetic passion and insight by Virginia Stem Owens in her book *And the Trees Clap Their Hands: Faith, Perception, and the New Physics*. She maintains that nature should be regarded not mechanistically but dynamically and that the biblical language about the participation of

---

13. H. Wheeler Robinson, *Inspiration and Revelation in the Old Testament* (New York and London: Oxford Univ. Press, 1946) 16.

nature in human creatureliness should not be regarded as "mere metaphor" but as metaphor that corresponds with reality. "And still the mute mountains, the dumb desert, the dying stars wait for us to provide a throat for their thanksgiving."[14] This view, I believe, is consonant with the biblical creation story, and we can be thankful for studies like this that help us to appreciate the poetic dimensions of the text.

But I now turn to a special matter in the creation drama, the movement from the greening of the earth to the climactic creation of life, preeminently human life. Hebrew has a special expression for "living being": *nepeš ḥayyâ*. This expression is not applied to the vegetation that greens the earth on the third day of the drama. Today we make a distinction between animate things (trees, plants) and inanimate things (rocks, water, soil), but the biblical narrator does not make this distinction. Rather, the expression "living being" is reserved for the new forms that appear in the second movement, and strikingly these new creatures (living beings) first appear in connection with the waters, the remnant of the waters of chaos.

It would be unwise, in my judgment, to make too much of this association of emerging life with the waters, as though the Bible anticipated modern views of evolution. The connection of emerging life with the waters is undoubtedly a coincidence. Nevertheless, the reader sees that something radically new appears in the case of marine beings (fish, sea monsters) and the flying creatures that soar over the waters (birds, winged creatures). For the first time in the story, creatures are called "living beings," *nepeš ḥayyâ* (Gen. 1:20). At the executive command of the Creator, the waters generate marine creatures (and if one follows the LXX, birds too: "Let the waters bring forth reptiles having life, and winged creatures flying above the earth in the heavenly firmament"). Moreover, this momentous development is marked by a dramatic pause during which the Creator gives these creatures a special blessing that grants dominion to them in their medium of water or air (1:22).

The narrator's climactic interest, however, is reserved for the *nepeš ḥayyâ* ("living beings") created on the last day of the drama: the animals according to their species ("kind") and the supreme earthling known as *'ādām,* "humanity, human being" (1:26-27). It is evident that the story intends to show an affinity between these earthlings—animals and humans. They were created on the same day (a subtle literary indication of affinity), and later on the story states that they share the same table in a peaceable kingdom, for they eat the vegetation that was prepared at the climax of the first movement of the creation drama.

The characteristics of this kind of *nepeš ḥayyâ* include:

14. Virginia Stem Owens, *And the Trees Clap Their Hands: Faith, Perception, and the New Physics* (Grand Rapids: Eerdmans, 1983) 132.

mobility:	they creep upon the face of the earth
sexuality:	they are capable of reproducing their species
breath:	they are animated by (divine) breath
blood:	they all share the mysterious potency of vitality, for "the blood is the life"

The narrator clearly wants to say that these earth creatures created on the same day belong together. In a sense they are relatives, if that means that they are related as God's creatures who live in the same *oikos* ("house"; *oikos* is the Greek term from which the English word "ecology" comes). But if all these animals are equal, then, to recall a line from George Orwell's *Animal Farm,* some are "more equal than others." The climax of the story is the creation of *'ādām* ("human being"), consisting of "male and female" equally. In various ways the narrator stresses that the human, though related to the animal, has a special role in God's creation.

The creation of human beings is preceded by a solemn announcement, a resolution that the Creator announces in the heavenly council:

Then God said: "Let us make human beings [*'ādām*] in our image, after our likeness, and let them have dominion over the fish of the sea, the birds of the sky, the cattle and all wild beasts, and everything that moves upon the earth."

So God created humanity [*'ādām*] in his own image, in the image of God he created it; male and female he created them. (Gen. 1:26-27)

Moreover, during another dramatic pause the Creator confers a special blessing on human beings (not on the land animals) to reproduce and to have dominion over the earth as those who are made in the "image of God."

The expression "image of God" is applied only to human beings, never to animals, and thus is crucial for understanding what makes humans different from animals. This subject alone deserves a full discussion (see chap. 8 below), and here I can only allude to some of its dimensions. The image refers to something distinctive in human being that makes possible a sense of awe and wonder, which could lead to prayer and relationship with God. The image refers to those special dimensions of human nature that lift humans above the animal plane: imagination, freedom to be and to become, responsibility and guilt, intellectual inquiry, artistic appreciation. The image refers, above all, to the God-given commission to "image" God on earth, that is, to be the agents who represent and realize God's benevolent and peaceful sway on earth.

This would be an appropriate point to launch into a discussion of human responsibility and ethical obligations. But my major interest here is in the concerns that scientists and theologians have in common, and one of these is clearly the novelty of life, especially human life, on this planet. One comes inevitably, then, to the evolutionary hypothesis and its relation to the biblical creation faith. Remember the premise of this discussion: that one should not confuse the descriptive language of science and the poetic language of the Bible, which are based on different modes of perception and yield different kinds of knowledge. At the same time, one should be able to appreciate that those who speak these languages (and sometimes in the same person) share common interests.

In this case, the common interest is the sheer novelty of life—*nepeš ḥayyâ,* to use the biblical terminology. Nothing that has been said about the Genesis creation story necessarily argues against an evolutionary hypothesis, provided that hypothesis stays within the limitations of the language of science. Indeed, there are striking points of contact: the emergence of biological life (*nepeš ḥayyâ*) in the waters; the appearance of life on the land (earth) with its special characteristics of mobility, breathing, sentience, and so forth. Further, the appearance of the human (*'ādām*) is a novelty, even though the human and the animal are interrelated.

It may be helpful in this connection to quote in part a portion of Judge Overton's decision in the 1982 Arkansas case:

> Although the subject of origins of life is within the province of biology, the scientific community does not consider origins of life a part of evolutionary theory. The theory of evolution assumes the existence of life and is directed to an explanation of how life evolved. Evolution does not presuppose the absence of a creator or God.[15]

SUMMARY

In this discussion I have tried to show that one should not put religion and science in opposition, even though they use different languages and give different kinds of knowledge. Moreover, I have suggested that religion, in order to find a secure haven from modern thought, should not retreat into an area of "experience" that is unrelated to the cosmos in which we live and move and have our being. The time has come for theologians and scientists to dialogue with each other, realizing that they share common interests. These interests include the mystery of the origination of the cosmos, the mystery of order that is sustained in the face of the threat of chaos, and the mystery of the emergence of life, especially human life, on this planet.

15. Quoted in *Is God a Creationist?* 77.

First and last, however, the view of creation expressed in the opening chapter of Genesis presupposes a commitment of faith—identification with a believing and worshiping community. The Genesis story speaks to and for people who have made such a commitment and who, like Luther before the Diet of Worms, say, "Hier stehe Ich, Ich kann nicht anders" ("Here I stand, I cannot do otherwise"). This stand of faith does not call for a sacrifice of the intellect, a blind faith in something irrational and absurd. On the contrary, it welcomes the exciting vistas of modern science and the opportunity to dialogue with scientists who also stand humbly before these mysteries.

CHAPTER 7

Human Dominion
over Nature

Some time ago an article appeared in the *New York Times* under the arresting title, "Think Rhinoceros, or All Is Lost."[1] The author's initial question, "Who needs a rhinoceros?" most readers could quickly answer in the negative. This animal, surely one of the homeliest in God's creation, does not claim our attention outside a zoo. But within a couple of sentences the author was calling into question our whole way of life. "Unless you take your Adam and Eve straight, you cannot believe that man came into a lonely world. Nor without those species that preceded them would mankind ever have happened. Earth has always been for sharing." He went on to observe that most species of plants and animals were well established before humankind assumed its tyrannical role of "tearing down, robbing, and polluting the earth." He suggested that human destiny on this planet is ominously threatened by the fate of the whooping crane or the snow leopard and "the passing of the last rhinoceros." Even the ant came in for praise, to the detriment of human beings. The article concluded with praise for Thoreau, the famous naturalist who declared that "in wildness is the salvation of the world."

It would be unjust to dismiss the "rhinoceros essay" as merely an expression of a romantic back-to-nature movement à la Thoreau. Today, as a result of enterprising initiative that has conquered the wilderness and subjected nature to human control, the United States faces a major ecological crisis. This crisis is manifest in debates about strip-mining, food and world population, the use of energy resources, disposal of waste, and so

1. Daniel L. McKinley, *New York Times,* Sunday, July 18, 1971.

on. As we know well, hardheaded, scientific realists, who are unaffected by the romanticism of Thoreau, have emphasized the gravity of the crisis, even in eschatological terms. Time is running out, we hear from members of the Club of Rome and from others. Now is the time for repentance, that is, a change of lifestyle. One can almost hear with new accent the words of an ancient prophet: "An end! The end has come upon the four corners of the land. Now the end is upon you" (Ezek. 7:1ff.).

From the time the Pilgrims landed on the soil of the New World and began to push back the wilderness, Christianity has had a great influence in shaping our way of life. Indeed, some would go so far as to maintain that the present crisis is traceable to Christian sponsorship of the view of human dominion over nature expressed in the passage about the *imago Dei* (Gen. 1:26-28). For instance, Lynn White, Jr., takes this position in a well-known and much-discussed essay.[2] He maintains that Christianity in the Latin West bears "a huge burden of guilt" for the ecological crisis, because our lifestyle in Western civilization has been profoundly shaped by a biblical theology that establishes a sharp dichotomy between human-kind (history) and its environment (nature). In sharp contrast to paganism and most Asian religions, Christianity "not only established a dualism of man and nature but also insisted that it is God's will that man exploit nature for his proper ends." He concludes by nominating Francis of Assisi, "the greatest spiritual revolutionary in Western history," as the patron saint of the ecological cause, for in vain "he tried to substitute the idea of the equality of all creatures, including man, for the idea of man's limitless rule of creation." Christianity's culpability was also discussed at a theological conference held in Claremont, California (1970), again with reference to the doctrine of the image of God. The *New York Times* (May 1, 1970) carried an article with the bold headline: "Christianity Linked to Pollution. Scholars Cite Call in Bible for Man to Dominate Life."

This indictment of Christianity makes good headlines, even though the case may not stand up under examination. It is undoubtedly true, however, that Christianity in the West has to some degree accommodated to the new economic climate that superseded medieval life. Strikingly, Karl Marx could speak a word of appreciation for capitalism, which in its own way is "permanently revolutionary," for it has produced "a stage of society compared with which all earlier stages appear to be merely *local progress* and idolatry of nature." His further comments in the *Grundrisse* well describe the modern enterprising spirit:

---

2. Lynn White, Jr., "The Historical Roots of Our Ecologic Crisis," *Science* 155 (1967) 1203–7; repr. in *The Environmental Handbook* (ed. Garrett De Bell; New York: Ballantine, 1970) 12–26.

Nature becomes for the first time simply an object for mankind, purely a matter of utility; it ceases to be recognized as a power in its own right; and the theoretical knowledge of its independent laws appears only as a stratagem designed to subdue it to human requirements, whether as the object of consumption or as the means of production.[3]

It is understandable that Christians, in the new age dominated by technology and the profit motive, would turn to biblical texts to find a warrant for the new way of life that has reached its highest peak of achievement in the New World. If Christianity has both shaped and been shaped by the revolutionary spirit of the modern age, it is time to seek a new understanding of the biblical texts in their appropriate biblical contexts and to learn anew what it means for people to be the image of God. In what follows I shall address the question of the role of *'ādām* ("humanity") in God's creation, with special attention to the related passages Gen. 1:26-28 and Ps. 8:5-8 [6-9].

THE DISTINCTION BETWEEN
NATURE AND HISTORY

In an important essay that appeared in the mid-sixties as a forerunner of our current ecological concern, Gerhard von Rad issued a call for a more balanced theological understanding of humankind in relation to its natural environment. He emphasized that ancient Israel had "a phenomenal sense of history"; for "it was above all in the realm of political history that the Hebrew of Old Testament times became aware of the sovereignty of God." But he went on to say that "we are nowadays in a serious danger of looking at the theological problems of the Old Testament far too much from the one-sided standpoint of an historically conditioned theology" and ignoring or neglecting "the greater part of what the Old Testament has to say about what we call Nature."[4]

We approach the task of a "theology of nature" in a post-Cartesian period, which means that inevitably we bring to biblical interpretation distinctions that did not exist in Israel's experience. The vocabulary of the Old Testament does not contain words that are equivalent to our terms "history" and "nature." What we distinguish as two separate realms constituted for Israel a single realm of Yahweh's sovereignty, as one can see from the exodus story, where both "natural events" (the driving back of

---

3. Quoted by Spencer Pollard in his review of Marx's *Grundrisse, Saturday Review,* August 7, 1971, p. 27.

4. Gerhard von Rad, "Some Aspects of the Old Testament World-View," in *The Problem of the Hexateuch and Other Essays* (trans. E. W. Trueman Dicken; New York: McGraw-Hill, 1966) 144. The essay appeared in German in 1964.

the Reed Sea, manna in the wilderness, etc.) and "historical events" (the liberation from Egyptian bondage, victory over the Amelekites, etc.) are regarded equally as signs of Yahweh's activity. The same easy shift from what we would call nature to history occurs in some of Israel's psalms that praise Yahweh as creator. This shift is evident, for instance, in Psalm 33, which belongs to the genre of the hymn. The psalmist's hymnic praise is motivated by Yahweh's power as creator of heaven and earth:

> By the word of the Lord the heavens were made,
>   and all their host by the breath of his mouth.
> He gathered the waters of the sea as in a bottle;
>   he put the deeps in storehouses.
> Let all the earth fear the Lord;
>   let all the inhabitants of the world stand in awe of him.
> For he spoke, and it came to be;
>   he commanded, and it stood firm. (Ps. 33:6-9, NRSV)

The psalmist considers immediately how the Creator's sovereignty is manifest in the realm of historical affairs: God is the one who "fashions" the hearts of human beings, who brings the counsels of the nations to naught, and whose "eye" is upon all people. Here the movement of praise proceeds smoothly, without any distinction, from the Creator's sovereignty over heaven and earth to divine sovereignty over human affairs, both constituting the unified area of God's control.

Since the 1960s scholars have called into question one of the favorite themes of past biblical theology, namely, that Yahweh was known and confessed as the God of history and that history was the primary mode of God's revelation.[5] Extending this criticism beyond the Old Testament, Bertil Albrektson has challenged the prevalent view that the religions of neighboring peoples were simply "nature religions." From Mesopotamian sources he adduces evidence that testimonies to divine activity in history were not peculiar to ancient Israel. In the end, however, Albrektson has to admit that "the idea of divine acts in history" in Israel on the one hand and in Mesopotamia on the other "may well have occupied a rather different place in the different pattern of beliefs."[6] That is true. The sporadic evidence adduced stands in contrast to the fundamental role of historical remembrance in the Israelite cult (Deut. 26:5-9) and, as von Rad observes, to Israel's "stubborn need to push forward to the perception of far-reaching

5. See James Barr, "Revelation through History in the Old Testament and Modern Theology," *Int* 17 (1963) 193–205; Brevard S. Childs, *Biblical Theology in Crisis* (Philadelphia: Westminster, 1970) 39–44, 62–66.

6. Bertil Albrektson, *History and the Gods: An Essay on the Idea of Historical Events as Divine Manifestations in the Ancient Near East and in Israel* (Lund: Gleerup, 1967). Quotation from p. 115.

historical continuities," as in the historical works of the Old Testament.[7] Nevertheless, Albrektson's study is a healthy reaction to the one-sided emphasis on history in Old Testament theology. At times this emphasis has been carried to the extreme of saying that Israel's "conception of the world is so little influenced by religion that it was rather an obstacle than an aid to faith";[8] and some theologians, influenced by Bultmann, have made faith existential to the point that "nature" is left out of account.

I do not see how, in the situation today, one can avoid the distinction between history and nature or a Cartesian distinction between mind and matter (subject and object), even though such distinctions are alien to the Old Testament. George Hendry, who emphasizes this point, has proposed that "a better answer to Descartes would be, not to attempt to rescind the bifurcation of reality which he introduced, but rather to inquire whether, by placing the particular problem with which he was concerned in a larger framework, the two perspectives could be combined in a stereoscopic vision, to which the doctrine of creation might appear in a new light."[9] Granted that, in the last analysis, such a "stereoscopic vision" is possible for God alone, the question is whether some intimations of it may be provided by Israel's experience of divine reality.

One of the best discussions of this subject, generally overlooked in recent biblical theology, is H. Wheeler Robinson's chapter on "The Hebrew Conception of Nature" in his posthumous *Inspiration and Revelation in the Old Testament*.[10] It is noteworthy that immediately after his initial statement about the unity of God's creation, he slips into the distinction between nature and history and gives theological primacy to the latter. "Yahweh's ultimate relation to things is a derivative from his primary relation to men."[11] One cannot ignore this epistemological starting point if indeed, as the Old Testament witnesses throughout, Yahweh reveals himself as personal will in relationship to a covenant people, rather than in natural processes (Baalism). The Old Testament speaks of Yahweh in bold anthropomorphisms and intolerantly avoids the theriomorphisms found in surrounding cultures. Moreover, the primary motifs for expressing the faith of Israel, such as the promise to the ancestors, exodus and covenant

7. Gerhard von Rad, *Wisdom in Israel* (trans. James D. Martin; Nashville: Abingdon, 1972) 289ff., esp. 290 n. 3.

8. Edmund Jacob, *Theology of the Old Testament* (trans. Arthur W. Heathcote and Philip J. Allcock; New York: Harper & Row 1958) 146. He quotes favorably the verdict of Victor Monod (*Dieu dans l'univers* [Paris: 1933] 16) that "the material universe is only the temporary and removable setting of the divine-human drama. It does not possess permanent worth" (p. 149).

9. George S. Hendry, "Eclipse of Creation," *TToday* 28 (1972) 406–25. Quotation from p. 423.

10. This work, published in 1946 (Oxford: Clarendon), constituted the prolegomenon to Robinson's projected Old Testament Theology. The chapter to which I refer is on pp. 1–16.

11. Ibid., 2.

(treaty), and the kingdom of God, are derived from social and political experience. Once this starting point is granted, however, it is important to hear Robinson's further elaboration:

> History supplied a revelation of God which Nature, notwithstanding all its rich content and variety, could never afford. Yet the conception of the God who works in history is inseparably linked to His manifestation in natural phenomena. He is what Nature, as well as history, reveals himself to be, and Nature is His peculiar language.[12]

This "peculiar language," which is used in the anthem of praise sung by the heavens (Ps. 19:1-3[2-4]), proclaims the "glory" (*kābôd*) of the Creator, or as Paul puts it, "Ever since the creation of the world his eternal power and divine nature, invisible though they are, have been understood and seen through the things he has made. So they are without excuse" (Rom. 1:20, NRSV). Here it is impossible to deal with the various connotations of "nature's language" as perceived by Israel's interpreters: Torah writers, psalmists, prophets, and sages. Robinson refers to several aspects of Israel's theology of nature: the aesthetic appreciation of natural phenomena as reflected, for instance, in the Song of Songs; the awesome awareness of the many mysteries in nature, which will not disclose its secret to the human's inquiring search (the book of Job); the awareness of the marvelous order of nature in which every aspect of God's earthly creation has its own *mîn* ("species, classification"; Gen. 1:11) and in which the whole is governed by regularity (Gen. 8:22, 9:13ff.; cf. Jer. 5:24); and the view that material objects are "alive," animated, as though having a psychical life of their own—a view that is strange to the modern notion of nature as dead and mechanical. "Nature is alive through and through, and therefore the more capable of sympathy with man, and of response to the rule of its Creator and Upholder, on whom it directly depends."[13] This does not imply, as we shall see, "a democracy of all God's creatures," as Lynn White, Jr., seems to advocate in the name of Francis of Assisi. Nonetheless, a kinship clearly exists between humanity and nature. Indeed, "earth has always been for sharing," to think once again of the threatened rhinoceros.

THE TRANSCENDENCE OF THE CREATOR

There is one limit, however, beyond which Israel's theology of nature cannot go. While heaven and earth reveal the "glory" of Deity, Israel

12. Ibid., 4.
13. Ibid., 16.

refused to suggest that the creation is a direct self-revelation of Yahweh, as though it were an emanation of God's being or as though God were a power immanent within it. As creator, God transcends the whole creation. This means, first, that the creation language of the Bible "unquestionably connotes origination."[14] The initial word *rē'šît,* especially when Gen. 1:1 is read (as it should be) as an independent sentence, points to "the absolute beginning of the world."[15] Second, the world is absolutely dependent on the Creator. This dimension of God's creative work is admirably expressed in Ps. 104:27-30, where the verbs in the Hebrew imperfect indicate continuous action (*creatio continua*):

> These all look to thee
>> to give them their food in due season.
> When thou givest to them, they gather it up;
>> when thou openest thy hand, they are filled with good things.
> When thou hidest thy face, they are dismayed;
>> when thou takest away their breath, they die
>>> and return to their dust.
> When thou sendest forth thy spirit they are created,
>> and thou renewest the face of the ground. (RSV)

Were it not for the sustaining and upholding power of the Creator, the creation would lapse into chaos. The regularities of nature—"seedtime and harvest, cold and heat, summer and winter, day and night" (Gen. 8:22)—are not based on laws of a self-existent cosmos; rather, they are signs of the faithfulness and dependability of the Creator who, according to the Priestly theologian, has made an "everlasting covenant" with "every living creature of all flesh that is on the earth" (Gen. 9:16, NRSV).

Israel was not unique in the formulation of myths that expressed these two aspects of creation. Various ancient myths told about origination, that is, the creation of individual human being or the creation of the world as a whole; and some myths expressed the dependence of the world upon the God who insured the regularity of the seasons and the annual renewal of fertility. Mediated to Israel through Canaanite culture or through the cosmopolitan atmosphere of the Davidic-Solomonic court, these myths belong undoubtedly to the prehistory of Israel's creation faith.[16] Recognizing that Israel borrowed mythical material and shared humanity's elemental

---

14. Hendry, *TToday* 28 (1972) 420. See above, pp. 89–93.

15. Walther Eichrodt, "In the Beginning," in *Israel's Prophetic Heritage: Essays in Honor of James Muilenburg* (ed. Bernhard W. Anderson and Walter Harrelson; New York: Harper & Row, 1962) 1–10. See also Claus Westermann, *Genesis* (trans. John J. Scullion; Continental Commentary; 3 vols.; Minneapolis: Augsburg, 1984–86) 1.93ff.

16. This prehistory receives great emphasis in Claus Westermann's *Genesis*. See esp. 1.19–47.

experiences, one may ask at what point Israel's worldview differed from its neighbors.

Gerhard von Rad locates the point of difference in Israel's strict prohibition of images: "any likeness of anything that is in heaven above, or that is in the earth beneath, or that is in the water under the earth" (Exod. 20:4)—in other words, in the whole realm of creation, pictorially conceived. Ancient religions, he points out, gave a central place to cult images, for in some sense the deity was present in the image; the image was a means of contact between God and human life, a source of blessing and saving power.

Without the gods, and without concrete representations of them, human beings would be lost in the world. Yet the mystery of godhead bursts out all around them. From it they may gain a blessing and bring order and purpose into their lives; apart from it they could not exist. In the sphere of human life there is an infinite variety of points at which divinity shines through, and every point in the human world is at least potentially a point of divine intrusion, an expression of Deity, and to this extent a means of communication between God and human beings. This understanding of the situation makes possible the extraordinary tolerance that idol cults extend to one another.[17]

From the Mosaic period on, however, Israel was intolerant of images. This aniconic faith received its supreme expression in the prophecy of Second Isaiah. Proclaiming the unfathomable wisdom and inexhaustible power of Yahweh, the Creator, the prophet asks:

> To whom then will you liken God,
>   or what likeness [*dĕmût*] compare with him? (Isa. 40:18, NRSV)

After a satire on the foolish manufacture of idols, once again the question is asked:

> To whom then will you compare me,
>   or who is my equal? says the Holy One.
> Lift up your eyes on high and see:
>   Who created these?
> He who brings out their host and numbers them,
>   calling them all by name;
> because he is great in strength,
>   mighty in power,
>   not one is missing. (Isa. 40:25-26, NRSV)

17. Von Rad, *Problem of the Hexateuch,* 147.

According to the prophet, Yahweh is the transcendent God: the Creator who originated the universe and whose sovereign power undergirds the whole historical drama from beginning to end. The world is under the sole control of the God who "declared the end [*'aḥărît*] from the beginning [*rē'šît*]" (Isa. 46:10).

THE CROWNING OF HUMANS AS *IMAGO DEI*

In the light of this perspective, what is the meaning of the affirmation that humankind is the image (*ṣelem*) or likeness (*děmût*) of God? For an answer, I will now turn to Gen. 1:26-28 and the related passage in Ps. 8:5-8[6-9]. In the history of interpretation these texts have received emphasis out of all proportion to the weight given them in the Old Testament itself, where they stand virtually alone.

Some kind of relationship exists between these two passages, which is not surprising since both reflect the liturgical usage of the Jerusalem cult. It is difficult to say whether Psalm 8 is older than and possibly influenced the formulation of Gen. 1:26-28, or whether the latter existed first, perhaps in the form of a cultic legend used in the Jerusalem Temple, and as such provided the inspiration for the psalmist's composition. Probability favors the first alternative.

Psalm 8 is a hymn that begins and ends with an exclamation of praise to Yahweh, whose "name" is majestic throughout all the earth. The hymnic invocation at the beginning is expanded by an elaboration, the purpose of which is to portray Yahweh's majesty in the heavenly realm. Unfortunately, the meaning of the hymnic expansion (vv. 1a, 2[2a, 3]) is not clear in the Hebrew original. The psalmist apparently draws upon mythical language, perhaps Canaanite in origin, to portray Yahweh's sovereignty in the cosmic sphere.[18] In any case, the subsequent theme of the coronation of humankind is placed in the context of Yahweh's transcendent sovereignty. The main part of the hymn begins in v. 3(4) with *kî* ("when," "for") and provides the motive for earthly praise, corresponding to the praise that resounds in the cosmic temple (cf. Isa. 6:1-4). When looking up at the starry vault, the work of Yahweh's "fingers," and the heavenly bodies that Yahweh has set in their ordered place, the psalmist marvels that the Cre-

---

18. At least three matters seem to stand out: (a) Yahweh's splendor is "above" (*'al*) the heavens; (b) Yahweh has established a "bulwark" (*'ōz*) in the heavenly sphere; and (c) from this citadel, situated above the heavenly vault, Yahweh subdues his foes. Mitchell Dahood maintains that the psalmist poetically employs mythical language, as in Ps. 89:10-11(11-12), to portray Yahweh's cosmic majesty. He compares the Canaanite myth of Baal, who vanquishes his adversary *Yamm* (Sea) and afterward builds a heavenly palace. See Dahood, *Psalms* (AB, 3 vols.; Garden City, N.Y.: Doubleday, 1965–70) 1.49–51.

ator is mindful of this comparatively small and transient creature, a "human being" (*'ĕnôš, ben-'ādām*) (cf. Job 7:17-18). The question, however, does not stand by itself but provides the lead into the contrasting statement that follows: such an insignificant and transient creature, yet one who is so richly endowed with glory and honor! Hence the hymn continues with a transition that in Hebrew is marked by an "adversative *waw*," to be translated as "but, yet, nevertheless":

> Yet you have made him to fall short slightly from divine beings,[19]
> and with glory and honor you have crowned him.
> You have caused him to rule over the works of your hands,
>   everything you have put under his feet:
>   small and large cattle—all of them,
>   also the beasts of the field,
>   birds of the heaven, and fish of the sea—
>   whatever courses through the ocean paths. (Ps. 8:5-8[6-9])

The hymn concludes with a refrain that echoes the opening exclamation of praise.

The creation account in Gen. 1:1—2:3 once may have served a liturgical purpose.[20] In its present form, however, it is detached from a cultic setting and stands in the so-called Priestly work, which starts from the creation of the world and from this universal scope narrows down genealogically to Israel, reaching its climax in the establishment of the tabernacle and the constitution of the people as a worshiping community. This chapter is not hymnic praise, as Psalm 8 is, but theological reflection on the cosmic implications of Israel's knowledge of God mediated through its historical traditions and rites of worship. The climax of Genesis 1 is the creation of humankind (*'ādām,* "human being"), an event that, in terms of the present seven-day scheme, occurs on the same day as the creation of other living creatures according to their species: cattle, beasts of the earth, and creeping things. In this context the solemn announcement is made, apparently in the heavenly council, of God's resolution to create humankind "as our image, according to our likeness" (v. 26). The preposition here translated "as" (*bĕ*) refers to the function of human beings; hence

---

19. In this translation I assume that *'ĕlōhîm* refers not to God directly but to the divine beings (Septuagint: *angeloi*) of the heavenly court (so NAB); NEB translates "a god."

20. Paul Humbert maintains that the Priestly creation story was a festival legend for the seven-day Feast of Tabernacles with which the New Year began, on the analogy of the Babylonian *Enuma elish,* which was the myth-libretto for the *akitu* or Babylonian New Year festival. See "La relation de Genèse 1 et du Psaume 104 avec la liturgie de Nouvel-An israélite," *Opuscules d'un hébraïsant* (Neuchâtel: Université de Neuchâtel, 1958) 166–74.

God's decision is to give humankind dominion over fish, birds, cattle, wild animals, and land reptiles.[21]

The affinities between these two passages, Ps. 8:5-8[6-9] and Gen. 1:26-28, are strong. (1) Both passages apparently presuppose the view of the heavenly council (the "sons of God" or *'ĕlōhîm*-beings) within which, as in the Babylonian *Enuma elish,* the decision to create humankind is announced. (2) Both passages bring human beings into close proximity to the status of *'ĕlōhîm.* The Priestly account states that humankind is created as the image of *'ĕlōhîm* ("God" or "gods," i.e., heavenly beings). The psalmist uses a circumlocution: humankind is made slightly inferior to *'ĕlōhîm.* (3) Finally, in both passages, humanity's high position in God's creation carries with it the power to exercise dominion over the animals. The question is: What does the motif of the *imago Dei* say or imply concerning human dominion over the natural environment?

There is, however, one major difference. The clearest evidence of the independence of Psalm 8 is the motif of the coronation of human beings: "with glory and honor you have crowned them [him]."[22] Here there is no suggestion that human dominion is based on a divine blessing that empowers humans to multiply and subdue the earth, as in the Priestly story (Gen. 1:28). Rather, human dominion over the earth is a consequence of Yahweh's elevating humankind to a royal position. One could argue that the verb "crown" is intended here in a general sense, as in Ps. 103:4, which states that Yahweh crowns a person with steadfast love and mercy. But the language of Psalm 8 suggests royal investiture. Human beings are crowned with "glory and honor," terms that are used of an earthly king (Ps. 45:4-5[5-6]; 110:3). Yahweh has "caused them [him] to rule" (*māšal*), a verb that is also used of a reigning king (Isa. 19:4; Mic. 5:2). And Yahweh has put everything "under their [his] feet," like booty (cf. Ps. 2:8). H.-J. Kraus remarks appropriately in this connection: "The Creator and world ruler Yahweh assigns the world to the human being as to a king

---

21. The prepositions *bĕ* and *kĕ* can be reversed, as in 5:3, which makes precise interpretation difficult. One should not place too much emphasis on the translation of *bĕ* as "in," for the preposition is used with various meanings in the Old Testament. It can be used to express "the quality or manner in which an entity shows itself" (KB, 102), and probably it should be so construed in this case, that is, "as our image." So Gerhard von Rad, *Genesis* (trans. John H. Marks; OTL; rev. ed; Philadelphia: Westminster, 1972) 57–58. Notice that the parallel preposition in Gen. 1:26-27 (*kĕ*) has the same use in Isa. 40:23: "[he] makes judges of the earth as nothing."

The words "over all the earth" in v. 26 (RSV) represent a defective text that is to be restored according to the Syriac and the animal sequence in vv. 24, 25, 28: "over all wild animals on earth" (see NEB and NAB).

22. In the Hebrew of Ps. 8:4-6(5-7) the pronouns are masculine singular ("him," "his"); one may render in English the inclusive meaning by shifting to the plural ("them," "their") as in NRSV.

installed by God."[23] There is little doubt that the language of Psalm 8 is the language of royal theology used in the Jerusalem court (and used more openly than in the parallel passage in Genesis 1). According to the psalmist, human beings are invested with a royal splendor that not only raises them above the animals but also draws them into the sphere of God's royal rule. The "glory and honor" that belong to the Creator (Ps. 29:1, 104:1) are reflected to a degree in humankind's majestic position on earth. The name of Yahweh is glorious on earth *through* the human being who is crowned as God's viceroy.

THE MYTHICAL "FIRST BEING"

Who is this "being" that is described in such exalted terms? Does the psalmist refer to everyman? Or to a particular person who represents the divine rule on earth? Since so many of the psalms are colored by the language of royal theology, it is possible that there is some influence from ancient mythical views that portrayed the king as "the son of God" or "the creation of God." In Ezek. 28:11-19, for instance, the king of Tyre is portrayed as "royal first man." According to the myth there once lived in Eden, the garden of God located on the sacred mountain, a glorious being who, from the day of his creation, was "the signet of perfection, full of wisdom and perfect in beauty." The primordial man is described as a royal figure who wore a pectoral studded with precious stones. The *Urkönig* ("first king") walked freely in the garden of God, which was adorned with flashing gems ("stones of fire"). But his wisdom and beauty went to his head and the Creator expelled him from the sacred mountain and hurled him to earth. In Ezekiel's interpretation, the mythical tragedy is a portrayal of the fall of Tyre.[24] It may well be that this myth lies behind the questioning of Job:

> Were you the first man born?
> Were you created before the hills?
> Have you listened in on the council of God?
> Have you sole possession of wisdom? (Job 15:7-8, NJPSV)

Scandinavian scholars have adduced these passages to support the view that the statements of Psalm 8 about the coronation of humankind originally referred to the king or, more properly, to the primordial king (*Urkönig*) who, as God's creation, was invested with royal splendor. Aage

23. H.-J. Kraus, *Psalms* (trans. Hilton C. Oswald; Continental Commentary; 2 vols.; Minneapolis: Augsburg, 1988–89) 1.183.
24. See H. G. May, "The King in the Garden of Eden," in *Israel's Prophetic Heritage*, 166–76; also John L. McKenzie, *Myths and Realities* (Milwaukee: Bruce, 1963) 154–56, 175–81.

Bentzen is a major advocate of this position. He maintains that this psalm belongs in a circle of psalms that presuppose a cultic drama celebrated at the New Year festival when worshipers reactualized the divine battle against powers of chaos (Sea, Rahab, Leviathan). In Psalm 8, he says, "the poet contemplates the Heavens as the bulwark created by the Lord against all his enemies. This work of Yahweh is greater than any other work of His, even greater than the First Man, who was created to be King of God's World."[25] This view is seconded by Helmer Ringgren, who insists that the words of Ps. 8:4-8[5-9] refer to the king, who acted in a representative capacity for the people.[26]

There is much to be said for the corporate or representative conception of "man," especially when the psalm is considered in the context of the royal theology of Jerusalem, which was heavily influenced by ancient Near Eastern views of king and temple. One could support the royal interpretation of Psalm 8 by appeal to Ps. 80:17[18], where the poetic parallelism makes the meaning clear:

Let your hand be upon the man [*'îš*] at your right hand,
the son of man [*ben-'ādām*] whom you have strengthened for yourself!

Here the psalmist refers to the king who is seated "at the right hand" of God (Ps. 110:1) and who is "made strong" through his election or adoption as God's son (Ps. 2:7). Further, the ascription or dedication of Psalm 8 to David, according to the superscription, may indicate that this was one of the psalms to be used in the cult. In any event, David was regarded as "a leading and archetypal figure in Israel," as Christoph Barth points out, one "in whom their own existence as the people of God had found an expression that was valid for all time."[27] Finally, it is noteworthy that elsewhere the dominion of the king is said to include rule over animals as well as over humanity, for instance in Jer. 27:4-6 (NRSV):

Thus says the Lord of hosts, the God of Israel: This is what you shall say to your masters: It is I who by my great power and my outstretched arm have

25. Aage Bentzen, *King and Messiah* (London: Lutterworth, 1955) 12. See pp. 42–43, where he discusses Ezek. 28:12-19.

26. Helmer Ringgren, *The Messiah in the Old Testament* (SBT 1/18; London: SCM, 1956) 20: "At first sight these words seem to refer to man in general or to Adam, but there is reason to believe that they were originally said about the king. Since the creative acts of God and man's dominion over creation were actualized in the annual Festival, it is conceivable that the proclamation of that dominion was repeated and addressed to the king, who, so to speak, played the role of Adam as the representative of mankind."

27. Christoph Barth, *Introduction to the Psalms* (trans. R. A. Wilson; New York: Charles Scribner's Sons, 1966) 65. Barth calls attention to the fact that "in the prayers of an individual the king is always more or less closely associated with him, while in the prayers of the king the individual Israelite is included at the same time" (p. 26).

made the earth, with the people and animals that are on the earth, and I give it to whomever I please. Now I have given all these lands into the hand of King Nebuchadnezzar of Babylon, my servant, and I have given him even the wild animals of the field to serve him.

But the fact that in Psalm 8 "royal" dominion is over animals, birds, and fish, not over people and animals, should warn against a messianic interpretation of the psalm. The royal figure of Psalm 8 is *not* empowered to overcome his enemies, as elsewhere in royal psalms (Ps. 2:7-9), but rather to have dominion over the everyday aspects of the world, which include hunting and fishing, pasturing of flocks, use of meat for food, and so forth. The most natural reading of "man" and "son of man" (*'ĕnôš, ben-'ādām*) is that the parallel terms refer to mortal man, everyman (as in Job 25:6; Isa. 51:12; 56:2, etc.), who despite his transience and limitation is elevated to a position of honor and glory in God's creation. This sense is brought out nicely in the REB:

What is a frail mortal, that you should be mindful of him,
a human being, that you should take notice of him?
Yet you have made him little less than a god,
crowning his head with glory and honour. (Ps. 8:4-5[5-6])

If the king used this language in the cult, it must have had the meaning of the king's prayer in Ps. 144:3-4, where the parallel terms *'ādām* and *ben-'ĕnôš* refer not to his royal status but to his identification with transient humanity:

O Yahweh, what is a human being [*'ādām*]
that you are mindful of him,
a human individual [*ben-'ĕnôš,* "son of man"]
that you think of him?
A human being [*'ādām*] is like a breath,
his days like a passing shadow.

Psalm 8 does employ royal terminology, and perhaps the myth of royal first man is in the background. But the psalm represents an early stage in the "democratization" of the royal theology of the ancient Near East. It is appropriate to refer to John Calvin's illuminating commentary on Psalm 8, where the democratization of royal rule is interpreted as human dominion over the ordinary aspects of the everyday world:

For there is no man so dull and slow-witted, but if he will open his eyes, he may see it is by the wonderful providence of God that horses and oxen yield their service to men; that sheep bear wool to clothe them with; and that all kinds of cattle yield even their flesh to feed them. The more visible the proof of this dominion is, the more it becomes us to be touched with the sense of God's grace, as often as we either eat meat, or enjoy other comforts.[28]

The messianic interpretation of the psalm in the New Testament (Heb. 2:5-18), which was influenced by the Septuagint translation, picked up overtones that were present in the psalm from the first.[29]

DEMOCRATIZATION OF THE *IMAGO DEI* IN PRIESTLY TRADITION

In view of the close affinities between Ps. 8:5-8[6-9] and Gen. 1:26-28, one would expect to find some evidence of the language of royal theology in the Priestly creation story as well. This expectation, however, is not amply rewarded. The Genesis passage does describe human dominion over the earth with verbs that can be used in the context of royal theology. This is true of the verb used in 1:26, *rādâ* ("tread," "rule"), which is used of the king in Ps. 110:2 ("rule in the midst of your foes!") and Ps. 72:8 ("May he have dominion from sea to sea"). It is striking that, with the exception of this scant linguistic evidence, the motif of the coronation of humankind, which figures so prominently in Psalm 8, is absent from Genesis 1.

Nevertheless, some Scandinavian scholars insist that the mythical first man or *Urkönig* is the subject of the Genesis passage. Aage Bentzen writes:

> The first man in Genesis 1:26-28 is described as the first ruler of the world. In the first Creation Story—the "gospel" of the New Year, we hear the blessing spoken by God at the enthronement of the first Royal Couple of the world. Man is to "rule" over all living creatures.[30]

Comparing the first pair with the Babylonian king, who was regarded as "the image of God," he concludes that the "royal" pair were divine (*göttlich*). In support of this view, he adduces the curious passage in Ps. 45:6[7] where, according to the received text, the king is addressed as *'ĕlōhîm,* "God":

> Your throne, O God, endures forever and ever.
> Your royal scepter is a scepter of equity;
> You love righteousness and hate wickedness. (Ps. 45:6-7a, NRSV)

---

28. John Calvin, *Commentary on the Psalms* (rev. trans. by T. H. L. Parker; London: James Clarke, 1965) 1.95.

29. See the illuminating article by Brevard S. Childs, "Psalm 8 in the Context of the Christian Canon," *Int* 23 (1969) 20–31.

30. Bentzen, *King and Messiah,* 17.

This mode of address, however, which belongs to extravagant court style, is the only instance of its kind in the Old Testament. There is no clear evidence that Israel adopted the whole conception of "sacred kingship."[31]

The question of royal theology in the Priestly creation story prompts a consideration of the statement that humankind is created as "the image of Elohim." In recent years biblical theologians have challenged the spiritualizing interpretations that have been influential in the Christian tradition, according to which the "image" is the spiritual capacity of human beings: reason, will, freedom, conscience, moral consciousness, immortal soul, self-transcendence, and so on. Without denying that the "image" points to human relationship to God, some have called attention to the corporeal aspect of *ṣelem,* which is softened somewhat in the parallel term *dĕmût* ("pattern, likeness"). For instance, Köhler asserts that the "image" means that human beings, in distinction from the animals, have an upright form that enables them to have dominion over their environment. "With the additional words 'in our form, to look like us' [humankind] is raised above the beasts and made to approach nearer to God."[32] It is doubtful, however, that the intention of the text is to stress the external, physical form of human beings in such a one-sided fashion. Theologians have rightly insisted that the separation between the bodily and the spiritual is alien to the Old Testament and that therefore the image refers to the whole person. The image is not something *in* the human person but is the human person itself. Gerhard von Rad, stressing the corporeality of the image, maintains that the language indicates human *function* in the totality of a person's bodily, historical being.

> Just as powerful earthly kings, to indicate their claim to dominion, erect an image of themselves in the provinces of their empire where they do not personally appear, so man is placed upon earth in God's image as God's sovereign emblem. He is really only God's representative, summoned to maintain and enforce God's claim to dominion over the earth.[33]

This is an illuminating interpretation, but unfortunately it finds no clear support in the Old Testament. The various usages of *ṣelem* show only that the term is used for something concrete like a statue (Num. 33:52; 2 Kings 11:18; Amos 5:26; Ezek. 7:20), a copy (1 Sam. 6:5, 11; Ezek. 16:17 [*ṣalmê zākār,* "images of men"—idols]), or a drawing of male figures sketched on

---

31. This matter is discussed judiciously by Martin Noth, "God, King, and Nation in the Old Testament," in *The Laws in the Pentateuch and Other Essays* (trans. D. R. Ap-Thomas; Philadelphia: Fortress Press, 1967) 145–78.

32. Ludwig Köhler, *Old Testament Theology* (trans. A. S. Todd; Philadelphia: Westminster, 1957) 147.

33. Von Rad, *Genesis,* 60.

a wall (Ezek. 23:14). One thinks especially of the *ṣelem* set up by Neb-uchadnezzar, before which all people were to bow down lest they be cast into a fiery furnace (Daniel 3). These instances show that in the ancient world a sharp distinction was not drawn between an original and its copy; a copy was regarded as something more than a mere resemblance.

The idea of "representation" deserves more exploration. Following the lead of Bentzen, but without necessarily adopting his conclusion, one might well inquire whether extrabiblical sources throw any light on the meaning of *imago Dei.*

Studies of Mesopotamian and Egyptian texts tend to support von Rad's thesis concerning the functional or representative character of the "image." Scholars have drawn attention to various Akkadian texts in which "image" (*ṣalmu*) is used of the king. In the context of the *Königsideologie* of the ancient Near East, the term is said to describe the relationship of the king to the deity and specifically his function as the god's representative in his royal office. It is argued, however, that the dominant ancestry of the Gene-sis *ṣelem* is the court style of ancient Egypt where, beginning especially with the 18th Dynasty, Pharaoh was called "the likeness of Re," "image of Re," "living likeness on earth," and so on. Strikingly, the usage often appears in creation contexts. The word of Amon Re to Pharaoh Amenophis III is especially pertinent: "You are my beloved Son, produced from my members, my image which I have established on the earth. I have made you to rule the earth in peace." H. Wildberger and W. H. Schmidt, who quote and discuss the above texts and others,[34] have concluded indepen-dently that Gen 1:26 stands on the whole much closer to Egypt than to Mesopotamia, although the Genesis passage has been "democratized" by being referred to humankind or *'ādām.*

One may concede that ancient mythical views lie behind Gen. 1:26-28, just as they lie remotely behind the opening portrayal of chaos (1:2). Using mythical language, the Priestly writers affirm that humankind stands in close relationship to God (the heavenly council) and is the agent of the divine rule on earth. The myth, however, has been changed in reinterpreta-tion. The writer stresses the transcendent majesty of God and thereby establishes a sharp differentiation between Creator and creature. Any lin-gering doubt about the writer's democratization of the image is dispelled by Gen. 5:3, where the same writer uses the terms "image" and "likeness" to describe the relationship between Adam and his son Seth. "When Adam had lived a hundred and thirty years, be became the father of a son in his likeness (*dĕmût*), according to his image [*ṣelem*], and named him Seth"

---

34. See H. Wildberger, "Das Abbild Gottes," *TZ* 21 (1965) 245–59, 481–501 (esp. pp. 484ff.); and W. H. Schmidt, *Die Schöpfungsgeschichte der Priesterschrift* (Neukirchen-Vluyn: Neukirchener Verlag, 1964) 136–42. This view is discussed and rejected by Westermann in his *Genesis* (1.15–54), but his negative arguments are not convincing to me.

(NRSV). Here the metaphor used in regard to human relationship to God is applied to the relationship between father and son in society. Just as a human being is God's representative and thus the sign of God's rule on earth, so the son is the representative of the father, one in whom, in some sense, the father appears.[35]

The democratization of the motif is clear in the Priestly description of human dominion: "Then God said: 'Let us make human beings as our image, according to our likeness, and let *them* have dominion'" (Gen. 1:26). What is involved here is not a single man, the Adam of the "book of generations" (5:1a), but rather a collective whole, that is, humankind or humanity. Accordingly, the jussive verb in 1:26 ("let them have dominion") is in the plural, as are the imperatives of the blessing in v. 28 ("be fruitful, multiply, fill the earth, tread down, dominate"). Furthermore, this corporate meaning is evident in the shift of pronouns from "him" to "them" in the sentence that reports the execution of God's resolution (v. 27):

> So God created human being as his own image,
>   as the image of God he created *him;*
>   male and female he created *them.*

Dominion is given to humankind as a whole and therefore to *man and woman.* Here the Priestly view departs from royal theology found in Egypt, for it is not said that Pharaoh *and* his wife represent together the image of God. In this respect Psalm 8 stands much closer to royal theology; for despite its democratization of the dominion motif, it speaks of *'ādām* in the singular and makes no reference to male and female.

GOD'S REPRESENTATIVE ON EARTH

In summary, Psalm 8 and the related passage in Genesis 1 are evidences of the new situation that prevailed in Israel when, with the rise of David, Israel accepted the alien institutions of temple and king and came under the influence of the royal theology of the ancient Near East. In both cases, though in different degrees, the mythical views were transformed when brought into the context of Israel's faith, which from the very first emphasized the incomparability of Yahweh and prohibited any image or likeness of God. In Psalm 8 the royal theology is at least implicit. The coronation of humankind is seen in the context of Yahweh's rule in the heavenly palace from which he comes out to rout his foes—the powers of chaos who manifest their uncanny influence in the threats of disorder. If my interpretation is right, the royal theology has already been democratized,

---

35. Cf. Schmidt, *Schöpfungsgeschichte,* 144.

so that the *'ādām* of the psalm is not the king but everyman. *'Ādām* is Yahweh's viceroy on earth, having a status only slightly inferior to divine beings. Through human dominion Yahweh's name becomes glorious on earth.

The situation is different in Gen. 1:26-28. Here the democratization of royal theology has been carried to its conclusion, leaving only vestigial remains, especially the motif of the image of God that entitles humanity to have dominion over the earth. *'Ādām* is the collective whole of humanity, differentiated according to male and female. Perhaps the Priestly writers could use the motif of the "image" boldly, without fear of its pagan meaning, because their theological presentation is based on the holiness and transcendence of God and the sharp distinction between Creator and creature. The psalmist may have been more reticent about using this motif directly in a context clearly influenced by royal theology, and therefore resorted to a paraphrase. Both biblical passages represent different responses to the mythical view of kingship.

Israel's interpreters make one fundamental exception to the iconoclasm inherent in the Mosaic faith and eloquently expressed by Second Isaiah: it is humanity who is crowned with honor and glory reflecting the splendor of God; it is humanity who is created as the image of God. Though an ephemeral creature in comparison to the stars, *'ādām* is the one elevated to be God's representative on earth, the one with whom God enters into personal relationship, and the one in whom the praise of the whole creation can become vocal.

> There is only *one* legitimate image through whom God is manifest in the world and that is humankind. It is of the most far-reaching significance that Israel, who so passionately rejected all image worship so as not to fall into idolatry, and who evidently would not accord the title *ṣelem 'ĕlōhîm* ["image of God"] even to the king, proclaimed, in the boldest reinterpretation of the image theology of the environment, that humankind is the form in which God is actually present.[36]

This is what prompts the hymnic praise of the psalmist. It is not just that the Creator pays attention to this transient human creature. Far more than that: the Creator's grace is displayed by elevating human beings to a supreme place in the creation, crowning them as kings and queens and putting the whole earth at their disposal.

SUMMARY

I conclude, then, that it is essentially correct to say that the Judeo-Christian heritage stresses human dominion over the earth rather than a

---

36. Wildberger, *TZ* 21 (1965) 249ff; cf. Schmidt, *Schöpfungsgeschichte,* 144.

primitive or romantic attitude toward nature. If the *imago Dei* has contributed to our ecological crisis by warranting conceptions that derive intellectually from the Enlightenment or economically from freewheeling capitalism, then it is time to understand what the biblical language intends to say. It is clear from the context of Genesis 1 that God's elevation of human beings does not entitle us to exercise power in an unlimited and autonomous manner by exploiting and subjugating nature. True, the verbs used of human dominion in Gen. 1:26-28 may have a violent meaning in other contexts.[37] But violence does not appear in this context, where, according to the Priestly story, human dominion is to be exercised in a situation of paradisiacal peace and harmony in which there was to be *no killing*. Not only were animals and humans created together on the sixth day of creation, indicating their interdependence, but together they "share the same table" upon which the Creator provides their common food, plants and fruits (1:29-30).

Even when this rule was relaxed in the Priestly narrative at the time of the flood, with the result that permission was given not only to eat the green plants but "*everything*" (Gen. 9:3), there was a clear recognition of the sacredness of life (blood), both animal and human. Under strict limitations, animals may be slaughtered for food; but the prohibition against one killing a fellow human being is as absolute as at the time of creation. Furthermore, these same writers declare that the Noachic covenant is an "everlasting covenant," predicated unconditionally upon God's sovereignty and embracing not only humankind but also the birds, cattle, wild animals, "and every living creature of all flesh" (9:8-17).

Thus the special status of humankind as the image of God is a call to responsibility, not only in relation to other humans but also in relation to nature. Human dominion is not to be exercised wantonly but wisely and benevolently so that it may be, in some degree, the sign of God's rule over the creation. Some of Israel's laws place restrictions on the careless harming and spoiling of nature, for instance the law prohibiting the taking of a mother bird (Deut. 22:6), or the command not to muzzle an ox while it treads the grain (Deut. 25:4). Modern military leaders who have carried out the defoliation of trees as an act of warfare could well ponder the implications of the law in Deut. 20:19-20 (NRSV):

> If you besiege a town for a long time, making war against it in order to take it, you must not destroy its trees by wielding an ax against them. Although you may take food from them, you must not cut them down. Are trees in the field human beings that they should come under siege from you?

37. The verb *rādâ* can mean to "tread, trample" as in the treading of the winepress (Joel 3:13[4:13]); the other verb, *kābaš,* can refer to acts of forcible subjection such as rape (Jer. 34:15; Esth. 7:8).

The Yahwist's story in Genesis 2 emphasizes that *'ādām* is to be a caretaker of God's garden, to "work" and "protect" it (Gen. 2:15). This custodianship involves working upon and changing what is given as well as the conservation of natural resources.

It would be going too far to say that, according to Israel's creation theology, the world is created only for the sake of humankind. The Priestly creation story reaches a climax with the announcement that "God saw *everything* that he made" and gave the approving verdict, "very good" (Gen. 1:31). It presents a picture in which every creature, including the human being, is assigned its proper place in God's creative order and, by performing the assigned function, serves and glorifies the Creator. Psalm 104, which is closely related to Genesis 1, announces that in wisdom Yahweh made *all* of his creatures (v. 24) and declares that Yahweh "rejoices" in his manifold works (v. 31).

It would be wrong to suppose that one can simply turn to the Bible to find a solution to the ecological dilemma. When understood in the full context of Israel's creation theology, however, the biblical motif of human dominion over nature calls into question present practices of exploitation and summons people to a new responsibility. The Priestly creation story suggests that human beings, *if* they will, may perform their proper role in the order and harmony of the creation to the glory of the Creator. But it is precisely that qualification, "if they will," which introduces the contingent element in the Priestly edition of the Pentateuch, necessitating the supplementary stories of paradise lost (Genesis 3) and the flood (Gen. 6:11-13).

CHAPTER 8

Relation between the Human and Nonhuman Creation in the Biblical Primeval History

Not too many years ago the word *ecology* would have been a good candidate for the parlor game known as "Fictionary," in which persons propose definitions—often humorously wild ones—of rare words. In recent decades, however, rapid social and scientific changes have brought this word into the active vocabulary of many people. Today it is commonly known that ecology, derived from Greek *oikos* ("house"), refers to the earthly habitation that human beings share with other living beings and specifically to "the mutual relations between organisms and their environment." The purpose of this essay is to explore in biblical perspective the relation between the human and the nonhuman creation.[1] As one whose specialization is Old Testament theology, I approach the task with modesty, for the subject belongs to the interdisciplinary field of environmental ethics, a field that is much broader than the interrelated theological disciplines.

Secular thinkers are just as aware as theologians, and sometimes more so, that the discussion takes place in a time of crisis—an eschatological situation. At such a time it is appropriate to turn to the Bible if for no other reason than that many of its writings—for instance, the eschatological preaching of the prophets of Israel on the imminent day of Yahweh (see Isa. 2:6-22) or the apocalyptic perspectives of the Gospel of Mark or the theology of Paul—speak to our contemporary sense of historical contin-

1. The controversy over this "man/nature dualism" thesis was stirred up by Lynn White, Jr., in his famous essay, "The Historical Roots of our Ecological Crisis," *Science* 155 (1967) 1203–7; repr. in *The Environmental Handbook* (ed. Garrett De Bell; New York: Ballantine, 1970) 12–26. See my response in chap. 7 above.

gency and future foreboding. In the community of faith, people also turn to the Bible in the conviction that it carries the weight of "Scripture" and hence is a primary source for theological understanding.

This study focuses attention not on the Bible as a whole (speaking in Christian terms) but on the so-called Old Testament (Israel's Scriptures), and within that large body of literature attention will be restricted for the most part to the primeval history (Genesis 1–11). Admittedly, other portions of the Old Testament would claim attention if the subject were treated adequately, such as certain creation Psalms (8, 104), the creation theology of the prophet of the exile (Isaiah 40–55), or passages in wisdom literature (e.g., Job; Prov. 8:22-31). I turn to the primeval history because this is often the scriptural ground that is chosen for discussion of environmental ethics or ecological theology, whether for criticism of the "dualism of humanity and nature" allegedly implied in the Creator's grant of dominion to '*ādām* (Gen. 1:26-28) or to set forth a more balanced theological understanding of the relation between the human and the nonhuman creation.[2]

THE CONTEXT OF INTERPRETATION:
PRIESTLY SCHEME

An immediate problem that arises is the context in which texts are interpreted. Biblical texts have too often been used as warrants or *dicta probantia* for ethical or theological positions arrived at on other grounds. Here it is appropriate to recall some wise words spoken by Eugene Borowitz during a discussion of environmental ethics (1980 meeting of the American Theological Society). He observed that while the mandate for human domination over the nonhuman creation—the *dominium terrae*—is indisputably biblical, the imposition of this view on scriptural texts reflects the modern overthrow of religion and the emergence of secular perspectives based on the confidence that human beings can take the world into their own hands.

The appeal to isolated texts, apart from the biblical context within which they function, has often led to the "use" of the Bible for particular purposes, whether in the religious community or in the modern technological world. One of the salutary results of the World Council of Churches (WCC) conference held at the Massachusetts Institute of Technology in 1979 was the chastened recognition that we read the Scriptures in our own "social location." A portion of the conference report merits repetition: "If

---

2. See the essays in the January 1979 issue of the World Council of Churches journal *Anticipation* entitled "Burning Issues," especially those by Klaus Koch on "The Old Testament View of Nature" and by Gerhard Liedke, "Solidarity in Conflict." These essays were prepared for the WCC "Conference on Faith, Science, and the Future" held at the Massachusetts Institute of Technology, Cambridge, Massachusetts, July 1979.

we search the Scriptures, we find that the parts that move us most powerfully are those that address us where we are, that the concepts by which
we interpret the Scriptures are those that we have developed in a given
historical context."[3]

Clearly, we read the Bible "where we are": as people who are conditioned by the times in which we live and by the history that we share,
including our philosophical heritage (capitalism and its Marxist counterpart) and our scientific outlook. This sober realization does not, in my
estimation, mire us in interpretive relativism, as though the Scriptures and
other literary works are "like a picnic to which the author brings the words
and the reader the meaning," to invoke the celebrated words of Northrop
Frye.[4] To be sure, we come to the Scriptures in a particular time and place.
But the words of Scripture, spoken or written in their own context, may
criticize where we stand, limit our use of them, and challenge us with their
strange social setting and theological horizon. Further, some of the ethical
problems that are "burning issues" for us were not even anticipated in
biblical times. I refer to such matters as the overpopulation of the earth,
the potential exhaustion of natural resources, technology that changes the
face of nature, science that can interfere with biological processes, and a
startling new cosmology, resulting from the exploration of outer space.

It is important, then, not to read the *dominium terrae* (or for that matter
the whole creation story) as a self-contained entity, isolated from its
function within a larger literary context. One cannot separate Genesis 1
(creation) from Genesis 9 (flood)—two crucial passages from Priestly tradition—and that means that one must consider a given text in the context
of the whole primeval history. This contextual approach should restrain the
reader from seizing a particular text—say the passage about the *imago Dei*
or the passage about God's blessing upon humankind (Gen. 1:26-27 and
1:28)—and using it as a warrant for a theological or ethical position arrived at independently. Unfortunately, the matter does not rest there. The
question arises: What is the proper biblical context for understanding a
given passage in the primeval history *(Urgeschichte)?* Here one enters the
arena of hermeneutical debate. As I see it, there are three major hermeneutical possibilities, which I will summarize briefly.

One possibility is to view a particular text in the context of a tradition-
historical development that received its major impulse at an early stage,
long before the final formulation of the book of Genesis. As Klaus Koch
observes, "Genesis 1 is not the first word of the Old Testament nor the

3. Quoted by Roger Shinn in a paper presented to the American Theological Society (1980) 28.
4. See David C. Steinmetz, "The Superiority of Pre-Critical Exegesis," *TToday* 37 (1980) 37;
he in turn refers to E. D. Hirsch, Jr., *Validity in Interpretation* (New Haven, Conn.: Yale Univ.
Press, 1967) 1.

last." It is appropriate, he maintains, to begin not with the Priestly account of creation but with the older Yahwistic text (Genesis 2–3); for the Priestly account should not be removed from "its place in the history of Hebrew thought and literature." In other words, the proper context for understanding a text is a tradition-historical *process* that received its theological character at an early literary or preliterary stage. This view is indebted to Gerhard von Rad, who capitalized on the tradition-historical approach that emerged from form criticism. Von Rad stressed the creative role of the Yahwist in shaping the Israelite epic and in particular in relating the primeval history to the *Heilsgeschichte* of the Hexateuch. The Yahwist's work, according to von Rad, was decisive, even "canonical," for later stages in the literary development that led to the Hexateuch in its present form.[5]

In his massive commentary on Genesis Claus Westermann has advocated another hermeneutical possibility. Westermann maintains that the *Urgeschichte* is a relatively self-contained totality. As such it was given to both the Yahwist and the Priestly writers, not in the form of a literary prototype but in an ontologically based mythical structure that one can trace by phenomenological analysis in the ancient Near East and, indeed, all over the world. Although the primeval history and the ancestral history now serve as introductions to the *Volksgeschichte* that centers in the exodus, Westermann maintains that the relation of these separate "histories" to the center is that of concentric circles, the outer of which reaches into the horizon of universal human experience of possibility and limitation, harmony and conflict, *Sein* and *In-der-Welt-Sein*.[6] Gerhard Liedke seems to belong in this hermeneutical category. In a stimulating paper presented for discussion at the WCC conference mentioned above he treats Genesis 1 and 9 (creation and flood) as a mythic portrayal of the polarity between the original harmony of creation and the threat of conflict and violence. His book on "ecological theology," with its intriguing title *Im Bauch des Fisches* ("In the Belly of the Fish," a reference to the Jonah story), also moves fundamentally from the hermeneutical position of Westermann, under whom he wrote his dissertation and from whom he learned "what biblical theology can be for the church."[7]

5. See von Rad's classic essay of 1938, "The Form-Critical Problem of the Hexateuch," in *The Problem of the Hexateuch and Other Essays* (trans. E. W. Trueman Dicken; New York: McGraw-Hill, 1965) 1–78. Also, see the foreword to his commentary, *Genesis* (trans. John H. Marks; OTL; rev. ed.; Philadelphia: Westminster, 1972) 11.

6. See the introduction to Claus Westermann's *Creation* (trans. John J. Scullion; Philadelphia: Fortress Press, 1974) 1-15; repr. in *Creation in the Old Testament,* 90–101. His view is set forth fully in the treatment of the primeval history in his *Genesis* (trans. John J. Scullion; 3 vols.; Minneapolis: Augsburg, 1984–86), vol. 1, 1–73.

7. Gerhard Liedke, *Im Bauch des Fisches: Oekologische Theologie* (Stuttgart: Kreuz, 1979).

A third hermeneutical possibility takes advantage of some of the insights provided by the tradition-historical and phenomenological approaches but emphasizes the given *scriptural* context. According to this view, the literary and theological context within which the various units of the primeval history function is the final literary work (Torah, Pentateuch). Franz Rosenzweig observed that the siglum R, which scholars have used for redactor, should really signify *Rabbenu,* "our master," for it is from these hands that we have received the Scriptures in their final form—the form in which we read them today and the form in which they have been read for centuries. This redactional approach does not necessarily commit one to a particular view of the prehistory of the final text of Scripture. My own view, shared with many other scholars, is that the final form is that of the Priestly work (P), that this work conservatively retains older traditions within its framework, and that the work, published during the exile, is substantially the Torah book that Ezra brought back with him from the Babylonian exile (see Nehemiah 9). It is sufficient to say, however, that the basic context for interpreting the primeval history is not a previous history of traditions or a "prehistory" rooted in universal human experience; rather, the context is the literary framework of the final form of the Torah, into which older traditions have been incorporated for the sake of filling out and enrichment.

So much for hermeneutical review. One thing becomes clear, especially if one reads the scriptural tradition in its final redacted form: it is necessary to look beyond the first chapters of Genesis, and indeed beyond the book of Genesis itself, to discover the literary and theological context in which the various parts function. In its received form, the primeval history is part of a "history" or "story" that extends from creation to Sinai—and beyond. Within this larger whole the book of Genesis is unified by a genealogical structure: five times the formula "these are the generations of" occurs in the primeval history (2:4a; 5:1; 6:9 [cf. 5:32]; 10:1; 11:10); and five times in the ancestral history (11:27; 25:12; 25:19; 36:1; 37:2). But even more significant is the fact that the entire history—primeval history, ancestral history, and exodus-Sinai history—is "periodized" into a sequence of covenants, each of which is called a *běrît 'ôlām,* a "covenant in perpetuity."[8] This type of covenant, one should note, stresses the unilateral initiative and sovereign grace of the covenant maker, who "gives" or "establishes" the covenant, in comparison to the more bilateral covenant type in which the covenant initiator imposes conditions and sanctions on the other contracting party (Exod. 24:3-8).

---

8. On the genealogical structure and the periodization of history, see Frank M. Cross, "The Priestly Work," in *Canaanite Myth and Hebrew Epic* (Cambridge: Harvard Univ. Press, 1973) 293–325; see also chap. 4 above.

According to the Priestly scheme, the first period extended from the creation to the end of the flood. The period was concluded with a *běrît 'ôlām* between Elohim (God) and Noah, his family, and descendants (Genesis 9). This was a universal covenant in that it embraced all peoples (the offspring of Noah's sons) and an ecological covenant in that it included the animals and a solemn divine pledge regarding the constancy of "nature" (Gen. 8:21-22). The second period extended from Noah to Abraham, with whom El Shaddai (God Almighty) made a *běrît 'ôlām,* promising to "be God" to him and his descendants and granting the land as a "possession in perpetuity" (Genesis 17). The third period extended from Abraham to the sojourn at Sinai, at which time and place God fulfilled his pledge to "be God" by giving his personal name and tabernacling in the midst of the people—a cultic community. At this point the Sabbath is regarded as the sign of the *běrît 'ôlām* (Exod. 31:13, 16-17) between God and people. Thus the Sabbath, which was "hidden in creation" (Gen. 2:2-3) and which became a cultic reality at Sinai, provides both a literary and theological *inclusio* that binds together the whole history with its system of covenants. (See figure 3.[9]) As Frank Cross remarks: "While both the Noachic and Abrahamic covenants remained valid, each was provisional, a stage on the way to God's ultimate covenant and ultimate self-disclosure."[10] It is within this total literary and theological context that the primeval history now functions to provide the cosmic and universal vista within which the human story, and particularly the story of Israel, unfolds.

FROM CREATION TO CHAOS (FLOOD)

Having established the interpretative context, we turn now to the *Urgeschichte* itself. This initial phase of the unfolding story has a dynamic of its own: a movement from creation toward chaos and finally to a new beginning, indeed, a kind of new creation. The story starts with the creation of the habitable earth out of chaos; it moves to a cosmic catastrophe in which the world was threatened with a return to precreation chaos; and it reaches a climax with the new beginning based on the Creator's sovereign covenant pledge, which opens a future for human beings, animals and birds, and the whole earth. In this movement, the two crucial moments are the Priestly creation story and the Priestly edited version of the flood. Since these two passages, standing at the beginning and the climax, are decisive for understanding the story, I will consider each, albeit briefly.

In the carefully wrought and theologically reflective creation story (Gen. 1:1—2:3), several things claim attention. First, in this account the opposite

9. The chart is taken from my book, *Understanding the Old Testament* (4th ed.; Englewood Cliffs, N.J.: Prentice-Hall, 1986) 464.

10. Cross, *Canaanite Myth and Hebrew Epic,* 297.

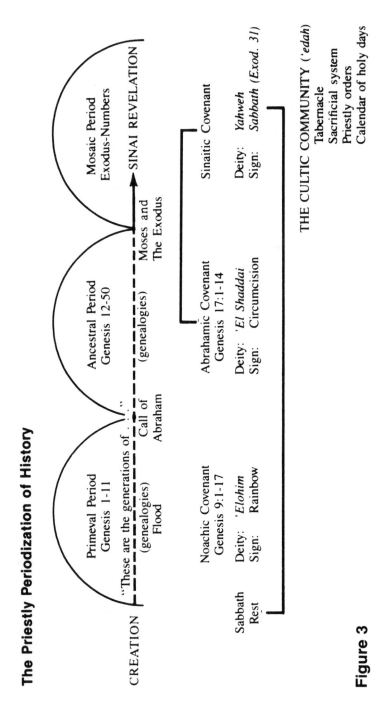

The Priestly Periodization of History

Figure 3

of creation is chaos, portrayed in terms of watery chaos and stygian darkness. The creation drama begins when, at the command of the Creator, light bursts upon the chaotic scene like a cosmic nuclear flash. Order is created out of chaos, but chaos is not eliminated; it is only pushed back or given bounds, as indicated by the placing of a firmament in the midst of the waters to separate the (lower) waters from the (upper) waters (Gen. 1:6-7). Chaos remains at the edge of creation, so to speak, as a threatening possibility. Psalm 104, which has many affinities with the Priestly creation account, portrays the contingency of creation in language that preserves more clearly the mythical view of the Creator pushing back or even subduing the powers of chaos:

> You set the earth on its foundations,
>   so that it shall never be shaken.
> You cover it with the deep as with a garment;
>   the waters stood above the mountains.
> At your rebuke they flee; at the sound of your thunder
>   they take to flight.
> They rose up to the mountains, ran down to the valleys
>   to the place that you appointed for them.
> You set a boundary that they may not pass,
>   so that they might not again cover the earth. (Ps. 104:5-9, NRSV)

Second, the creation drama occurs in two movements, each of which concentrates on the *earth,* a motif introduced at the opening of v. 2 where "earth" stands in the emphatic position: "Now the earth was in a chaotic state." In each three-day sequence (vv. 3-12 and 14-31) the movement is from heaven to earth, which increasingly becomes an orderly habitation. At the end of the first movement (third day), the narrative portrays the greening of the earth with vegetation: plants and trees according to their species (Hebrew: *mîn*). At the conclusion of the second movement (sixth day), the narrative portrays the creation of animals "according to their species" and finally the supreme earth creature, *'ādām,* to whom is given dominion over the earth. In view of the overall pattern of the account,[11] it is apparent that the emphasis falls not so much on anthropology, that is, the supremacy of humanity, as on ecology, that is, the earthly habitation that human beings share with other forms of "living being" (*nepeš ḥayyâ*). Although *'ādām* (human beings in the corporate sense) were made "in [as?] the image of God" and therefore were entitled and commissioned to have dominion over the earth as God's representatives,[12] they share

---

11. I work out this pattern in detail in chap. 3 above.

12. For a discussion of the functional or representative significance of *imago Dei* (a title also applied to kings in Near Eastern texts), see chap. 7 above, esp. pp. 126–29. Also von Rad, *Genesis,* 57–61.

the earth and its resources with other land creatures who, according to the dramatic sequence of the story, were created on the same climactic day. The earth-centered focus of the account is evident also in the way the cosmic regions are treated. There is no interest in the heavens (the number of heavens or God's celestial enthronement); even the sun, moon, and stars are treated only in terms of their relation to the earthly sphere. These bodies are not living beings, as in other ancient religions, but only luminaries that function to regulate times and seasons.

Finally, an important feature of the creation story is the theme of fertility—procreation. In this connection, it is important to consider the place of the divine blessing. The first movement of the story does not mention God's blessing. The greening of the earth occurs because God commands Earth to release its powers of fertility and "bring forth" (a maternal, childbearing verb, 1:12) vegetation of various species. In the second movement a major interruption occurs in the formulaic pattern at the point of the appearance of "living being" (*nepeš ḥayyâ*) or biological life. God commands the waters to "bring forth" (once again the maternal verb, 1:20) aquatic beings of various species and birds (apparently they were also to emerge from the waters; see LXX). To these creatures God gives a special blessing: "Be fertile and multiply" (1:22). Strangely, this is not true in the case of the land animals. Once again Earth is commanded to "bring forth" (the maternal verb, 1:24) *nepeš ḥayyâ* of various species: domestic animals, things that creep on the earth, and wild beasts; but no divine blessing is given them. Instead, the blessing is reserved for the supreme land being, *'ādām,* and of this being it is said explicitly (for the first time in the account) that "they" consist of "male and female" (*zākār ûněqēbâ*), an expression that is later emphasized in the Priestly recension of the flood story (7:13-16). To this earth creature the Creator gives a blessing that exceeds the one given previously to fish and birds (1:28).

How does this passage regarding God's conferral of the blessing relate to the previous passage concerning the creation of *'ādām* bisexually "in [as] the image of God"? Phyllis Trible is undoubtedly right in saying that the *imago Dei* in the aspect of sexuality does not pertain in a narrow sense to procreation: both sexes are equally created to image or represent God on earth and thus are to be coresponsible for maintaining the goodness of the earth.[13] In my estimation, however, it would be going too far to say that the creation of *'ādām* as "male and female" is unrelated to procreation, either in the context of the creation account or in the larger context

---

13. I refer to Phyllis Trible's paper presented to the William Rainey Harper Conference on Biblical Studies (University of Chicago, October 1979). See also her illuminating discussion in *God and the Rhetoric of Sexuality* (OBT; Philadelphia: Fortress Press, 1978) 1–30. For an opposing view, see Phyllis Bird, "'Male and Female He Created Them': Gen 1:17b in the Context of the Priestly Account of Creation," *HTR* 74 (1981) 129–59.

of the primeval history. It is hardly accidental that the creation of human beings, sexually differentiated, is immediately followed by a special divine blessing. Dominion over the earth apparently means, at least in part, the human capacity to multiply and fill the earthly *oikos* ("house"), even as the fish multiply and fill their habitat (waters) and the birds theirs (sky). In some sense, dominion over the earth is connected with population growth and diffusion—a theme that is taken up later in the aftermath of the flood (see the Table of Nations in chap. 10; also the Babel story in 11:1-9). In contrast, the Babylonian Atrahasis epic, which dates from the seventeenth century B.C.E., portrays the threat of overpopulation of the earth. In this long Babylonian poem, the gods send a massive flood to annihilate humankind, all other means of controlling the fertility of the human species having failed.[14]

The command to be fertile, multiply, and fill the earth has been amply fulfilled, as evident from the teeming population of the earth. In our time human dominion over the earth must mean seeking ways to hold population growth within the bounds that the earthly environment and economic well-being allow.

In the Priestly narrative and Priestly genealogical structure that govern the primeval history in its final form, creation and flood correspond. This is evident when one considers how the three features of the creation story discussed above are present in the flood story. I will indicate the correspondences briefly. First, just as the habitable earth was created out of chaos, according to the creation story, so the flood is portrayed as a catastrophe that threatened to return the earth to watery chaos, the *tōhû wābōhû* of Gen. 1:2. Indeed, the flood, viewed in Priestly perspective, was a *cosmic* catastrophe, brought about when "the fountains of the great deep [*tĕhôm rabbâ*] burst forth, and the windows of the heavens were opened" (7:11, NRSV), allowing the "waters below" and the "waters above" (cf. 1:6-7) to come together. Second, the flood story portrays the renewal of the earth as a new creation out of watery chaos. Dramatically the narrative moves with crescendoing force toward a literary climax. The rising flood waters threaten the return of the earth to chaos. Yet there is a fragile ark tossing on the turbulent waters! Umberto Cassuto's commentary can hardly be surpassed:

> We see water everywhere, as though the world had reverted to its primeval state at the dawn of Creation, when the waters of the deep submerged everything. Nothing remained of the teeming life that had burst forth upon the earth. Only a tiny point appears on the face of the terrible waters: the ark that preserves

14. The Atrahasis myth is summarized and discussed by Norbert Lohfink, S.J., "The Future: Biblical Witness to the Ideal of a Stable World," in *Great Themes from the Old Testament* (trans. Ronald Walls; Edinburgh: T. & T. Clark, 1982) 183–201.

between its planks the seeds of life for the future. But it is a mere atom and is almost lost in the endless expanse of water that was spread over the face of the whole earth. A melancholy scene that is liable to fill the reader with despair. What will happen to this atom of life?[15]

The turning point comes with the words: "But God remembered Noah and all the wild and tame animals that were with him in the ark" (8:1). Then the narrative moves in decrescendo: God caused a wind to blow over the chaotic waters (8:2; cf. the "wind of God" in 1:2); gradually the waters diminished until the dry land appeared again (8:5, 12-14; cf. the gathering of the waters in 1:9-10); and the return of the dove to Noah with a freshly plucked olive twig was a tender sign of the greening of the earth once more (cf. 1:11-12). The earth now becomes a permanent *oikos* for human and nonhuman creatures owing to God's pledge to maintain the constancy of the natural order (8:22). Finally, the ensuing divine address in chapter 9, which comes from Priestly tradition, highlights the divine blessing upon humankind. The blessing given to *'ādām* at the time of creation is reiterated in the time of the new creation: "be fertile, multiply, and fill the earth" (9:1 and 9:7).

The new creation, however, is not just a repetition of the first. Profound differences demand a different ordering of relations between the human and nonhuman creatures from that which prevailed in the time of creation. This is clearly evident in Gen. 9:2-6, which falls between the twofold reiteration of the divine blessing given originally at the creation (9:1 and 9:7). Animals who once lived in harmony with humans are now overcome with "fear and dread" of human dominion; and they are regarded as rivals and predators to be held responsible for the blood of *'ādām* (9:2-5a). Furthermore, human beings, to whom the earth was given to manage as children inherit a parental estate, are now at such odds with one another that a strict, apodictic law, predicated on the *imago Dei,* has to be issued against murder (9:5b-6). Thus the movement from creation to flood to a new beginning introduces a more tragic view of existence in comparison to the original state of creation. To appreciate this movement it is necessary to consider the theme that, in Priestly perspective, governs the interim between creation and flood: the disruption of the goodness and order of God's creation through violence.

THE NATURE OF VIOLENCE IN GOD'S CREATION

The preface to the flood story, which comes from the Priestly tradition, contains the solemn announcement:

15. Umberto Cassuto, *Commentary on Genesis* (trans. Israel Abrahams; 2 vols.; Jerusalem: Magnes, Hebrew University, 1961–64) 2.97.

> Now, the earth was corrupt before God,
>   the earth was filled with violence.
> God saw how corrupt the earth was,
>   for all flesh had corrupted its way on the earth. (Gen. 6:11-12)

The theme of "violence" (*ḥāmās*) is picked up immediately in God's first address to Noah:

> The end of all flesh has come before me,
>   for through them the earth is filled with violence.
> I am about to destroy them and the earth. (Gen. 6:13)

In Priestly language the expression "all flesh" may refer to all that is fleshy (including birds, fish, animals, humans), as in God's resolution "to exterminate all flesh under heaven that has the spirit of life" (6:17) or God's vow to "remember the everlasting covenant between God and every living being [*nepeš ḥayyâ*] of all flesh that is upon the earth" (9:16). If this is the case in the passages quoted above (6:12 and 13), the text indicates a general corruption that permeates both the human and the nonhuman creation.

Here it is appropriate to consider a striking difference between our conception of "life" and that found in the primeval history. We distinguish between inanimate things (such as stars, rocks, and seas) and animate life (such as trees, flowers, birds, and insects etc.). In the primeval history, however, the distinction is between those creatures that are *nepeš ḥayyâ* ("living being") and those that are not. In the creation story the vegetation that greens the earth (plants, trees) is not regarded as "living." Only during the second movement of the creation drama, on the fifth day, is *nepeš ḥayyâ* created (fish, birds); and, as we have seen, this momentous development in the story is accompanied by a special divine blessing (1:20-23). Also the animals according to their various species are called *nepeš ḥayyâ* (1:24). It is self-evident that human beings fall in this category, even though this usage is superseded by the special status of "the image of God." Note that in the Old Epic story of paradise, which has been incorporated into the Priestly work, *'ādām* is created as *nepeš ḥayyâ* from the *'ădāmâ* or "soil" (2:7), as are the birds and the animals (2:19).

Keeping this distinction in mind, one cannot trace the source of violence to "nature"[16] in a general sense. As we know well, tremendous violence does occur in the natural realm: earthquakes, floods, disease, volcanic fire and brimstone, and so on. Indeed, according to a modern

---

16. In this essay I have put the word *nature* in quotation marks in recognition of the fact that the Old Testament has no word for this term, which is laden with a philosophical history of its own.

view of nature, violence—the survival of the fittest—belongs essentially to the evolutionary process. But this surly face of nature receives no attention at all in the primeval history. The story of the deluge would seem to be an exception, especially if the biblical account is reminiscent of a natural calamity that attended the rampaging waters of the Tigris and Euphrates Rivers. But in the primeval history, the flood story does not function to illustrate natural evil; rather, the story is told to show the severity of God's judgment upon "all flesh." The portrayal of a world on the verge of returning to precreation chaos is analogous to Jeremiah's poetic vision of the awesome wrath of Yahweh. "As if struck by a mighty nuclear bomb," so the annotator of the RSV text remarks, "the earth has been returned to its primeval state: waste and void"—the *tōhû wābōhû* of Gen. 1:2.[17]

> I looked upon the earth, and lo, a chaotic waste *[tōhû wābōhû]*,
>   and unto the heavens, and their light was gone.
> I looked on the mountains, and lo, they were quaking,
>   and all the hills were trembling.
> I looked, and lo, there was no human being,
>   and all the birds of the sky had vanished.
> I looked, and lo, the fertile land was wilderness,
>   before Yahweh, before his burning wrath. (Jer. 4:23-26)

Moreover, while the animals were affected by the violence and corruption of the earth, the primeval history contains no suggestion that they were the source of the violence. It may be, as Benno Jacob suggests, that the animals were denied the Creator's blessing (in contrast to the fish and birds) because they were potential threats to human beings on the land (earth);[18] but there is not the slightest hint anywhere in the narrative dealing with the period from creation to flood that their predatory instincts led them into conflict with human beings for living space or for survival. On the contrary, the picture presented in the creation story is that of a paradisiacal peace in which human beings and animals live together in a peaceable kingdom. Those who have supposed that the *imago Dei* entitles human beings to exploit and destroy the animals overlook the fact that the *dominium terrae* is a call to responsibility. Made in the image of God, human beings are God's representatives, entitled to manage the Creator's earthly estate. The picture given in Psalm 8, which is somehow related to the Priestly creation story, is the same. The psalmist exclaims that humankind

---

17. See the *Oxford Annotated Bible* (1973) on Jer 4:23ff.

18. Benno Jacob, *Das erste Buch der Torah: Genesis* (Berlin: Schocken, 1934) 55–56; abridged translation, *The First Book of the Bible: Genesis* (trans. Ernest I. and Walter Jacob; New York: KTAV, 1974) 9.

is elevated to a high rank, just a little less than God (or the angels), and hence is "crowned" to rule wisely and benevolently over the works of the Creator's hands. It is in this sense that "all things" are subjected to human-kind. Notice that in the psalm, as in the Priestly creation story, the area of dominion is not explicitly all of "nature" but the nonhuman living crea-tures: the animals, birds, and fish (Ps. 8:5-8[6-9]).[19]

We come, then, to an uncomfortable point. In the primeval history the "violence" that corrupted "all flesh" is traced to the Creator's noblest creatures. The Priestly writers illustrate violence by including episodes from Old Epic tradition (J), thereby "fleshing out" the Priestly historical and genealogical scheme that extends from creation to flood. In the story of the Garden of Eden, a human couple rebel against their Creator. Wish-ing to reach out for divine prerogatives of knowledge and eternal life, they disrupt their relationship with God and hence their relationship with each other and with the soil (*'ădāmâ*), to which they are intimately related and on which they depend for existence. In the story of Cain, a brother pollutes the soil with the blood of his murdered brother. In the story of Lamech, the ancestor of those who originated the benefits of civilization (agriculture, music, metallurgy), the lust for power prompts a boast of measureless revenge. And in that strange story in Gen. 6:1-4, which almost defies understanding, the heavenly beings ("sons of God") breach the Creator's distinction between heaven and earth by seizing and having sexual inter-course with beautiful human maidens, thus fathering abnormal offspring.

These episodes do not illustrate exhaustively the range of violence. The Priestly writers have drawn from an Old Epic tradition that undoubtedly was once fuller and have adapted it and worked it into a new presentation, as one can see from the blending of so-called Priestly and Old Epic ele-ments in the flood story itself. Enough illustrations are given, however, to indicate the character of the violence. Notice, first, that the violence (sin) is not essentially connected with sex, though it may become manifest in the relation between the sexes (Genesis 3) or even lead to illicit sexual union (6:1-4). Second, the violence portrayed in the primeval history is not directed against "nature," that is, the natural environment or the animal world. The violence described occurs primarily in the human realm. Third, from the human realm violence spreads its corruption to the nonhuman sphere, so that it can be said of "all flesh" (human and nonhuman) that "through them the earth is filled with violence" (6:13). Notice that in the Old Epic tradition used by the Priestly writers, God's curse on the soil (3:17-19) is not intended as a direct curse on nature. God's word of judg-ment to *'ādām* is: "cursed is the soil [*'ădāmâ*] on your account," because of what you have done. It is human actions that contaminate the soil. The

19. See chap. 7 above.

serpent, though demythologized into a natural creature (another "wild creature that Yahweh God had made," 3:1), still retains something of his mythical role as an uncanny, sinister power of chaos (see chap. 12 below).[20]

In short, violence is a disease, as it were, that affects all those living in
the same *oikos*. How does one deal with this widespread and deep-seated
corruption of the earth (notice again the ecological accent in Gen. 6:11)?
In the perspective of Priestly tradition, which is dependent on Old Epic
tradition (see 6:5-7), the Creator resolved to tear down the house and start
all over with a saved and saving remnant of humans and animals.

A NEW CREATION: THE NOACHIC COVENANT

Translated into the terms of traditional theology, the problem here is
one of power in a "fallen world" or, perhaps better, a marred creation.
What is the source of the corruption? The Priestly narrators do not inter-
rupt the flow of the narrative to raise this question or to reflect on the
problem of evil (theodicy). One can say only that the creation story itself
does not allow one to trace the source of the problem to the Creator. The
marvelous order of creation, in which every creature, celestial and terrestrial, plays a role in a harmonious whole, receives the Cosmic Artist's
imprimatur: "very good" (1:31). The supplementation of the story of paradise lost (2:4b—3:24) to the creation story provided an opportunity for
later generations to reflect on the serpent as the embodiment of the mysterious, uncanny powers of chaos, especially in apocalyptic contexts (e.g.,
Isa. 27:1; Revelation 12); but even this story did not allow a thoroughgoing dualism of coeternal powers of good and evil. The primeval history
traces the source of "violence" to creaturely freedom. This freedom manifests itself as power: power to rebel against God ("You shall be as God,
knowing good and evil," Gen. 3:4), power to crush a fellow human being
under the illusion of impunity (4:8-10), power to exalt human revenge to a
measureless degree (4:23-24).

This creaturely power, as portrayed in the primeval history, is ambivalent. It is not bad in itself but is potentially creative. It leads to a new
human independence, some would say even a new maturity (Genesis 3). It
makes possible agriculture: the extraction of life-sustaining produce from
the soil (4:1-16). It leads to the cultivation of aesthetic sensibilities: music
and the arts (4:21). It enables human beings to use natural resources, for
instance, in forging instruments of bronze and iron (4:22). If one looks

---

20. For further discussion of the symbolic significance of the serpent, see my *Creation
versus Chaos: The Reinterpretation of Mythical Symbolism in the Bible* (New York: Association, 1967; repr. Philadelphia: Fortress Press, 1987) 144–70, esp. 155–59; idem, "Sin and the
Powers of Chaos," in *Sin, Salvation and the Spirit* (ed. Daniel Durken; Collegeville, Minn.:
Liturgical Press, 1979) 71–84.

beyond the flood story, it finds expression in technology of a sort: the revolutionary use of artificial stone (brick) for building a city (11:1-9). Yet for some strange reason, this power corrupts even the finest human achievements. The preface to the flood, found in Old Epic tradition (J), traces the problem to a curious perversity in human nature (6:5-6). The Priestly writers incorporate this older Epic view into their covenantal theology. Human beings, created to image or represent the rule of God in their exercise of dominion, have corrupted the earth with violence.

We have seen that the primeval history moves from creation through ecological catastrophe into a new beginning. The nonhuman creation is involved in this movement as well. Just as the animals are affected by the violence that corrupted "all flesh," so they are involved in the saving divine purpose expressed in God's favor toward Noah. With a fine touch the narrative describes the animals turning to Noah, as though by their own impulse in the face of catastrophe. "Two by two *they came to Noah* into the ark, male and female, just as God commanded Noah" (Gen. 7:9). It is tempting to find in the story at this point the anticipation of Paul's testimony that the nonhuman creation (nature) is "groaning in travail"— sharing with human beings the bondage to decay and waiting with them for the promised deliverance (Rom. 8:19-23).

According to the Priestly account, the new creation is based on God's covenant with Noah, anticipated at the beginning of the flood story (Gen. 6:18) and established at the end (9:8-17). Deserving of attention are several theological features of this ecological covenant that embraces all human beings, animals and birds, and the whole natural order.

First, the Noachic covenant is a guarantee of the constancy of the natural order, upon which all *nepeš ḥayyâ* depend. The Priestly writers appropriately include and emphasize the motif of God's resolution found in the Old Epic tradition (J), Gen. 8:21-22. In the Priestly elaboration of this motif in Genesis 9, the constancy and regularity of nature are guaranteed by the Creator's "everlasting covenant," the sign of which is a natural phenomenon: the rainbow that appears after the storm. No human violence can be great enough to upset indefinitely the order and balance of "nature."

Second, the new creation involves the repopulation of the earth. We have seen that the motif of fertility and dispersion through the earth dominates the creation story, where it is emphasized by a special divine blessing. The purpose of Noah's taking the animals and birds into the ark in pairs, male and female (*zākār ûněqēbâ,* 7:9), is to preserve the seed of *nepeš ḥayyâ.* God's command to Noah, according to the Priestly formulation, is emphatic (6:19-20). This is clearly the purpose of the preservation of Noah and his wife, his sons and their wives. It is appropriate, then, that the new creation is inaugurated by a repetition of the divine blessing given to *'ādām,* "male and female," at the time of the original creation: "Be fertile, multiply, and fill the earth" (9:1, 7). The remainder of the primeval history (the Table of Nations in Genesis 10 and the story of the Tower of Babel in 11:1-9) deals with this theme. In a time of catastrophe, when the earth is on the verge of chaos, God preserves a remnant with which to make a new beginning.

Finally, the new creation opens up a new horizon: the future. It should be emphasized that this horizon is not the result of any change in the human condition. The Old Epic tradition had affirmed that God's resolve never again to curse the soil or destroy everything that lives was made despite the tendency of human thinking (8:21-22), the very tendency that had precipitated God's ominous judgment in the first place (6:5-8). The Priestly writers restate this theme in terms of God's *běrît 'ôlām* ("everlasting covenant"). As mentioned previously, this type of covenant (unlike the more reciprocal Mosaic covenant) is unilateral in character, resting solely on God's commitment, not on the human fulfillment of conditions. The verbs used are verbs of theocentric initiative: God "establishes" (6:18, 9:9, 11, 12, etc.) the covenant with Noah and his posterity, and with every *nepeš ḥayyâ* with him. The future is open because of God's grace, not because of fragile, weak, creaturely "living being." Just as God "remembered" Noah and the remnant with him in the ark (8:1), so God will "remember" the covenant in perpetuity (*běrît 'ôlām*) with "all flesh."

> Whenever the rainbow is in the clouds and I see it,
> I will remember the everlasting covenant between God
> and every living being of all flesh that is on the earth. (Gen. 9:16)

In the first and last analysis, the hope for the human and nonhuman creation is grounded in the *sola gratia* of God's universal, ecological covenant.

HUMAN RESPONSIBILITY IN THE NOACHIC COVENANT

In conclusion I note once again that the new creation, according to the Priestly account, bears the marks of tragedy. This is evident, first of all, in the broken relation between human beings and animals. For the first time the narrator recounts that "fear and dread" fall upon the animals as though they regarded *'ādām* as a predator who wages war against the animal kingdom, including wild animals, birds of the sky, everything that creeps on the soil, and the fish of the sea (9:2). A new word is spoken, which contrasts with the provision made for humans and animals at the time of creation (1:29-30): "Into your power they are given" (9:2, end of verse).

Human beings are reminded, however, that their power is not absolute. These creatures may be killed for food but not wantonly; indeed, there must be reverence for life as evidenced by the prohibition against eating flesh with blood, the vital element (9:4). Moreover, in the new era the broken relation between human beings persists, as is evident in the exercise of human power that results in the taking of another human life. With great force it is announced that human life is sacred to God: therefore both animals and human beings will be held accountable for the life of a human being. Precisely in this context, where the limitations on power are announced, the motif of the *imago Dei* is repeated in order to emphasize the God-given status and role of *'ādām* in the creation:

> Whoever sheds the blood of a human being,
>   by a human being his blood will be shed,
> for in the image of God God made humankind. (Gen. 9:6)

Even though the new creation has a tragic dimension, owing to the continuing problem of power, human beings do not cease to be who they are: creatures made in God's image who are called to represent God's rule on earth. This "imaging" of God is to be manifest not only in reverence for human life, protected by apodictic law against murder, but also in proper reverence for the nonhuman creation. It may well be, as Klaus Koch has suggested, that one should not disregard the ritual law concerning slaughter of animals, which also belongs essentially to the universal Noachic covenant, without finding some way to express reverence toward this part of God's creation. For animals too are *nepeš ḥayyâ,* and "every *nefesh* has its direct connection to God and its own value which does not depend on human will or pleasure."[21]

As indicated at the beginning of this essay, the biblical primeval history does not specifically address many aspects of the ecological crisis. Indeed, many Americans, who believe that all problems are capable of solution, will be distressed by this part of Scripture, which shows that the problem of power persists not only in the time after the original creation but also in the time after the new creation. (The story of the Tower of Babel comes shortly after the flood in the sequence of the primeval history. See chap. 10 below.) The biblical account, however, does not encourage a fatalistic view of history. On the one hand, it portrays a world in which God is sovereign, a world in which people cannot escape divine judgment in consequence of their acts of violence. On the other hand, human beings are called to responsibility: to exercise dominion within the rule of God. Inherent in being the "image of God" is the role of being God's represen-

---

21. Koch, "The Old Testament View of Nature," 50.

tative on earth. Human beings, regardless of their ethnic identity or religious community, are called to an ecological task: to be faithful managers of God's estate, or, as stated in Gen. 2:15, to till and keep God's garden. The dimension of chaos has not been erased from God's creation; indeed, human beings in their freedom can act to unleash the powers of chaos. Human responsibility, however, is grounded in God's covenant, which is universal and ecological. Its sign is the rainbow after the storm: a phenomenon of the natural order known to all human beings.

Hope for the human and nonhuman creation has traditionally been grounded in the so-called *protoevangelium* of Gen. 3:15, which allegedly anticipates the ultimate messianic victory over the evil that mars God's creation. This is a precarious textual foundation on which to base hope, and few today would build on it. If, however, one interprets the opening chapters of Genesis in the literary context that embraces a movement from creation to flood and to the new beginning that lies beyond, there are grounds for hope in the Noachic covenant, which the Creator has established not only with Noah and his descendants but also with *the earth.*

> Then God said [to Noah]:
> "This is the sign of the covenant that I am making between
>   me and you [plural],
> as well as every living being that is with you, for
>   endless generations.
> My bow I have set in the clouds, and it shall be a covenant
>   sign between me and the earth." (Gen. 9:12-13)

The Noachic covenant opens up the horizons of the future by predicating the hope of the human and nonhuman creation on the unconditional commitment of the Creator to humankind, to nonhuman creatures, and to the order and regularity of "nature."

CHAPTER 9

Creation and the
Noachic Covenant

The superb forty-sixth psalm, which was the basis of Martin Luther's well-known hymn of the Reformation, contains a line that rings with both unshakable trust and ominous foreboding. Right after the affirmation that God is a "mighty fortress," "a bulwark never failing," as Luther paraphrases, comes the confession in the familiar KJV:

> Therefore will not we fear, though the earth be removed,
> and though the mountains be carried into the midst of the sea.

This poetic contemplation of the ominous possibility that the earth will undergo such profound changes that chaos will return finds a sympathetic response in our technological world. It is gradually dawning on us that the earth's resources are not inexhaustible, and that we cannot continue the exploitation of our natural environment much longer without suffering nature's severe backlash. Furthermore, modern technology, conscripted for military service, has brought about a historical crisis in which nuclear disaster could reduce the earth, or large portions of it, to a radioactive wasteland. As I write this essay many people in various parts of the world, awakened to this frightening possibility, are demonstrating against the nuclear arms race.[1]

The crisis, of which scientists are often more aware than theologians and practitioners of religion, is totally inclusive: it affects humanity, non-human forms of life, and the earth itself. People inevitably raise the ques-

---

1. Elements of this essay derive from chap. 8 above.

tion: Who or what is to blame for this unprecedented ecological crisis? In a celebrated essay Lynn White, Jr., ventured to say that the Judeo-Christian tradition bears "a huge burden of guilt" for having espoused a view of creation that places humanity at the peak of God's creation and endows it with dominion over the earth. He even nominated Francis of Assisi, "the greatest spiritual revolutionary in Western history," to be the patron saint of the ecological cause, for in vain "he tried to substitute the idea of the equality of all creatures, including man, for the idea of man's limitless rule of creation."[2] Since the Bible is inevitably read and interpreted in a particular social location, however, it makes more sense to trace the roots of the crisis to the economic and political revolution that marked the transition from medieval life to the modern age. Karl Marx observed that capitalism introduced a sharp dichotomy between human beings and their natural environment, in which "nature becomes for the first time simply an object for mankind . . . [not] a power in its own right."[3] Given the sociological matrix of biblical exegesis, it is understandable that in the new age dominated by technology and free enterprise many people have turned to the Bible to find warrants for the new way of life that some nations, especially the United States, now enjoy to the full.

In any event, the time has come to seek liberation from a "root metaphor" that is mechanistic and technological and to regain an artistic appreciation of creation and the dwelling of human and nonhuman beings in it.[4] If this is to happen, we most also liberate ourselves from a literalistic (and hence rationalistic) view of the biblical creation tradition, which in the past has led to unnecessary conflict between science and religion (see chap. 6 above). The rediscovery and refurbishing of the biblical creation tradition can take place only if we reject a hermeneutic that accommodates to a rationalistic, technological world and instead cultivate an artistic, poetic appreciation of the creation story. Viewed as story or narrative, the creation tradition opens up new horizons of ecological, ethical, and philosophical/theological understanding.

CREATION AND FLOOD IN THE
CONTEXT OF COVENANT

To begin with, the story of creation found in Gen. 1:1—2:3 belongs to and functions within a larger narrative context, the so-called primeval

2. Lynn White, Jr., "The Historical Roots of Our Ecological Crisis," *Science* 155 (1967) 1203–7; repr. in *The Environmental Handbook* (ed. Garrett De Bell; New York: Ballantine, 1970) 12–26. For a biblical-theological response to this thesis, see chap. 7 above.

3. Quoted by Spencer Pollard in his review of Marx's *Grundrisse, Saturday Review* (August 7, 1971) 27.

4. See Gibson Winter's provocative book, *Liberating Creation: Foundations of Religious Social Ethics* (New York: Crossroad, 1981), where this challenge is set forth forcefully.

history set forth in the opening chapters of Genesis (Genesis 1–11). It may be, as some scholars maintain, that the creation story once circulated independently and served as a liturgical reading for a religious festival, perhaps the celebration of the New Year. Whatever its prehistory, the literary piece has been placed within a scriptural setting. Its meaning depends on its function in the larger setting of the Torah which has been given to us in final form by so-called Priestly redactors. The creation story has too often been torn out of its native scriptural context and used as a warrant for ethical or philosophical views arrived at on other grounds. One should avoid this "modern use of the Bible." The basic interpretive rule is: read the creation story in its own narrative context.

When one reads the creation tradition in this manner, it is clear that creation belongs to a "story" or "history" that moves dramatically from the "first things" to a universal, ecological crisis; from creation "in the beginning" to the flood in the days of Noah—and beyond. The literary and theological correspondences between the creation story and the flood story, both of which come from Priestly writers in their final form, are striking.[5] It is instructive to read the key theological passages, Genesis 1 and Gen. 9:1-17, side by side, so that one can sense the connections. According to the Priestly creation story, the habitable earth was created out of chaos— the watery, turbulent abyss portrayed in Gen. 1:2; the corresponding story portrays the flood (*mabbûl,* a technical term for cosmic waters) as a cosmic catastrophe that threatened to return the earth to watery chaos. Genesis 1 portrays the Creator making a living space for humans and animals by pushing back the waters so that the dry land may appear; correspondingly, the flood story portrays the renewal of the earth when God caused a wind (8:1; cf. the "wind of God" in 1:2) to blow over the chaotic waters with the result that the dry land appeared and the earth began to green again.

Both stories emphasize the God-given blessing upon humankind and the commission to have dominion over the earth. Indeed, the blessing on Noah and his descendants, "Be fertile, multiply, and fill the earth" (9:1, 7), is linguistically the same as the blessing given at creation (1:28). The motif of the *imago Dei* (1:26-27 and 9:5b-6) also provides an important link of continuity. Numerous other linguistic affinities between the two passages become evident when one studies them carefully, especially in the original language. The Priestly tradents clearly intend that the two should be taken together, as the obverse and reverse of the same coin. The covenant between the Creator and Noah, with which the flood story culminates, is the narrative goal that is in view. The story starts with the creation

---

5. "Story" and "history," both covered by one word in some languages (as in German *Geschichte*), are closely related. Here I cannot go into the question of whether or how far "historical" elements are present in, for example, the flood story.

of the habitable earth out of chaos; it moves to a cosmic catastrophe in which the earth was on the verge of returning to precreation chaos; and it reaches a climax with the new beginning—indeed, the new creation—based on the Creator's covenant pledge that opens a future for human beings, animals and birds, and the whole earth.

When one interprets the creation story contextually, several matters leap to attention. First, the Creator's purpose is to provide living space for a great variety of living beings. Stylistically the creative drama is composed of two movements, in each of which the movement is from heaven to earth (*'ereṣ,* a word that stands in the emphatic position in the prologue to the creative acts, 1:2).[6] The first movement, consisting of four creative acts in three days, culminates in the greening of the earth with vegetation (1:3-13). The second movement, likewise consisting of four creative acts in three days, reaches a climax in the appearance of earth creatures, animals and humans (1:14-27). The wonderful order and regularity of the cosmos, in which every creature, animate and inanimate, has its assigned place and function in a marvelous whole, evokes aesthetic feelings of wonder and reverence. Indeed, the narrators observe that the Creator, like a cosmic artist, surveyed the symmetry and design of the completed work and perceived it to be *ṭôb mĕ'ōd,* "very good" (1:31).

The beauty of the earth, however, lies primarily in its functional value. The story intends to show that the Creator's purpose is to provide the earth, and its surrounding cosmic environment, as a well-ordered and well-furnished habitat for living beings to appear and flourish. The Creator's activity is directed toward order, not chaos. This theme would have had special appeal in the period of the exile, when the Priestly Torah was given its final literary shape. Speaking to a people threatened with the powers of meaninglessness and chaos, an exilic prophet could proclaim that Yahweh, the God of Israel, is the one:

> who created the heavens
>   (he is God!),
> who formed the earth and made it
>   (he established it;
> he did not create it a chaos,
>   he formed it to be inhabited!) (Isa. 45:18, NRSV)

This God does not say to people "seek me in chaos" (45:19). The earth, then, is a God-given habitat, an *oikos* ("house")—designed for use by living beings.

Second, the story shows that the earth is created as a habitat for both human and nonhuman creatures equally. The emphasis falls not so much

6. The literary pattern is worked out in detail in chap. 3 above.

on anthropology as on ecology, on the earthly habitation that human beings share with other forms of "living beings" (*nepeš ḥayyâ*). It is striking that the creation account applies the expression "living being" not to the vegetation that greens the earth at the end of the first movement of the creative drama but to the new forms that appear in the second movement. The reader senses that something radically new appears in the case of the water beings (fish, sea monsters) and the flying creatures that soar over the waters (birds, winged creatures). For the first time in the story, these creatures are called "living beings" (*nepeš ḥayyâ*, Gen. 1:20), novelty signaled by a special divine blessing that grants dominion to these creatures in their medium of water or air (1:22). The narrative's climactic interest, however, is reserved for the *nepeš ḥayyâ* created on the sixth day: the animals according to their species (*mîn*, "kind"; see 1:24-25) and the supreme earthling known as *'ādām*, "human being, humanity" (1:26-27). Even though the story reaches its climax in the creation of *'ādām* and reserves the divine blessing for this earth creature, the narrators show in various ways that animals and humans belong together and share a common "house."

It is significant that, according to the dramatic sequence, animals and humans are created on the same day, a subtle literary indication of affinity. Moreover, the conclusion of the story states that animals and human beings are to share the same table: the vegetation provided in the first movement of the creation drama (1:29-30). Indeed, one should note that the Creator initiated a "peaceable kingdom" in which there was no violence, not even the killing of animals. When the narrative moves from creation to flood, again humans and animals share the same "house," the ark or houseboat in which all living beings according to their species huddle together to escape the waters of chaos. To be sure, God's special favor is bestowed on Noah, who is the representative ancestor of humankind according to ethnic groupings. But with a fine literary touch, the narrators portray the animals turning to Noah, as though led by their native attraction to human beings, in the face of catastrophe.

Two by two they came to Noah into the ark, male and female,
Just as God commanded Noah. (7:9)

The fish are not mentioned because they live in another habitat and, in any case, are not threatened by water. This picture of a remnant of animals, birds, and human beings living together in a house that tosses on the cosmic waters of chaos (the *mabbûl*) is not far removed theologically from Paul's testimony in the New Testament that the nonhuman creation longs to share with humankind the redemption from "the bondage of corruption" (Rom. 8:19-23).

Third—and this point has already been anticipated—when one reads the creation story in its scriptural context it becomes clear that God's covenant embraces the whole of creation. In the Priestly scheme that governs the Torah in its final form, the genealogical movement from creation through the times of primeval and ancestral history and on to the Sinai sojourn is periodized into a sequence of covenants.[7] Three major periods— from creation to Noah, from Noah to Abraham, from Abraham to Moses —are concluded with a covenant, each of which is characterized as a *běrît 'ôlām,* an "everlasting covenant" or a "covenant in perpetuity." The first period, the one with which I am concerned here, culminated in the Noachic covenant, the covenant in perpetuity between the Creator and Noah along with his sons, who are regarded as the ancestors of the major ethnic groupings that populated the earth. This covenant, one should note, is anticipated at the opening of the Priestly flood story (Gen. 6:18) and is actualized at the conclusion (9:8-17), thereby forming a literary and theological *inclusio* that unifies and rounds off the story. The covenant not only includes all humankind, for—as we have seen—Noah and his wife are regarded as the ancestor and ancestress of all peoples that dwell on earth (cf. 10:1), but also embraces "every living being of all flesh" (6:19), that is, all creatures that are regarded as *nepeš ḥayyâ,* "living being."

> Then God said to Noah and his sons who were with him:
> "As for me, I am establishing my covenant with you,
> 　　and with your posterity to come,
> and with every living being with you—
> the birds and the animals and all the wild beasts
> that are with you,
> 　　all that came out of the ark. . . ."[8] (9:8-10)

The Noachic covenant, then, is universal in the widest sense imaginable. It is fundamentally an ecological covenant that includes not only human beings everywhere but all animals—"every living being [*nepeš ḥayyâ*] of all flesh that is upon the earth" (9:16, repeating what was said in 6:19). Furthermore, this covenant includes the earth itself, for it is based on a solemn divine pledge never again to disturb the constancy of nature so radically that precreation chaos almost returns. In this regard the Priestly narrative has built on Old Epic tradition, which included a poetic passage:

---

7. See Frank M. Cross, "The Priestly Work," in *Canaanite Myth and Hebrew Epic* (Cambridge: Harvard Univ. Press, 1973) 293–325. I elaborate on this matter in chap. 4 above.

8. At the end of the verses quoted, where I have placed ellipsis points, the received Hebrew text adds the phrase "every beast of the earth," thus stressing the involvement of nonhuman creatures in the Noachic covenant. The repetitious phrase, however, is lacking in the Greek translation of the Old Testament (Septuagint) and has probably crept into the text by scribal error.

Throughout all the days of the earth,
   seedtime and harvest,
   cold and heat,
   summer and winter,
   day and night,
shall never cease. (8:22)

The regularities of "nature," then, are not based on the mechanical laws of an autonomous self-contained system (a "cosmos" in the Greek sense) but are the constancies that express the Creator's covenant faithfulness. Living beings flourish in an environment that is dependable and trustworthy because, as a prophetic interpreter puts it, God has established "a covenant with day and night and the orders of heaven and earth" (Jer. 33:25).

GOD'S UNCONDITIONAL COMMITMENT TO CREATION

So far we have seen that the creation story belongs to a larger narrative that reaches its theological climax with the Noachic covenant, and that in this narrative perspective creation is embraced within covenant. The word "covenant" symbolizes commitment of one party to another. What is the nature of God's commitment to the creation?

I noted earlier that the Noachic covenant, according to the Priestly scheme that governs the Torah, is classified as an "everlasting covenant" (*běrît 'ôlām*) or "covenant in perpetuity." This type of covenant differs from the Mosaic covenant as interpreted by Deuteronomic theologians, who have given us the book of Deuteronomy and have edited the history work extending from Joshua through 2 Kings (the so-called Deuteronomistic History). The Deuteronomic covenant is one in which a party is bound to the covenant maker, who imposes conditions and sanctions (blessings for obedience, curses for disobedience). It is a covenant initiated by a powerful party who extends help and protection to the weaker one, but it is a reciprocal relationship and, above all, is conditional upon faithfulness to legal stipulations. The Priestly covenant, however, is one in which God is bound by God's own commitment, regardless of the actions of the covenant recipient.[9] Although legal obligations are given in the Noachic covenant, the permanence of the covenant is based on the unconditional commitment of God to the human and nonhuman creation, for better or for worse. In this view, hope for the future does not rest on human performance or improvement, a weak reed on which to lean since human beings do not

---

9. For a discussion of these two kinds of covenant, see George E. Mendenhall, "Covenant," *IDB* 1.714–23. He distinguishes between covenants in which God is bound and covenants in which the people are bound.

seem to change, a somber note that was struck in the Old Epic flood tradition (Gen. 8:21) and that reverberates in today's wars and rumors of wars.[10] Rather, hope is based on God's absolute commitment to the creation.

The Creator's unconditional commitment to creation, according to the biblical narrative, is made in the face of violence that threatens the earth with chaos. The Priestly recension of the flood story begins with the solemn announcement:

> Now, the earth was corrupt before God,
>   the earth was filled with violence,
> God saw how corrupt the earth was,
>   for all flesh had corrupted its way on the earth. (Gen. 6:11-12)

In the Priestly view the worldwide catastrophe of the flood was not unmotivated, nor was it a capricious natural calamity (an "act of God" in the sense of modern insurance policies). Rather, violence had so marred and corrupted the earth that God's judgment came for the purpose of cleansing the earth and making a new beginning.

In the story, "all flesh" has corrupted its style of life and "through them the earth is filled with violence" (6:13). In Priestly vocabulary the expression "all flesh" refers to all that is fleshy, including birds, animals, and humans, as in God's resolution "to exterminate all flesh under heaven that has the spirit of life" (6:17) or God's final vow to "remember the everlasting covenant between God and every living being of all flesh that is upon the earth" (9:16). The language suggests that violence is a disease, as it were, that contaminates all those beings, human and nonhuman, that live in the same earthly *oikos* ("house"). A lifestyle based on violence, as we know well today, cannot be contained or confined. Violence affects not only human beings; it also permeates the nonhuman realm of animals, birds, and fish. It pollutes the earthly environment. We are dealing here with the problem of power—power that corrupts.

Although the story indicates that violence corrupted "all flesh," that is, the human and the nonhuman creation, there is no suggestion that violence is rooted in "nature," the nonhuman creation. The natural realm manifests tremendous violence: "nature red in tooth and claw"; earthquake, wind, and fire; disease, plague, and pestilence. Indeed, according to a modern view of nature, violence (power) belongs essentially to the evolutionary process in which the fittest beings struggle to survive. In the biblical

---

10. *Surrender in the Falklands,* according to an editorial in the *Boston Globe* (June 16, 1982), "ends a war that demonstrated that even in this nuclear age men don't change, that on the tiniest speck of land in the most remote part of the earth armies can battle for the most contrived and anachronistic reasons of national honor and for the basest reasons of domestic politics."

narrative, however, the violent aspect of nature receives virtually no attention. Even the flood itself, which may be reminiscent of a natural calamity caused by rampaging waters of the Tigris and Euphrates Rivers, is not recounted to illustrate natural evil but to symbolize narratively the severity of God's judgment. Furthermore, the biblical narrative provides not the slightest hint that animals were driven by their predatory instincts into conflict with human beings for living space and for survival. Indeed, as we have seen, the picture presented in the creation story is that of a paradisiacal peace in which humans and animals live together and share earth's resources. The biblical story makes the reader face one uncomfortable truth: the violence that corrupted "all flesh" is traced to the noblest creatures of God's creation, those whom God elevated to the highest position of honor and responsibility.

Here I will not go into the details of the dramatic biblical story as it unfolds from creation to flood. Suffice it to say that the Priestly writers, who have given us the primeval history in its received form, show what violence is by including illustrative episodes from Old Epic tradition. In the story of the Garden of Eden, a human couple, desiring to be like God, rebel against their Creator and, in doing so, disrupt their relationship with each other and with the soil from which they were taken and to which they will return (Gen. 2:4b—3:24). In the story of Cain, brother murders brother (4:1-16). In the story of Lamech, lust for power prompts a boast of measureless revenge (4:17-24). And in the story of the heavenly beings, "sons of God" breach the Creator's distinction between heaven and earth by having intercourse with human maidens (6:1-4). These episodes are only illustrations taken from a much wider human tradition that could easily be extended to the present. Enough illustrations are given, however, to show that the problem of violence is rooted in the misuse of God-given freedom, that this perversity is manifest especially in humankind's exercise of power, and that the corruption of power spreads from the human to the nonhuman sphere, so that it may be said of "all flesh" that "through them the earth is filled with violence" (6:13).

The total sweep of the biblical story from the original beginning to the new beginning after the flood brings before the reader two important aspects of the biblical doctrine of creation: first, the "deed-consequence" syndrome belongs not only to the social order but to the creation, and second, the created order cannot be violated without severe consequences which, in religious perspective, signify the judgment of God.[11] The flood

11. This is the thesis of Hans Heinrich Schmid in his essay, "Schöpfung, Gerechtigkeit und Heil," ZTK 70 (1973) 1–19; abridged translation by Bernhard W. Anderson and Dan G. Johnson as "Creation, Righteousness, and Salvation," in Creation in the Old Testament (ed. Bernhard W. Anderson; IRT 6; Philadelphia: Fortress Press, 1984) 102–17. By concentrating on this dimension of creation he is able to claim that "creation theology" is the full, encompassing horizon of biblical theology.

story portrays vividly the paradox of human culpability and divine judgment. On one hand human beings bring upon themselves catastrophe by their false lifestyle and violent ways; yet, on the other, this consequence is seen to be the judgment of God.

The prophet Jeremiah also dealt with the paradox of human freedom and divine sovereignty. Catastrophe, he proclaimed, is indeed the consequence of human actions. "Have you not done this to yourself," he asked, "by forsaking Yahweh your God?" (Jer. 2:17). Yet he could also perceive the consequences of human action to be the judgment of God, a backlash so severe that, as in the case of the flood story, the earth seemed to be on the verge of returning to precreation chaos. His poetic vision is not alien to the experience of many modern people.

> I looked upon the earth, and lo, a chaotic waste
> [tōhû wābōhûu],
>   and unto the heavens, and their light was gone.
> I looked on the mountains, and lo, they were quaking,
>   and all the hills were trembling.
> I looked, and lo, there was no human being,
>   and all the birds of the air had vanished.
> I looked, and lo, the fertile land was wilderness,
>   before Yahweh, before his fierce indignation. (Jer. 4:23-26)

A commentator on the RSV remarks appropriately at this point: "As if struck by a mighty nuclear bomb, the earth has been returned to its primeval state: waste and void," the tōhû wābōhûu portrayed in Gen. 1:2.[12]

The biblical storytellers and poets are realists, not dreamers. As the biblical story shows, human beings do have the terrible power to pollute the earth with their lifestyle. They do have the capacity for violence to the degree that the earth is threatened with a return to chaos. This is the precarious possibility of human history. Nevertheless—and this "nevertheless" is characteristic of the Noachic covenant—the Creator remains unconditionally committed to the creation, and moves history from chaos toward a new age, indeed, a new creation in which the relations among human beings, nonhuman creatures, and their environment will be reordered. The rainbow, which is the sign of the new age of God's covenant promise, has an ambivalent poetic meaning. In one sense, a "rainbow" represents a natural phenomenon, visible after a storm as a sign of the dawning of a new day. In another sense, "bow" symbolizes a weapon of war, which God has, so to speak, set down as a sign of peace. One of my students has put it well: "By this act of unilateral divine armament,

---

12. *The New Oxford Annotated Bible* (1973) on Jer. 4:23-26. The commentator is Victor R. Gold.

God casts judgment on the arrogant and petty violence of man and woman, of which the *Ur*-history (and beyond) provides numerous examples."[13]

THE EXTENSION OF HUMAN DOMINION IN THE NOACHIC COVENANT

The biblical story, then, moves toward a new age and a new humanity, of which Noah is the representative. The final question is: What is the role of humanity within the Creator's covenant with creation? We have already seen that in one sense human beings and nonhuman creatures are equal. Both are *nepeš ḥayyâ*, "living being"; both share the same earthly habitat; both depend on earth's regularities and resources. Yet equality of status before God does not mean equality of position and responsibility. To quote the well-known words from George Orwell's *Animal Farm*, "All animals are created equal, but some animals are more equal than others." In the biblical story, the being who is "more equal" than other earth creatures is *'ādām*, "human being," consisting of both "male and female." The creation story, articulated in two movements, reaches a dramatic climax with God's resolution:

Let us make humanity [*'ādām*] in our image,
 after our likeness,
and let them have dominion over the fish of the sea,
 over the birds of the air,
 over the cattle and over all wild beasts,[14]
 and over all crawling things that move on the earth. (Gen. 1:26)

The special status of *'ādām* is also a special commission. For no sooner is the divine intention realized in a creative act than a divine blessing empowers man and woman, who together share the divine image,

Be fertile, multiply,
 Fill the earth and subdue it!
Rule over the fish of the sea,
 over the birds of the air,
 and over every living creature that moves on the earth. (Gen. 1:28)

As we have seen previously, this theme of the creation story is recapitulated at the climax of the primeval history, when the earth emerges from the

13. Hugh J. Matlack, a Th.M. student at Princeton Theological Seminary, in an essay on Gen. 9:1-17, Spring 1982.
14. The received text reads here "and over all the earth." The notion of *dominium terrae* certainly fits the context, but at this point the text requires an animal sequence, not a general reference. Accordingly, following the Syriac, I read here "all wild beasts."

waters of chaos and a new creation dawns. At this juncture the divine blessing on humanity is repeated in practically the same language (9:1, 7; cf. 1:28), and once again the truth is underscored that *'ādām,* made in the image of God, has a special status and function in God's creation (9:6; cf. 1:26-27).

The expressions "image of God" and "likeness of God" occur only in the Priestly recension of the primeval history (but cf. Isa. 40:18). This is not the place for an extended discussion of these terms; suffice it to say that they intend to affirm that *'ādām* is created to be God's representative on earth, just as a child represents the parent on a family estate.[15] A helpful parallel occurs in ancient Babylonian and Egyptian texts that describe the king in similar language. For instance, in an Egyptian text the deity addresses Pharaoh Amenophis III: "You are my beloved Son, produced from my members, my image which I have established on the earth. I have made you to rule the earth in peace."[16] Here the emphasis is on the king's role in the royal office, his function *ex officio.* Analogously, in the biblical texts the image refers not to something *in* human nature (reason, will, conscience, immortal soul, etc.), but to the role of *'ādām,* consisting of male and female, in their bodily, historical being. Viewed in this perspective, *'ādām* is not an autonomous being, at liberty to rule the earth arbitrarily or violently. On the contrary, human dominion is to be exercised wisely and benevolently so that God's dominion over the earth may be manifest in human action. In his commentary on the book of Genesis, Gerhard von Rad writes:

> Just as powerful earthly kings, to indicate their claim to dominion, erect an image of themselves in the provinces of their empire where they do not personally appear, so man is placed upon earth in God's image, as God's sovereign emblem. He is really only God's representative, summoned to maintain and enforce God's claim to dominion over the earth. The decisive thing about man's similarity to God, therefore, is his function in the nonhuman world.[17]

Humanity did not forfeit or lose this God-given role in the period "after the Fall," to use the language of Christian theology. To be sure, the new creation after the flood was not just a repetition of the original creation. The narrative shows that the new creation bears the marks of tragedy owing to the misuse of human freedom and the spread of violence. Therefore, there must be a reordering of relations between the human and non-

15. The same language is found in the Priestly genealogy in Genesis 5, which states that Adam fathered a son "in his own likeness, after his image" (5:1). Here the idea is not just physical resemblance. The son, as the heir, not only looks like but acts like the father.

16. I cite and discuss this text in chap. 7 above; see pp. 127–28.

17. Gerhard von Rad, *Genesis* (trans. John H. Marks; OTL; rev. ed.; Philadelphia: Westminster, 1972) 60.

human creation, which contrasts with the peaceable kingdom that prevailed at first. This reordering is spelled out in a passage that comes between the *inclusio* of 9:1 and 9:7 where the divine blessing given at creation is renewed. Here animals, who once lived in harmony with humans, are now overcome with "fear and dread" of human dominion; and they are regarded as rivals and predators who are to be held responsible for the blood of *'ādām* (9:2-5a). Furthermore, human beings, to whom the earth was given to manage as children inherit a parental estate, are now at such odds with one another that a strict, apodictic law, predicated on the *imago Dei,* has to be issued against murder (9:5b-6; cf. Lev. 24:17). Nevertheless, even in this new situation, in which may be heard the "groaning of creation" (cf. Rom. 8:22-23), human beings do not cease to be who they are: creatures who are made in the image of God and who are therefore called to the high responsibility of representing or "imaging" God's rule on earth.

In this new situation a new word is spoken that contrasts with the evenhanded treatment of humans and animals at the time of creation (Gen. 1:29-30). The new word of God is: "Into your power they are given" (9:2, end of verse); "I give you everything" (9:3, end of verse). This extension of human dominion, however, is immediately qualified by two heavy restrictions, each of which is introduced by an emphatic Hebrew particle (Hebrew: *'ak,* "only," "however," at the beginning of vv. 4 and 5). First, there is a prohibition against eating animal flesh with its blood. Meat may be eaten only if an animal is properly slaughtered, for blood is regarded as sacred to God. The life of any *nepeš ḥayyâ* is precious, not because it has value in itself but because of its relation to the Creator. Second, there is a prohibition against the violent shedding of human blood on the grounds that *'ādām* is made in the image of God. Both animals and humans are held responsible before God for the taking of human life.

Thus human beings are reminded in the strongest terms, precisely at the time when their dominion over the nonhuman creation is extended, that their power is not absolute but is subject to the judgment of God. Indeed, the Noachic covenant demands a reverence for life, for every *nepeš,* animal or human, has value by virtue of its relation to God. It may well be, as some have suggested, that in our time, when meat has become a necessary staple for many human beings, some way must be found to express reverence toward animals, consonant with the demand of the Noachic covenant. For, as the creation story shows, animals also have a place, along with human beings, in the *oikos* that God has created and furnished, and they have value in relation to the Creator. Above all, the Noachic covenant demands respect for the sanctity of human life. Each person, each human *nepeš,* is precious, not because of intrinsic value but because of the Creator's relation to and claim upon human life as expressed in the *imago Dei.* The Noachic covenant has far-reaching ethical implications, especially in our time when many people have become inured to violence and when indiscriminate bloodshed can mount to genocide. It is inconceivable that a nuclear holocaust, in which multitudes of human beings would be vaporized and the remainder subjected to the torture of slow, agonizing death, could be squared with the permissions and prohibitions of the Noachic covenant.

In summary, the Noachic covenant endorses the call to human responsibility that is inherent within the creation story. To be sure, hope for the future is not grounded in human ability or human wisdom, for the biblical story, both in Old Epic tradition and in the Priestly reworking of that tradition, shows that there is a stubborn perversity in human nature (see Gen. 6:5 and 8:21). Nevertheless, God is committed irrevocably and unconditionally to the creation, and God's will is that there should be order, not chaos, on the earth. Human beings, created in the image of God, are commissioned to represent God's will for *šālôm* ("peace, well-being, harmony") on earth.

The biblical story, as far as I have traced it in the so-called primeval history, is unfinished. The story unfolds into a continuing history, an open-ended future in which God not only upholds the order of creation but continues to work creatively in the history that takes place on earth. God, who created in the beginning, creates the "new thing." The prophet of the exile, so-called Second Isaiah, announced that one should not look backward but forward:

> Don't remember the beginning of things,
>   the things of old don't consider!
> Behold, I am going to make something new;
>   now it sprouts up, don't you perceive it? (Isa. 43:18-19a)

Within the spacious horizons of the Noachic covenant, to which this prophet also refers with exquisite poetry (Isa. 54:9-10), the future is not closed but open. Standing under the rainbow arch of God's promise, whose source is lost to human view at both the beginning and the end, human beings are called to responsibility as God's representatives. Indeed, they are summoned to participate actively in God's continuing creation.

CHAPTER 10

The Tower of Babel:
Unity and Diversity
in God's Creation

The whole earth once had a single language and the same speech.	11:1
Now, it happened that when people migrated in the east, they came upon a plain in the land of Shinar and they settled there.	11:2
They said to one another:	11:3
"Come, let's mold bricks and bake them with fire!"	
So, they used bricks for stone, and bitumen they used for mortar.	
Then they said:	11:4
"Come, let's build for ourselves a city, and a tower with its peak in the sky, and let's make a name for ourselves, lest we be scattered over the surface of the whole earth!"	

But Yahweh came down to see the city and the tower that the   11:5
human beings were building.
Then Yahweh said: 11:6
"Look, the people are one and all of them have one language;
and this is how they have begun to act! Now everything they plan
to do will be attainable.
Come, let's go down and there confuse their language so that they 11:7
won't understand one another's speech!"
So, Yahweh scattered them from there over the surface of the whole 11:8
earth and they discontinued building the city.

That is why its name is called Babel, for there Yahweh confused the 11:9
language of the whole earth; from there Yahweh scattered them
over the surface of the whole earth. (Gen. 11:1-9)

165

The incentive for composing this essay in biblical theology is a work by Andrew M. Greeley, a representative of the Center for the Study of American Pluralism at the University of Chicago. In a chapter dealing with "A Theology of Pluralism," Greeley points out that the American vision of society, as articulated in James Madison's *Federalist Papers,* was one that sought to preserve and foster diversity in the midst of a national unity. The adjective "American," he observes, functions as both a hyphen (-) and an equal sign (=), as in the compounds American-Italian, American-Irish, African-American, American-Japanese, and so on. To be an American is not to be absorbed into a homogenized society; rather, the Madisonian view calls for a coalition of groups, within which persons find their identity and through which they participate in the common life. The time is overdue, Greeley maintains, for a theology of pluralism that deals not only with the diversity found in "the far-off corners of the world" but also with the pluralism that is "just down the street." At one point he declares that the Babel story, as traditionally interpreted, has been an obstacle to developing a theology of pluralism.[1]

At that point Greeley prompted my reply as a biblical theologian. In this study I propose to respond to his challenge by considering the Babel story theologically and, in so doing, to show that the biblical exegesis ought to move beyond the analysis that has dominated past biblical scholarship toward synthesis—that is, appreciation of how a particular text functions in the larger whole of the biblical narrative in its final formulation.

The story of the building of Babel or Babylon (Gen. 11:1-9) is, indeed, important for a theology that considers, on the one hand, our common humanity as creatures of God and, on the other, the manifold pluralism in the Creator's purpose. Taken by itself, the story portrays a clash of human and divine wills, a conflict of centripetal and centrifugal forces. Surprisingly, it is human beings who strive to maintain a primeval unity, based on one language, a central living space, and a single aim. It is God who counteracts this movement toward a center with a centrifugal force that disperses them into linguistic, spatial, and ethnic diversity.

The Babel story reflects the concrete realities of ancient Mesopotamia, a cradle of civilization. It includes true-to-life details that accord with archaeological knowledge, such as the use of kiln-fired bricks to compensate for the lack of natural stone in the Mesopotamian plain, and the construction of tiered temple-towers, like the famed ziggurat of Babylon known as Etemenanki.[2] These archaeological details, however, are ingre-

---

1. Andrew M. Greeley, *The Communal Catholic* (New York: Seabury, 1976), 151–62.

2. See Hugo Gressmann, *The Tower of Babel* (New York: Jewish Institute of Religion Press, 1928); and André Parrot, *The Tower of Babel* (trans. Edwin Hudson; New York: Philosophical Library, 1955).

dients of an artistic portrayal that transcends the ancient cultural setting and hence becomes a paradigm of human life in all times and places. Accordingly, the story stands at the climax of the primeval history (Genesis 1–11), whose meaning and scope are universal. Better than the English designation "primeval history" is the German term *Urgeschichte;* for the element *Ur-* refers not only to what lies in the distant past (primeval) but also to what is constitutive of history itself (primal).

The narrative has often been regarded as the story of tragic failure, of the loss of the unity that God intended for his creation. Greeley observes that "the great theologians of the Middle Ages concluded—largely from the tower of Babel myth—that if it were not for sin there would be no diversity in the human condition. The fantastic pluralism we find in the cultures of the world, in other words, is at best a necessary evil intended not by God but caused by human sinfulness."[3] In one way or another this negative interpretation has survived in Christian circles to the present day. For instance, Jacques Ellul, a layman of the French Reformed Church, insists in his provocative study of the motif of "the City" that the story is a paradigm of humankind's declaration of independence from God and that it is essentially related to the story of the Fall. The City, he maintains, is the locus of evil in human history and is "the great enemy of the church."[4]

There is a measure of truth in these gloomy interpretations, for the Old Epic tradition surely deals with the persistence of sin. Such interpretations, however, are one-sided and not sufficiently contextual. For one thing, in the larger perspective of the *Urgeschichte* the diffusion and diversification of humankind clearly represents God's positive intention. In the beginning God lavished diversity on the creation, as is apparent from the creation story with which the Bible begins; and God's creative blessing, renewed after the flood, resulted in ethnic pluralism (Genesis 10). Furthermore, eschatological portrayals of the consummation of God's historical purpose do not envision a homogenized humanity but human unity in diversity. According to the Isaianic vision of the last days (Isa. 2:1-4), when the peoples ultimately join in a vast pilgrimage to Zion, the City par excellence, they will come as nations with their respective ethnic identities. When the Spirit was given at Pentecost, according to the New Testament account (Acts 2), human beings "from every nation under heaven" heard the gospel, each "in his own native language" in the city of Jerusalem, including a host of strange peoples: Parthians, Medes, Elamites, and so on.

The Babel story contains a peculiar dialectic. Human beings strive to maintain unity, God's action effects diversity. Human beings seek for a

---

3. Greeley, *Communal Catholic,* 153.

4. Jacques Ellul, *The Meaning of the City* (trans. Dennis Pardee; Grand Rapids: Eerdmans, 1970). See pp. 10–20.

center, God counters with dispersion. Human beings want to be safe with homogeneity, God welcomes pluralism. How is one to understand these centripetal and centrifugal tendencies? I will reexamine this question by considering, first, the Babel story as a discrete narrative unit and, second, how this pericope functions in the narrative context of the primeval history. In the end, having seen the part in relation to the whole, one may be able to understand how the story illumines a theology of pluralism.

THE BABEL STORY AS A LITERARY UNIT

Considered by itself, the Babel story is a masterpiece of narrative art. In very brief compass and with an amazing economy of words, the narrator has produced a symmetrical literary structure that is well-rounded and complete. The quasi-independence of the pericope is indicated, on the one hand, by its dissonance with the previous Table of Nations (chap. 10), in which linguistic, territorial, and ethnic diversity is already realized; and, on the other, by the ensuing Shemite genealogy (11:10-26), which clearly belongs to a different literary genre, comparable to the entries extracted from the so-called *tôlĕdôt* ("generations") document (5:1). This is a pericope in the literal sense of the Greek term: one can "cut all around" it— clip it from its context—and it has its own integrity.

It is not possible here to consider the various stylistic features which show that this story is an inspired work of art, like a poem. Various scholars have helped us to understand that it is a finely wrought literary achievement.[5] For my immediate purpose it is important to notice that the story occurs in two movements that balance each other, as shown in the translation at the beginning of this essay.

The story begins with a brief introductory line that describes the situation, once upon a time: "The whole earth once had a single language and the same speech." In the first movement, which consists of a narrative report (v. 2) and discourse (vv. 3-4), human beings are the actors. In the course of their nomadic wanderings from an undesignated source, they came upon a plain in "the land of Shinar" or Babylonia (cf. 10:10), and there they settled down. Determining to make their settlement permanent and to preserve their family-like unity of language, they worked with energy and resourcefulness, as indicated by the twofold resolution introduced by a call to action: "Come [*hābâ*], let's make bricks" (v. 3); "Come [*hābâ*] let's build a city" (v. 4). Their ability to make artificial stone (kiln-

---

5. See Isaac M. Kikawada, "The Shape of Genesis 11:1-9," in *Rhetorical Criticism: Essays in Honor of James Muilenburg* (ed. Jared J. Jackson and Martin Kessler; PTMS 1; (Pittsburgh: Pickwick, 1975) 18–32; and J. P. Fokkelman, *Narrative Art in Genesis* (Amsterdam: Van Gorcum, 1975) 11–45.

fired brick) was a creative accomplishment; and this technological break-through spurred them to build a city, whose distinctive feature was an impressively high tower. If one assumes that the tower was a ziggurat, not just a military fortress, they were apparently a religious people—not un-like Christians who down through the centuries have built in the center of their cities a cathedral with a lofty spire.

In the second movement of the story (vv. 5-8), Yahweh is the actor. This section is also composed of narrative report (though, in this case, of Yahweh's action) and discourse. From the heavenly abode Yahweh "came down" to examine the antlike enterprise of human beings, ridiculously microscopic from a cosmic perspective. Like the human discourse preced-ing, Yahweh's discourse is also twofold: "Behold [*hēn*], the people are one" (v. 6), and therefore the possibilities of centralization stagger the imagination; thus, "Come [*hābâ*], let's . . ."—the language deliberately echoes that of the resolute builders—frustrate the project (v. 7). This part of the story reaches a climax (v. 8) with another narrative report about how Yahweh intervened, not by causing the tower to topple on the people but by "scattering" them "from there" over the surface of the whole earth so that they had to stop building the city, including the tower as its distinctive feature.

The story ends with a line (v. 9), introduced by the narrator's "there-fore," that gives an ironic twist to the whole. Those who wanted to make a name for themselves received a memorial, but it was a name (*šēm*) of shame. Here Babel does not mean "gate of the god(s)," as in Akkadian (*bab-ilim*), where the term suggests that the temple center was the ompha-los where heaven and earth meet and where human beings experience contact with the divine; rather, by a Hebrew wordplay, Babel is understood to mean "confusion" (*bālal*, "confuse, confound"). Moreover, the narrator concentrates on the center (*šām,* "there"), and the name (*šēm*) that the people sought to make for themselves. The people who wanted to settle securely "there" (v. 2), in one metropolitan and religious center, were scattered "from there" over the face of the earth (v. 9). Thus the ending recapitulates the beginning, though by way of reversal.

In short, the whole story is governed by a chiastic structure, a double movement that proceeds toward a climax point (in this case, the interven-tion of Yahweh) and that follows a path of reversal toward the starting point, though with an ironic twist. The movement may be diagrammed in this fashion:

Introduction: the original situation (v. 1)
    Human action:
        a. Narrative report (v. 2): wanderers settle in the plain
        b. Discourse with twofold invitational exclamations (vv. 3, 4)

Divine action:
  a. Narrative report (v. 5): investigation of the building
  b. Divine discourse with twofold invitational exclamations (vv. 6, 7)
  c) Narrative report of divine action (v. 9): dispersion
Conclusion: return to the beginning but on a new level of meaning (v. 9)

If one grants that the text in its received form is a unity, what motivated the actors in the drama? On this question the text is ambiguous. The builders apparently did something wrong, but this is not stated outright, nor is their sin specified. Moreover, Yahweh was apparently worried about what human success might lead to (v. 6; cf. 3:22!), but the text itself gives no reason for divine intervention, and I am not sure that it is proper to go beyond the text and try to explain it on the basis of ancient mythical views from the history of religions. The exegetical problem is to understand the text in its present form, rather than to explain it by a hypothetical reconstruction of its prehistory.[6] The narrative does not attempt to fill in the gaps and resolve all tensions prosaically, leaving nothing to the imagination; rather, the hearer is invited into the story's dimension of depth and mystery. Here it is appropriate to recall Erich Auerbach's discussion at the beginning of his *Mimesis,* where he contrasts the style of the Homeric story of Odysseus's scar ("uninvolved and uninvolving") with that of Genesis 22 ("The Testing of Abraham"), which invites the reader to enter the story and fill in the gaps.[7]

Since the Babel story is fraught with ambiguity and has various levels of meaning, it is not surprising that interpretations vary. On the one hand, Christians tend to favor a maximum interpretation: the human beings were motivated by a Promethean impulse to storm the heavens and to be like God. The story portrays human hubris and divine nemesis. In his study of narrative art in Genesis, J. P. Fokkelman says: "I deliberately choose a maximizing reading, for here the heavens must be retained for the sake of contrast to 'the earth, the whole earth,' which is definitely relevant in a narrative containing a short but fierce struggle for power between man and God." In the phrase "its top in the heavens," he insists, the word *šāmayim* ("heavens") must be given its full significance "because the very function of this word is to reveal the action and intentions of the people as *hubris.*"[8]

On the other hand, a line of Jewish expositors, beginning with Josephus (*Ant.* 1.4.1), advocates a more modest view: the intention of the builders

6. In his commentary, *Genesis* (Göttingen: Vandenhoeck & Ruprecht, 5th ed. 1951, 6th ed. 1964), Hermann Gunkel analyzes the story into two recensions: a City version and a Tower version (pp. 92–101); but this analysis does injustice to the symmetry of the literary unit.

7. Erich Auerbach, *Mimesis* (trans. Willard R. Trask; Garden City, N.Y.: Doubleday Anchor, 1957) 3–23. See further my essay, "The Contemporaneity of the Bible," *Princeton Seminary Bulletin* 62 (1969) 38–50, esp. 46–47.

8. Fokkelman, *Narrative Art in Genesis,* 19–20.

was to gather the people into a centralized location, thereby resisting God's purpose that they should multiply, fill the earth, and subdue it. According to this interpretation, the description of the tower as reaching into the heavens means nothing more than an impressively high structure such as Canaanites built (Deut. 1:28; 9:1)—in modern terms a skyscraper. For instance, Nahum Sarna objects to the view that the story implies "an attempt to storm heaven in insolent rebellion against God." Adducing various references, biblical and extrabiblical, to show that the expression "with its top in the sky" means nothing more than a tower of great height, he declares that the sin of the generation was not that of hubris but something quite different: "it actually consisted of resistance to the divine will that the children of men be dispersed over the whole world."[9]

This is admittedly a difficult interpretive dilemma. Interpreters inevitably bring something to the text as they are caught up in its movement, though it would be an oversimplification to suppose that this "input" depends on whether one is Christian or Jew. In any case, it is noteworthy that the motivation of the builders is indicated in both positive and negative terms in v. 4: "Let us make a name for ourselves [positive], lest we be scattered over the face of the earth [negative]." Claus Westermann finds in this verse a mixture of motives that to him is evidence that the story has undergone a tradition-historical development. According to his form-critical analysis, the original human resolve (v. 4a) was simply "an expression of the will to greatness, something 'over and above'" ("Ausdruck des Willens zur Grösse, zum Überragenden").[10] Whether human motives can be sorted out so neatly and logically is open to question. Furthermore, when one gives attention to the stylistic unity and symmetry of the story in its present form, it is clear that the theme of "scattering" is intrinsic to it, occurring three times in strategic places: the first part (v. 4b), the second part (v. 8), and the conclusion (v. 9). The positive and negative aspects of the motivation—making a name and fear of dispersion—belong essentially to the paradigmatic portrayal of the human situation.

In his book *When Man Becomes God,* Donald Gowan has presented a study of the hubris theme in the Old Testament.[11] His thesis is that this theme appears most clearly in connection with the state which has the

---

9. Nahum M. Sarna, *Understanding Genesis* (New York: Schocken, 1966) 63–77; quotation from 72. This view is also advocated by Benno Jacob, *Das erste Buch der Torah: Genesis* (Berlin: Schocken, 1934); abbreviated English edition, *The First Book of the Bible: Genesis* (trans. Ernest I. and Walter Jacob; New York: KTAV, 1974); and Umberto Cassuto, *A Commentary on the Book of Genesis* (trans. Israel Abrahams; 2 vols.; Jerusalem: Magnes, 1961–64), vol. 2.

10. Claus Westermann, *Genesis* (trans. John J. Scullion; Continental Commentary; 3 vols.; Minneapolis: Augsburg, 1984–86) 1.546.

11. Donald E. Gowan, *When Man Becomes God: Humanism and Hybris in the Old Testament* (PTMS 6; Pittsburgh: Pickwick, 1975).

potential of arrogating unto itself the powers that belong to God, as we well know from manifestations of totalitarianism in recent times. He calls attention to passages like Isa. 14:1-21 and Ezek. 28:1-19, where the urge to grasp equality with God is exemplified by the tyrant who, to use mythical language, attempted to ascend to heaven and sit in the assembly of the gods or who likened himself to the *Urkönig* ("primal ruler") in the Garden of Eden on the mountain of God. For such tyrannical hubris, there is nemesis; the pride of nations leads to their fall. Gowan, however, hesitates to regard the Babel story as a clear example of the hubris motif. "We conclude that intimations of concern about usurpation of God's place and power are present, but in a subdued form. Although it is open to several interpretations, it is essentially the kind of negative judgment of urban culture which has appeared in many forms from the nomads to the free-land advocates of late twentieth-century America."[12] This reserved judgment with respect to the Babel story is justified, in my estimation. Gowan could have pointed out that not once do Israel's poets and prophets use the Tower of Babel as a symbol of Babylon's overweening pride that led to destruction.

It is noteworthy that the Babel story contains no suggestion of royal or imperial motivation—in contrast to another tradition (Gen. 10:8-12) that speaks of Babel as one of Nimrod's royal cities and a base for imperial expansion. On the contrary, the people are described as acting in democratic concert: "Come, let us. . . ." The text gives no intimation that the project was under the leadership of a king like those Babylonian rulers who engaged in architectural works to make a name, as we know from ancient royal inscriptions; nor is there any hint that the builders surrendered their primitive democracy to an aggressive leader like Nimrod who promised political security and imperial renown. Their motivation was deeply human and "democratic" in the broad sense of the term. The builders surely sought material glory and fame; but more than this, they sought dominion over the limitations of their environment. Animals are gregarious, but they do not build cities. The city is the symbol of humanity's creative freedom to rise above the natural environment and to come together in social unity. It is a place of security from powers of chaos that threaten from the outside world, the "wilderness." It is a place where people may raise a memorial, even a religious monument (a ziggurat or a cathedral) that, at least for a period, stands above the flux and contingency of history.

Yet the story portrays human freedom as a mixture of creativity and anxiety; therefore the words "lest we be scattered" are appropriately joined with the "name" that signifies dominion. Benno Jacob rightly stresses the

12. Ibid., 29.

anxiety that accompanies human aspiration and gregariousness. The builders, he says, "do not want to force their way into the heavens, but to
huddle closely together on the earth where they fear getting lost."[13] Fear of
the unknown—the trackless wilderness, strange places and faces, the un-
certainties of the future—may impel a wandering people toward a center,
where they organize to build a city or to create a civilization. They may
eventually turn to a tyrant, like Nimrod, to carry out the policy of centralization. In the story Yahweh observes: "This is how they have begun to
act! Now everything they plan to do will be attainable" (v. 6). Whether this
human activity should be described as hubris or as sin is debatable. The
narrator simply portrays that dimension of life that underlies human
conflicts: fear of geographical dispersion, fear of linguistic and ethnic
diversity, fear of differences of race, religion, custom.

There is something very human, then, in this portrayal of people who,
with mixed pride and anxiety, attempted to preserve primeval unity. But
their intention to hold on to the simplicity of the primeval past collided
with the purpose of God, who acted to disperse them from their chosen
center.

THE BABEL STORY IN ITS NARRATIVE CONTEXT

I turn now to the second major concern. It is not enough to consider the
story by itself as a literary unity and to puzzle over some of its inner
tensions and ambiguities. The Babel story now functions in a larger narrative context. This given narrative context enhances the meaning of the
story itself and enables one to consider the theological issue of unity and
diversity, centralization and dispersion, in a broader perspective.

The mainstream of critical scholarship generally recognizes that the
Babel story is the climactic episode of the Old Epic tradition (the so-called
Yahwist Epic or J source) that portrayed world history from the creation of
the world to the call of Abraham and on. Even though the presuppositions
of past literary criticism (e.g., source criticism or form criticism) need
reexamination,[14] I see no convincing reason to dispute the major result of
past generations of research: namely, that large blocks of this Old Epic
narrative are embedded in the final formulation of the primeval history.
For theological exegesis, however, it is important to recognize that the
Priestly writer-editors (P), whom one should undoubtedly regard as the
final compositors and editors of the Pentateuch, have incorporated portions of this Old Epic into a new work for the sake of enrichment and
elaboration. Therefore, instead of analytically isolating so-called J and P

13. Jacob, *Genesis,* 301 (Eng., p. 79).
14. See chap. 4 above.

materials and commenting on them separately, as the major critical commentaries of the twentieth century do, the interpreter is obliged to take seriously the final synthesis of the tradition. In the case at hand, this means that one should consider the "ethnological framework" within which the Babel story functions, that is, the *tôlĕdôt* ("generations") scheme that provides the outline of the Priestly composition as a whole in the book of Genesis.[15]

The Babel story immediately follows the Table of Nations (chap. 10). There is an obvious seam between these two traditions. The Babel story begins with the assertion that people spoke the same language; the Table of Nations, however, indicates that already the family of Noah had proliferated into a diversity of ethnic groups that were dispersed spatially. How is one to understand this dissonance?

Some light is thrown on the question by studying the editorial procedure used by the Priestly writers in appropriating blocks of Old Epic tradition. Not surprisingly, these writers give primacy to Priestly material, but at appropriate places add the Old Epic tradition that harks back to an earlier point in the Priestly outline and, to a certain extent, is parallel. For example, the writers begin with the Priestly creation story (1:1—2:3);[16] then, after the *tôlĕdôt* formula (2:4a), add a block of Epic material (2:4b—4:26) that at the outset duplicates and parallels the Priestly account of the creation of human being (*'ādām*), male and female. That is, the story resumes from an earlier point. Also, in chapter 5 the writers present the *tôlĕdôt* of Adam up to the birth of Noah's sons, then resumptively introduce a block of Epic material (6:1—7:8) that at its outset (6:1) reaches back to an earlier, indefinite point in time. Similarly, after the flood story the writers continue with the (basically) Priestly Table of Nations, then add the Babel story, which resumptively reverts to an earlier time before the proliferation of Noah's sons into ethnic and linguistic groups. In proceeding thus, the redactors attempted to preserve the traditions and, at the same time, to enrich and fill out the Priestly outline. In the specific case of the Babel story, the redactors may have supposed that this episode provided an etiology of the ethnic pluralism portrayed in chapter 10, where the primary emphasis is on spatial distribution. Be that as it may, the Babel story is supplemental. It adds a dimension that is necessary for a full understanding of the interaction of the divine and human purposes in the *Urgeschichte*. Gerhard von Rad rightly observed—though without pursuing fully the implications of his remark—that "the chapters must be read together, because they are intentionally placed next to each other in spite

15. See Frank M. Cross, "The Priestly Work," in *Canaanite Myth and Hebrew Epic* (Cambridge: Harvard Univ. Press, 1973) 293–325.
16. The reason for saying that the creation story ends at 2:3, not 2:4a, is set forth in "A Stylistic Analysis of the Priestly Creation Story" (chap. 3 above).

of their antagonism."[17] What needs to be said further is that the intention of the Priestly writers is evident in the way they combine materials that once had an independent meaning, with the result that the whole is greater than—or at least different from—the sum of its parts.

When one surveys the block of materials dealing with the postdiluvian period, that is, 9:18-19 ("The sons of Noah who went forth from the ark were . . .") through the Babel story (11:1-9), it is evident that the "scattering" motif is prominent. Indeed, the dispersion verb (*pûş,* or its related form, *nāpaş*) is a motif that runs through the whole section, appearing in various modulations in 9:19 and 10:18, as well as three times in the Babel story (11:4, 8, 9). This motif is introduced in a passage found at the conclusion of the flood story:

> Now, the sons of Noah who disembarked [*hayyôşě'îm*] from the ark were Shem, Ham, and Japheth,
>   Ham being the father of Canaan.
> These three were sons of Noah,
>   and from them the whole earth was scattered [*nāpěşâ*]. (Gen. 9:18-19)

In the present narrative context, these verses clearly have a transitional function: they lead from the flood story to what follows. The verses, however, provide a good illustration of the analytical procedure of twentieth-century critical scholarship. Without exception, source critics (Wellhausen, Gunkel, Driver, Noth, Westermann, et al.) have assigned this passage to J, except for the last part of v. 18 ("Ham being the father of Canaan"), which is regarded as a subsequent, harmonizing addition. The reasons for this analysis are as follows. (1) P has already mentioned Noah's sons by name, once at the beginning (6:10) and again in the course of the story (7:13), and it seems overly repetitious to mention them again at the end. (2) The proper starting point is to divide the story into its component strata; and since J, up to this point, has not mentioned Noah's sons by name, it is appropriate to assign these verses to J and to regard them as J's introduction to the genealogy of Noah's sons, now incorporated into chapter 10 (the Table of Nations). (3) The "scattering" verb (*nāpěşâ*) occurs in other passages that must be assigned to J. Westermann quotes with approval Gunkel's dictum: "The expression has its setting *[Sitz]* in the story of the building of the tower."[18]

None of these arguments is convincing to me. I will take them in chiastic order. First, it is doubtful whether the occurrence of a single verb is sufficient basis for source analysis. There is no a priori reason why the

---

17. Gerhard von Rad, *Genesis* (trans. John H. Marks; OTL; rev. ed.; Philadelphia: Westminster, 1972) 152.

18. Westermann, *Genesis,* 1.486.

Priestly writers could not have used this verb, one that is prominent in the vocabulary of an approximate contemporary, Ezekiel, who frequently speaks of the scattering of the people as the prelude to their later unification on the land (e.g., Ezek. 11:16-21; 12:15; 20:33-38). If one were to focus on linguistic niceties, one should give equal attention to the participial expression "those who went forth [*hayyôṣĕ'îm*] from the ark" in 9:18, which corresponds to the same formulation in the preceding Priestly material (9:10: *yôṣĕ'ê hattēbâ*).[19] In short, style and vocabulary provide no firm basis for analysis in this instance. Second, methodologically one should begin with "the functional unity" of the story in its present form, as George Coats has argued in his study of the Joseph novella, and only then turn to the question of sources or traditions. "To reverse the procedure and begin with a division of the story into its component sources begs the question about structure and unity."[20] Third, the repetition of the names of Noah's sons has a special function in this case, namely, *resumption*—harking back to the beginning of the story for the purpose of carrying the narrative forward. The resumption not only recapitulates but adds a note of contrast that is intentionally emphasized in the sentence formulation: "These three sons of Noah—yet from them the whole earth was repopulated."

This transitional passage has no suggestion of scattering being an act of divine judgment, as in the Babel story (see also Isa. 33:3). On the contrary, ethnic diversity is understood to be the fruit of the divine blessing given at the creation (1:28) and renewed in the new creation after the flood (9:1, 7). From the "one" (Noah) God brought into being "the many" through the ordinary course of human increase and population expansion. This is the sense of the "scattering" verb (*pûṣ*) in 10:18, where the expansion of the Canaanites is in mind. In accordance with this positive view, the Priestly writers summarize the revised Table of Nations by using a synonymous verb: "These are the families of the sons of Noah, according to their genealogies, by their nations, and from these the nations branched out [*niprĕdû*] after the flood" (10:32).

I conclude, then, that in the present context the passage 9:18-19 provides a literary bridge from the story of the flood proper to the postdiluvian period. Contrary to Gunkel and Westermann, the "scattering" verb does not have its effective setting in the Babel story but in its present narrative context, where it introduces the leitmotif of the ensuing section, in which the Priestly writers have absorbed Old Epic tradition into their

19. Cassuto draws attention to this "verbal parallel" in his *Genesis*, 2.148. Likewise Jacob observes (*Genesis*, 259) that v. 18 prepares for the following story by echoing the "identical" expression in v. 10.

20. George W. Coats, *From Canaan to Egypt: Structural and Theological Context of the Joseph Story* (CBQMS 4; Washington, D.C.: Catholic Biblical Association, 1976) 7–8.

overall presentation. How, then, is one to understand the combined viewpoints: one perceiving that God's blessing is manifest in manifold diversity, and the other suggesting that God's judgment is disclosed in the dispersal of human beings from a center?

At least this is clear: when one reads the Babel story in the total context in which it now functions, there is no basis for the negative view that pluralism is God's judgment upon human sinfulness. Diversity is not a condemnation. Long ago Calvin perceived this truth. Commenting on Gen. 11:8 ("So the Lord scattered them abroad"), he observed: "Men had already been spread abroad; and this ought not to be regarded as a punishment, seeing it rather flowed from the benediction and grace of God. But those whom the Lord had before distributed with honour in various abodes, he now ignominiously scatters, driving them hither and thither like the members of a lacerated body."[21] No longer is it necessary, however, to try to harmonize what "Moses" wrote. Tensions and dissonances in Scripture reflect a previous history of traditions extending from the early oral period to the final composition of the Priestly edition of the Pentateuch during the exile. The written form of the tradition that we have received undoubtedly bears the stigmata of oral performance. We know little about how the transmission of traditions was related to the sociology of ancient Israel,[22] and we are ignorant about the circumstances that occasioned the final literary formulation of the tradition. Before us we have only the end result of this process. The Priestly writers have given us a final composition in which the presentation of the primeval history, based on a genealogical scheme, is enriched with Old Epic tradition. Whatever excursions into the prehistory of the text are possible or necessary, theological exegesis begins and ends with the text in its final form.

Viewed in this light, the Babel story has profound significance for a biblical theology of pluralism. First, God's will for his creation is diversity rather than homogeneity. We should welcome ethnic pluralism as a divine blessing, just as we rejoice in the rich variety of the nonhuman creation: trees, plants, birds, fish, animals, heavenly bodies. The whole creation bears witness to the extravagant generosity of the Creator.[23] But something more must be added, and this the Priestly writers have done by including the Old Epic story of the building of Babel. Human beings strive for unity and fear diversity. They want to be settled and are fearful of insecurity. Per-

---

21. John Calvin, *Commentaries on the Book of Genesis* (trans. John King; 2 vols.; Grand Rapids: Eerdmans, 1948) 1.332.

22. See Burke O. Long, "Recent Field Studies in Oral Literature and Their Bearing on Old Testament Criticism," *VT* 26 (1976) 187–98; also my comments on this matter in chap. 4 above.

23. Andrew Greeley's chapter, from which this essay took its start, vividly treats this dimension of creation theology; see *Communal Catholic*, 152, 156.

haps they do not pit themselves against God in Promethean defiance, at least consciously; but in their freedom they are driven, like the builders of Babel, by a creative desire for material glory and fame and a corresponding fear of becoming restless, rootless wanderers.

This creative freedom is both the grandeur and the misery of humanity. On the one hand, it enables human beings to rise above the limitations of their environment and, with cooperative effort and technological ingenuity, to build a city that affords unity and protection. There is security for people who are of one kind: who speak one language, live at one center, and share one goal. On the other hand, their "will to greatness," which also reflects anxiety, prompts an assertion of power that stands under the judgment of the God whose creative purpose includes richness, variety, and proliferation. Human beings are, indeed, "members of a lacerated body"— a broken, fragmented humanity in which God's will for unity in diversity is transformed into conflicting division between peoples who speak different languages, live in separate territories, and belong to particular ethnic groups or nations. The ambition of the builders of Babel for human unity has been refracted into the conflicts of human history. The blessing of God, which produces a rich variety of peoples of different races, colors, tongues, nationalities, and living spaces, has been transformed into antagonistic division between peoples who speak different languages, live in separate territories, and belong to particular ethnic groups or nations. The human drive for unity has fearful possibilities and consequences, as Yahweh's judgmental word in the Babel story indicates: "Now everything they plan to do will be attainable!" The picture of a million people raising their hands in a single salute is an awe-inspiring—and frightening—vision.[24]

The primeval history, however, leads beyond the Babel story toward the call of Abraham. Uprooted from his Mesopotamian homeland and moving by faith into the unknown, Abraham represents a new people who, in contrast to the builders of Babel, do not strive to make a name but whose name is "made great" by God's blessing (Gen. 12:1-3). Abraham is the paradigm of a new people through whom all the families of humankind are to experience blessing, not by surrendering their ethnic identities but by being embraced within the saving purpose of the God who rejoices in the diversity of the creation. It is significant in this connection that a Christian apocalyptic writer portrays the consummation of history by showing that the present diversification of society is a prelude to an ultimate unity-in-pluralism, when a vast and diverse people "from every nation, from all tribes and peoples and tongues" will join in a concert of praise to God (Rev. 7:9-12, RSV).

24. The allusion is to the display of popular unity that attended the death of Mao and the acclamation of his successor. Other examples could easily be found from history, ancient and modern.

CHAPTER 11

"The Lord Has Created
Something New":
A Stylistic Study of
Jeremiah 31:15-22

At the conclusion of a poem in the "Little Book of Consolation" (Jeremiah 30–31) the announcement is made that Yahweh has created something new to signify the new age into which a sorrowing, despairing people is invited to enter. The received Hebrew text of Jer. 31:22 reads (KJV):

kî bārā' YHWH ḥădāšâ bā'āreṣ	For the Lord hath created a new thing in the earth,
nĕqēbâ tĕsôbēb gāber	A woman shall compass a man.

This announcement, introduced by the motive particle *kî* ("for"), is the climactic line of the poem. Here the poet speaks about God's innovation, something so marvelous that it should motivate a response to the gracious invitation. Unfortunately, however, the second colon, which specifies the "new thing" (*ḥădāšâ*) indicated in the first colon, is not clear. Though venturing a translation, Arthur Weiser observes that the final words constitute "ein ungelöstes Rätsel" ("an unsolved riddle"). John Bright says that "the meaning is wholly obscure" and suggests that it would be wiser to leave the colon blank rather than try to translate it. Wilhelm Rudolph, among other scholars, maintains that the text in its present form makes no sense and should be emended.[1]

---

1. Arthur Weiser, *Das Buch der Propheten Jeremia* (ATD 20/21; Göttingen: Vandenhoeck & Ruprecht, 1959) 290; John Bright, *Jeremiah* (AB 21; Garden City, N.Y.: Doubleday, 1965) 282; Wilhelm Rudolph, *Jeremia* (HAT 12; Tübingen: Mohr [Siebeck], 1958) 290.

It may be that the Hebrew text has become corrupt in the course of transmission.[2] But before resorting to the desperate expedient of textual emendation, it may be worthwhile to take another look at the problem from the standpoint of a stylistic study of the text in its context.

AN APPEAL TO DAUGHTER ISRAEL

The troublesome words occur in the immediate context of an appeal to Israel, addressed as "Virgin" and "Daughter," to return home (31:21-22). The summons to return involves a geographical movement: a movement away from captivity along the very route (marked with guideposts) of the journey into exile, and a movement toward the homeland, specifically "her cities" (v. 21). There is also the suggestion that coming home involves a return to a faithful relationship to Yahweh, for the Virgin/Daughter is addressed: *habbat haššôbēbâ* ("O wandering daughter"). Thus she is asked, with double entendre, why she wanders to and fro (*'ad-mātay tithammāqîn*),[3] both in the sense of getting lost on the homeward journey and in the sense of continuing in her faithless straying from the covenant relationship with Yahweh, (v. 22a). The appeal to "return," in the double sense of returning home to the land and of returning home to her covenant loyalty with Yahweh, who gives the people Israel a future, is followed by the inducement: "For Yahweh has created something new." Here the "prophetic perfect" is used to announce the future that is already present, in the sense that it is anchored in the certainty of God's intention. Appropriately the creation verb *bārā'*, which is used only in connection with divine creativity (e.g., Gen. 1:1), is employed here—as in Second Isaiah (Isa. 48:6-7; cf. 65:17-18)—to announce the new creation, the new age that will be inaugurated "on the earth" or "in the land" (*bā'āreṣ*).

The prophetic *novum* itself is described in three Hebrew words: (1) the subject *něqēbâ*, which refers to a female, whether human or animal (Gen. 1:27, 6:19); (2) the verb *těsôbēb* (polel of *sābab*, "to turn," "go around," "encircle"), which means to "encompass" in various senses, such as enemies surrounding a city (Ps. 59:14 [15]), a liturgical movement around the altar (Ps. 26:6), or—in a theological sense—Yahweh's enfolding the people with protection (Deut. 32:10) or with covenant faithfulness (Ps. 32:7, 10); and, finally, (3) the object *geber*, which refers to a full-bodied male

---

2. The LXX at Jer. 38:22 has a different reading: *eōs pote apostrepseis, thygatēr etimōmenē; hoti ektisen kyrios sōtērian eis kataphyteusin kainēn, en sōtēria perieleusontai anthrōpoi* ("How long will you turn away, disgraced daughter? For the Lord has created salvation for a new planting; in salvation men will walk").

3. This hithpael form is a hapax legomenon (cf. qal in Cant. 5:6) and apparently means "to turn hither and thither," possibly to turn about in circles (like a lost person).

who is capable of military, sexual, and other responsibilities (Exod. 12:37; Deut. 22:5; Prov. 30:19; etc.). It has long been recognized that the difficulty lies not in translating the three Hebrew words but in understanding their meaning in the syntax of the sentence and, above all, their function in the given poetic context.

Here one should note the translation of the Vulgate:

> Usquequo deliciis dissolveris filia vaga?
> quia creavit Dominus novum super terram:
> femina circumdabit virum.

Jerome took the final words to be a mariological prophecy, referring to Mary's protective embrace of the Christ-child within her womb.

> The Lord has created a new thing on earth without seed of man, without carnal union and conception, "a woman will encompass a man" within her womb— One who, though he will later appear to advance in wisdom and age through the stages of infancy and childhood, yet, while confined for the usual number of months in his mother's womb, will already be a perfect man.[4]

According to this interpretation, the words are not just eschatological but messianic in a specific Christian sense. In the history of interpretation this influential view has taken its place along with a variety of others.[5]

The difficulty of the text is evidenced by various modern English translations, each of which takes a hermeneutical stand.

American Translation	How long will you hesitate, O backturning daughter?
	For the Lord has created a new thing on the earth—
	The woman woos the man!
JPSV	How long will you waver,
	O rebellious daughter?
	(For the Lord has created something new on earth:
	a woman courts a man.)

---

4. Quoted in the annotation of the NAB (New York: Kenedy, 1970) 1136. See Jerome: *PL* 28.255; 24.880–81. My colleague Karlfried Froehlich has pointed out that apparently the first patristic mariological interpretation of Jer. 31:22 was given by Marcellus of Ancyra (d. ca. 374 C.E.); see *PG* 25.250B (Ps. Athanasius). Following the translation of Aquila, not of LXX, he commented: "The Lord has created a new thing in the female [LXX: on the earth], that is, in Mary. For nothing new has been created in the female except that which was born from the Virgin Mary without intercourse, the body of the Lord."

5. For a summary of the *Nachgeschichte* of this text to the mid-nineteenth century, see L. Reinke, *TQ* 33 (1851) 509–63; idem, *Beiträge zur Erklärung des Alten Testamentes* 3 (1855) 60–69, 318–406. Later brief updatings of the discussion are found in Albert Condamin, *Le livre de Jérémie* (Ebib; Paris: Lecoffre, 1920) 227–28; and C. Shedl, "'Femina Circumdabit Virum,' oder 'Via Salutis'?" *ZKT* 83 (1961) 431–35.

RSV	How long will you waver,
	    O faithless daughter?
	For the Lord has created a new thing on the earth:
	    a woman protects a man.

NRSV	How long will you waver,
	    O faithless daughter?
	For the Lord has created a new thing on the earth:
	    a woman encompasses a man.

JB	How long will you hesitate,
	    disloyal daughter?
	For Yahweh is creating something new on earth:
	    the Woman sets out to find her Husband again.

NAB	How long will you continue to stray,
	    rebellious daughter?
	The Lord has created a new thing upon the earth:
	    the woman must encompass the man with
	    devotion.

NEB	How long will you twist and turn, my wayward child? For the Lord has created a new thing in the earth: a woman turned into a man.
REB	How long will you waver, my wayward child? For the Lord has created a new thing on earth, a woman will play a man's part.
AB	How long dillydally, O turnabout daughter? For Yahweh has created a new thing on earth: [A female shall compass a man (?)]

The interpretation given in these translations may be divided into two general categories:

First, some take *nĕqēbâ* and *geber* to refer generically to feminine and masculine human beings, respectively. Thus according to one view (cf. RSV), there will be such peace and security in the new age that women will no longer need male protection but, on the contrary, will protect the men. Admittedly, the verb *tĕsôbĕb* may connote protective encirclement, as in Deut. 32:10, which states that Yahweh encircled the people of Jacob and kept them as "the apple of his eye"; but this interpretation does not suit the context of the new age that is announced. A proper rejoinder is that if women need no protection in a time of peace and security, men should not need it either.[6] Others suggest that the new age will introduce a reversal of relationships, with the result that the woman will take the lead in "wooing" the man (cf. JPSV) or, by emending the verb, that the woman will "be

6. See J. Philip Hyatt, *IB* 5.1034.

turned into a man" (cf. NEB).[7] Even when these meanings are imputed to the verb, the sentence remains obscure. Is one to think that Israel, who had been acting like a timid woman, will act as a vigorous man? Or that there will be such a reversal of relationships that women will be the leaders? In none of these cases is the interpretation warranted by the context.

Second, other interpreters take the nouns *něqēbâ* and *geber* to refer to Israel and Yahweh respectively. In the new age there will be a great reversal: formerly, the Man (Yahweh) had encircled the Woman (Israel) with covenant fidelity, but the time will come when Israel will take the initiative to encompass Yahweh with devotion (cf. NAB).[8] Or the verb *těsôbēb* is construed as "to go looking for" (cf. JB) or is even emended to "return,"[9] with the translation "the woman returns to the man," that is, "the faithless woman Israel finally does return to Yahweh, her man, even though this has never happened before."[10] These interpretations have the advantage of suiting the context. But it is doubtful that the verb, unless emended, can be so construed; further, it is unusual for the word *geber* to be applied symbolically to Yahweh (cf. *rēaʿ* in 3:20; *ʾîš* in Hos. 2:2, 7 [4,9]).

William Holladay has offered a different interpretation.[11] He maintains that the verb *těsôbēb* is "plainly sexual" and that one should translate approximately: "the female embraces the he-man." The noun *geber*, he alleges, has the same meaning as in 30:5-7, which he interprets to mean that the soldiers of Judah are mocked for "acting like women" when God comes to wage battle against the people Israel. In the passage at hand, Jeremiah is said to have used the motif of femininity in two ways: first, to

---

7. Emending *těsôbēb* to *tissôb*, as proposed by Bernhard Duhm (*Das Buch Jeremia* [KHAT 11; Tübingen: Mohr (Siebeck), 1901] 251). Translating "the woman is turned into a man," he maintained that the sentence is a witty gloss, intended to remind the reader that Israel, who had been referred to shortly before as a man, is here regarded as a woman. Similarly John Paterson (*Peake's Commentary on the Bible* [rev. ed.; New York: Nelson, 1962] 556) suggests that the sentence is "a grammatical gloss where the copyist is indicating that the masculine (son) has been changed to the feminine (daughter) in 20, 21, 22."

8. The annotation to the NAB translation points out that the words "with devotion" are not in the Hebrew text but "are added for the sense."

9. The emendation of *těsôbēb geber* to *tāšûb lěgeber* was proposed by Condamin, *Jérémie*, 228.

10. Norman C. Habel, *Jeremiah-Lamentations* (Concordia Commentary; St. Louis: Concordia, 1968) 241. This general view was advocated long ago by Reinke (*Beiträge*, 318–406) and has been freshly revived by Edmond Jacob ("Féminisme ou Messianisme? A propos de Jérémie 31:22," in *Beiträge zur alttestamentlichen Theologie: Festschrift für Walther Zimmerli zum 70. Geburtstag* [ed. Herbert Donner, Robert Hanhard, and Rudolf Smend; Göttingen: Vandenhoeck & Ruprecht, 1977] 179–84).

11. William L. Holladay, "Jer xxxi 22b Reconsidered: 'The Woman Encompasses the Man,'" *VT* 16 (1966) 236–39; idem, "Jeremiah and Woman's Liberation," *Andover Newton Quarterly* 12 (1972) 213–23; idem, *Jeremiah: Spokesman out of Time* (Philadelphia: Pilgrim, 1974) 116–21. His interpretation of this passage is also set forth in his commentary, *Jeremiah* (Hermeneia; 2 vols.; Philadelphia and Minneapolis: Fortress Press, 1986–89) 2.195.

portray Israel in the wilderness (exile) as innocent, vulnerable, and "giddy"; and second, to portray weakness under combat, like the "warriors-become-women" referred to in an earlier passage (30:5-7; cf. 50:37; Nah. 3:13). "Israel is not only acting feminine in the wilderness but effeminate," and God intends to put a stop to such behavior. Therefore, in the new age God will reverse the masculine-feminine roles; God "will make the female rather than the male the initiator in sexual relations, so that the demoralized warriors-turned-to-women will no longer be under a curse. Next time women will take the lead." Holladay, who is sensitive to changing human relations in our time, warns against hastily jumping to the conclusion that this text is "an early anticipation of women's liberation." Rather, the prophet was using "the stock assumption of his time" to portray hope for the people in their helplessness; for "God will make even the people's presumed effeminacy into a strength."[12]

This novel interpretation has at least two problems. First, the interpretation hinges on understanding 30:5-7 as the mockery or curse of warriors who had become, in the view of a male-oriented society, as weak as women.[13] The text at hand, however, does not lend itself easily to this understanding. Elsewhere, Jeremiah used the image of childbirth to portray the anguish of the times, for instance in 6:24 (cf. 4:31; 22:23), where the impending invasion of the foe from the north evokes the consternation of the people, portrayed as the daughter of Zion:

> We have heard the news of it,
>   our hands fall limp;
> anguish has seized us,
>   pain like a woman in labor [yôlēdâ].

Similarly in 30:5-6 the pangs of "a woman in labor" (yôlēdâ) grip men—a metaphorical description of the general anguish and ashen fear in prospect of the day of Yahweh, which will be unlike any other day. Second, while Holladay's interpretation is consonant with the movement of the poetry from despair to hope, from weakness to strength, it does not provide a persuasive identification of the enigmatic *nĕqēbâ* and *geber* mentioned in 31:22. The virile term *geber,* in view of its various usages in the Old Testament and in the prophecy of Jeremiah (see 30:6 [parallel to *zākār*]; 22:30; 23:9 [parallel to *'îš*]), need not be restricted to "warrior."

A "pregnant" suggestion has been offered by Weiser, who observes that two words in the line, *bārā'* ("create") and *nĕqēbâ* ("female"), are related

12. Holladay, *Jeremiah: Spokesman,* 117, 120.

13. Holladay alludes to Delbert Hillers, *Treaty-Curses and the Old Testament Prophets* (BibOr 16; Rome: Pontifical Biblical Institute, 1964) who treats this theme, and calls attention to Jer. 50:37; 51:30; and Nah. 3:13, which reflect this type of curse.

to the creation account in Gen. 1:27ff., a literary (or liturgical) tradition that reaches back into a time much earlier than the final formulation of the Priestly work. He proposes that the final colon of 31:22 points to "the renewal of the creation blessing of fertility (Gen. 1:28; cf. Jer. 31:27), from which the people will arise anew."[14] This potentially fruitful proposal, however, does not take sufficient account of the literary context of the poem in which the enigmatic words occur. Stylistic analysis of the poem, I submit, may illumine the exegetical problem and contribute to theological understanding.

POETIC STRUCTURE AND MOVEMENT

The question immediately arises: What is the literary unit with which we are dealing? On the one hand, some literary critics maintain that the poetic unit is very brief: only two verses (vv. 21-22). For instance, Weiser remarks: "Previously it was Ephraim, the son, who was involved [31:18-20], but now it is the Virgin Israel; therefore v. 21 begins a new utterance [*Spruch*] that, by virtue of its content, stands apart from the surrounding material as an independent unit."[15] On the other hand, other literary critics maintain that these two verses are the concluding strophe of a larger poem: 31:15-22.[16] This important matter needs further consideration.

To begin with, it is noteworthy that 31:15-22 is surrounded on both sides by passages in which Yahweh speaks of the people Israel in the third person plural, using the pronouns "they," "them," "their." On one side, this is true of the poem about homecoming in 31:7-9 (10-14) and, on the other side, of the oracle in 31:23-25—each of which is introduced by the formula "thus says Yahweh." In the passage found between these units, however, Yahweh addresses the people as a woman, using the second person singular *feminine*. There is no real exception to this prevailing mode of address in v. 15, which refers to weeping Rachel in the third person, or in vv. 18-19, where Ephraim, her son, speaks in the first person. To these matters I shall return presently. Notice, however, that the verbs and pronouns at the end of the poem (vv. 21-22a), as at the beginning (vv. 16-17), all indicate feminine address.

The major reason for supposing that vv. 21-22 represent an independent literary unit is that v. 22b refers to Yahweh in the third person. Some go so

14. Weiser, *Jeremia*, 290. He suggests that "die nicht wieder rekonstruirbare Übersetzung" of LXX points in this direction.
15. Weiser, *Jeremia*, 289. This is also the view of Rudolph, *Jeremia*, 181, and of Holladay, who maintains, in personal correspondence, that vv. 21-22 are a separate poem that closes the whole cycle of chaps. 30–31 and do not belong closely with 31:15-20.
16. So James Muilenburg, "Jeremiah," *IDB* 2.834; also, Bright (AB), Condamin (EBib), Duhm (HKAT), Habel (Concordia), Hyatt (*IB*).

far as to suggest that here the text should be emended to read "I will create" ('*ebrā*');[17] but this is a purely conjectural way out of the difficulty. The reference to Yahweh in the third person stands securely in the text; and this has led scholars (e.g., Rudolph) to the conclusion that in these verses the prophet, not Yahweh, is the speaker, and therefore that this is a separate literary unit.

Admittedly, the identity of the speaker is uncertain. One should guard against expecting strict distinctions in poetry, however, especially in a context where one can draw no sharp line between the "words of Yahweh" and the prophetic bearer of those words (see 1:9). Sometimes the prophetic "I" fades imperceptibly into the divine "I," as in 23:13-15, where "to me" (v. 14b) seems to refer to Yahweh, not just to what the prophet "saw" (v. 13). Moreover, it is not uncommon in prayerful address to Yahweh for the second person form to be used along with the third person (17:13), and the same flexibility is possible in God's address to the people. It is noteworthy that the poem in 31:7-9 (+ 10-14) displays an alternation of persons: Yahweh is spoken about (v. 7) and is also the speaker (vv. 8-9); and the prophet summons the nations to hear Yahweh's word (vv. 10-12), but in the conclusion the divine "I" speaks (v. 13). So the change of grammatical forms in 31:21-22, from second person feminine address to third person masculine (v. 22b), is not conclusive proof that the prophet is the speaker here. In any case, a sudden change of speakers would not argue against the stylistic unity of the whole passage, 31:15-22, for this phenomenon is found elsewhere in Jeremiah's poetry (e.g., 5:1-14).[18] Even Rudolph, who maintains that the prophet is the speaker in vv. 21-22, recognizes that "substantively the verses are the conclusion, or better the summary, of everything that precedes."[19]

Under the assumption that the literary unit is 31:15-22, I now examine the structure of the passage in order to understand how the climactic strophe in vv. 21-22 relates to the whole.

The poem falls into four strophes, each of which contributes to the dramatic movement toward the concluding exhortation to return home. The first strophe (v. 15) is introduced by the formula "thus says Yahweh." In this case, the formula serves to set off the passage from the preceding poem (31:7-9 [10-14]), for the strophe contains nothing to suggest that it is a word of Yahweh. Indeed, this may have been an independent piece that

---

17. See *BHK*. This textual change was advocated by F. Giesebrecht, *Das Buch Jeremia 3/2* (Göttingen: Vandenhoeck & Ruprecht, 1907) 170. Elmer A. Leslie (*Jeremiah* [New York: Abingdon, 1954] 105) emends the text further and translates: "For I am about to create a new thing, in the land of [your] return."

18. Jeremiah's fondness for changing speakers abruptly is discussed by William L. Holladay, "The So-called 'Deuteronomic Gloss' in Jer. VIII 19b," *VT* 12 (1962) 494-98.

19. Rudolph, *Jeremia*, 181.

was appropriated for an introduction to Jeremiah's poem. It speaks of the disconsolate weeping of Rachel, the ancestral mother of Joseph (Gen. 30:24) and Benjamin (Gen. 35:18), heard at her grave in Ramah, with which Jeremiah, as a Benjaminite, was familiar.[20] The strophe is cast in a prevailing 3/2 *qînâ* ("lamentation") meter:

Strophe 1.   Hark! In Ramah is heard lament,   31:15
              bitter weeping;
              Rachel is weeping for her sons,
              refusing to be comforted for her sons,
              for [*kî*] they are gone.

In rhythmic language the poet plays on the theme of Rachel's weeping (*běkî, měbakkâ*) and the loss of her sons (twice repeated: *bānêhā . . . bānêhā*). The motive (*kî*) for her disconsolate grief is stated in one emphatic Hebrew word: *'ênennû,* "they are not!" But unlike Matt. 2:18, where Rachel's lament is remembered in a situation of abject motherly grief (Herod's slaying of the infants), here Rachel's refusal of consolation provides the occasion for Yahweh to speak, as indicated by the repetition of the formula "thus says Yahweh" at the beginning of v. 16.

The poem now shifts from the rhythm of lament to a prevailing 3/3 meter as Yahweh speaks comforting words to Mother Israel. Her sons are not gone forever; they will come home. The opening imperative echoes sounds from the preceding lament (*mině'î / mē'ănâ; qôlēk / qôl; mibbekî / běkî, měbakkâ*):

Strophe 2.   Restrain your voice from weeping,   31:16
              your eyes from tears!
              For [*kî*] there is reward for your labor:[21]
              they will return from the enemy's land;
              there is hope for your posterity: 31:17
              sons will return to their territory.

Here the key word, twice used, is *šûb,* "return." The poet clearly refers to a concrete return—from the land (*'ereṣ*) of the enemy to their own country (*gěbûl*), the land of Palestine. Thus there is hope for Rachel's future because she will have posterity (*'aḥărît*) and Israel will be rebuilt (cf. 31:4-5).

The third strophe is longer, for it contains a quotation within a quotation. At the beginning and end, Yahweh's words are cited (first person);

20. The tradition that Rachel's tomb was at Ramah (1 Sam. 10:2) is at variance with the later tradition, based on the parenthetical scribal remark in Gen. 35:19, which transferred it to the vicinity of Bethel (cf. Matt. 2:18), where it is venerated today. Ephraim and Manasseh were Joseph's sons, though the former gained ascendancy.
21. Omitting with the LXX the expression "oracle of Yahweh" (*ně'um YHWH*) at the end of the third and fifth cola.

but in between Yahweh quotes the confession of Rachel's son, Ephraim (first person), who penitently laments the folly of his youth:

Strophe 3.   I listened intently—   31:18
Ephraim was shaking with remorse:
"You disciplined me and I was corrected,
like an untamed calf.
Restore me so that I may come back,
for [*kî*] you are Yahweh, my God.

For after I turned away, I repented;   31:19
after I came to my senses, I slapped my thigh.[22]
I blush with shame, feel humiliated,
for [*kî*] I bear the disgrace of my youth."

Isn't Ephraim my precious son,   31:20
a child in whom I delight,
For [*kî*] as often as I speak against him,[23]
I am still very much concerned for him.
Therefore I yearn for him with my being,
I am filled with compassion for him —
the oracle of Yahweh.

Rhetorically, the last two lines display a wonderful balance and assonance, each being introduced by corresponding expressions ("as often as"/"therefore") and concluding with strengthened verbal forms (infinitive absolute plus imperfect):

kî-middê dabbĕrî bô
zākōr 'ezkĕrennû 'ôd
For as often as I speak against him,
I am still very much concerned for him.

'al-kēn hāmû mē'ay lô
raḥēm 'ăraḥămennû
Therefore I yearn for him with my being,
I am filled with compassion for him.

It is especially noteworthy, however, that the lament of Rachel's son adds another dimension to the verb *šûb,* which occurs in various modula-

---

22. This gesture of remorse is comparable to beating the breast or slapping the forehead.
23. Bright (*Jeremiah,* 282) maintains that in v. 20 *dabbĕrî bô* means literally "speak of him," not "speak against him" as usually translated, and he translates "as oft as I mention his name." Admittedly, the expression *dibbēr bô* may have either a friendly (cf. Num. 12:8) or a hostile (cf. Num. 12:1; 21:5, 7; Ps. 78:19) meaning. In the context of Yahweh's discipline of his son, "against" is appropriate.

tions (*hăšîbēnî*, "cause me to return," "restore me"; *'ăšûbâ*, "I will return"; *šûbî*, "my turning away"). Like the New Testament parable of the prodigal son in the far country (Luke 15), the return in this case has a double dimension: it is a geographical return (from exile), and a return to a relationship that was spurned in the folly of youth.[24] Since Ephraim's confession is contained within Yahweh's speech, one may wonder whether repentance was the condition of Yahweh's restorative action. The passage itself, however, especially when understood in the larger context of Jeremiah's preaching, hardly warrants an affirmative answer to this question. Like Hosea (chap. 11), Jeremiah portrays Yahweh's tender affection for Rachel's son, Ephraim, who is also Yahweh's firstborn (Jer. 31:9c); and he says that even when Yahweh disciplines his son he is nevertheless concerned for him and eagerly awaits any sign of his return. Even in Ephraim's time of separation and alienation, he remained Yahweh's "son" and could confess, "You are Yahweh, my God."

Yahweh's moving soliloquy is not left hanging in the air. At its conclusion, the poem returns to the central theme of Yahweh's bringing Rachel's sons home. Once again in the fourth strophe the poet uses the language of address in the second person *feminine,* as in vv. 16–17. Feminine language is dominant throughout the poem. Here, however, the poet shifts from the image of Mother Israel, to which the maternal ("womb") language in v. 20c may correspond,[25] to the related prophetic imagery of Israel as the Virgin/Daughter (Amos 5:2; Isa. 23:12; 37:22; Jer. 14:17; 31:4; etc.). Portrayed as a woman, Israel is summoned to return in the double meaning that has now become apparent in the poem: to return in a geographical sense from exile to the homeland along a well-marked highway, and to return in the deeper sense of coming home to the covenant relationship.

Strophe 4.   Establish for yourself path markers,   31:21
            set up for yourself guideposts [*tamrûrîm*]!
        Pay attention to the road,
            the path by which you went!
        Return, Virgin Israel,
            return to these cities of yours!

        How long will you go to and fro,   31:22
            O wandering daughter?
        For Yahweh has created something new,
        (. . .)

24. Cf. William L. Holladay, *The Root Šûbh in the Old Testament* (Leiden: Brill, 1958) 128–39, 152–53, who emphasizes the covenantal meaning of the verb ("repent"). He suggests (pp. 146–47) that the motif of return from exile in chaps. 30–31 is a later reinterpretation under the influence of Second Isaiah.

25. See Phyllis Trible, "God, Nature of, in the OT," *IDBSup* 368–69, who discusses "womb imagery" (*reḥem* and related words) with special reference to Jer. 31:20c.

For the time being I shall leave the final colon untranslated. Two matters, however, deserve special attention. First, the poet mixes the figural language of the sons of Israel returning home and of Israel, personified as a woman, coming back. This mixed figure, which may disturb some readers, is present elsewhere in Jeremiah's poetry. An excellent example is found in Jer. 3:12-13, 19-22a, poetry that is also addressed to the North (3:12a). The strophe begins in 3:12b with an address in the masculine singular, "Return faithless Israel!" (*šûbâ mĕšûbâ yiśrā'ēl*), and continues in v. 13 with an address to Israel in the feminine singular, "Only, acknowledge your guilt" (*'ak dĕ'î 'ăwōnēk*). In the ensuing strophe in 3:19-22a (I take the intervening verses to be a later supplement), Yahweh speaks of Israel as a daughter ("How I would set you [feminine singular] among my sons" [v. 19]) and at the same time as a faithless wife ("so you have been faithless [masculine plural] to me" [v. 20]). Finally, in vv. 21-22a it is the sons, whose weeping is heard on the bare heights (v. 21a; cf. Rachel's weeping), who receive the divine invitation: "Return, faithless sons!" (*šûbû bānîm šôbābîm*), whereupon they penitently confess their renewed faith in Yahweh (vv. 22b-25).

Second, in the final strophe of the poem in 31:15-22 the poet plays on the motif of the road (*mĕsillâ*) or the path (*derek*), a motif also found in Isa. 40:3. In the time of exile, this route led away from the promised land and away from the covenant relationship; in the time of restoration, the route will lead back to the land ("your cities") and to the relationship with Yahweh that is the basis of *šālôm* in the homeland. This observation adds force to the question in v. 22a, addressed to Israel in feminine terms, as to why she turns this way and that (*titḥammāqîn*), like one who is lost and goes in circles, both geographically and spiritually. Being gracious (cf. 3:12: *kî ḥāsîd 'ănî*), Yahweh summons his back-turning (*šôbĕbâ*) daughter to return and to take part in the new age.

THE NOVUM: CREATING A "NEW THING"

The invitation to return is motivated by the announcement that Yahweh will create (or, in the prophetic perfect, "has created") something new—the "new thing" (*ḥădāšâ*) of which the prophet of the exile also spoke (Isa. 43:19; 42:9; 48:6-7). But what specifically is the future *novum* that is announced in Jer. 31:22?

I approach this question by considering first the geographical locus of Yahweh's new act of creation: the innovation is to occur *bā'āreṣ*, "in the earth" or "in the land." It is noteworthy that almost all modern translations render the Hebrew word as "on/in the earth," thereby implying the broad terrestrial horizon of the creation story (Gen. 1:1) or Jeremiah's vision of chaos (Jer. 4:23-26). This consensus is surprising, for nothing supports it in the context of the Book of Consolation or in the poem itself. The theme of the collection as a whole is stated in the prefatory oracle:

> For lo! days are coming—the oracle of Yahweh—when I will restore the fortunes of Israel and Judah, says Yahweh; for I will bring them back to the land [*hā'āreṣ*] that I gave to their ancestors and they will take possession of it. (30:3)

It is generally recognized that this little book contains material that originally dealt with north Israel (Ephraim), the people who had gone into exile in 722 B.C.E. (e.g., the exquisite poem in 31:2-6). The preface indicates, however, that God's consolation is extended to Israel as a whole, north and south. The heart of the promise is the establishment of a new relationship, signified by the covenant formula, "You shall be my people and I will be your God" (30:22; 31:1; 31:33). But this promise is not purely spiritual; it involves return from exile and resettlement of the land of the ancestors (31:5, 12), the blessing of fertility and increase for land and people (31:4-5, 12, 14), and a situation of security and peace (31:4, 13). Furthermore, the particular poem under consideration gives no hint of a wide meaning of *'ereṣ*. On the contrary, the children of Rachel are summoned to come back from "the land of the enemy" (*mē'ereṣ 'ôyēb*) and to return to their own territory (*ligĕbûlām*, v. 16), to their own cities (v. 21). Thus in the light of the total and immediate contexts one has every reason to suppose that the "new thing" pertains to life in the promised land (see also 3:14, "I will bring you to Zion"; and 3:19, "a pleasant land, a heritage most beauteous of all nations").[26] The poet announces that in the land Yahweh will create a "new thing" to signify the future that God opens up for the people, in reversal of their former condition.

The specific character of this reversal is clarified, in my judgment, when one considers the overall structure of the poem. A characteristic literary device of Israelite poets is to sound a motif at the end that was announced at the beginning, in the manner of *inclusio*. Recalling my previous summary, I outline the design of the poem as follows:

> Mother Israel's grief (v. 15)
> Yahweh comforts Mother Israel (vv. 16-17)
>> The lost son, Ephraim, confesses (vv. 18-19)
>> Yahweh's soliloquy of affection for the son (v. 20)
> Invitation to the Woman, Israel, to return (vv. 21-22)

At the end, the poem returns to the theme struck at the beginning, but the correspondence is one of contrast. This is probably the reason for a striking play on words having the same sound but different meaning. At the

---

26. Rudolph (*Jeremia*, 180) properly translates "im Lande."

beginning, Rachel's grief was characterized as *tamrûrîm* "bitter" (v. 15a); but in the final strophe the poet uses *tamrûrîm* in a different and contrasting sense, namely, "road markers" that indicate the path of the homeward return (v. 21a). Thus bitterness is converted into hope. Moreover, the poet juxtaposes and associates two images: Rachel who weeps disconsolately because her sons are no more, and Virgin/Daughter Israel who takes part in the homecoming and the rejoicing over family reunion. The promise to Rachel in her grief is specific: no longer will she be bereft of her sons, for Ephraim is, in a special sense, God's beloved son and he will be restored to his mother at home. The motif of homecoming from exile is also found in 31:7-9, where Yahweh invites the returning people to sing aloud with joy.[27]

> With weeping they will come,
>   but with consolation I shall bring them.
> I shall direct them to streams of water,
>   in a smooth path where they will not stumble.
> For [*kî*] I am a father to Israel,
>   and Ephraim is my firstborn son. (31:9)

Viewed in this literary and theological context, the enigmatic concluding line about the *novum* begins to make sense. Weeping will be converted into rejoicing, for (*kî*) Yahweh has created something new, as in the original creation when the blessing of fertility and posterity was conferred on *'ādām,* consisting of "male and female" (*zākār ûnĕqēbâ*). Whereas Rachel, the Mother of Israel, was formerly deprived of her sons, she will have a posterity (*'aḥărît*), a future—as Yahweh explicitly promised in 31:17. It is probably true that the verb *tĕsôbēb* has a sexual—or, better, maternal—meaning: the Woman (Virgin Israel) will enfold a man (a son) as a sign of Yahweh's gracious gift of new life in the land. The use of *geber* ("man") in a context of fertility also occurs, interestingly, in Job's lament that the Night had announced the conception of a "man-child" (Job 3:3). Furthermore, the enigmatic words in the final colon of v. 22 may be analogous to the text of Gen. 4:1, where Eve, after the birth of her firstborn, hailed the arrival of new life with the exclamation: "I have begotten [*qānîtî*] a man ['*îš*] with (the help of) Yahweh!" Like the English word "beget" in its original sense, the verb *qānâ* means both "to acquire, get" and "to bring into being," indicating that Eve, though a creature, engages in creative activity with divine assistance.[28] It is Yahweh who opens the womb and

---

27. The following poem (31:10-14) may be a later expansion in the spirit of Second Isaiah. See, for instance, Muilenburg, "Jeremiah," *IDB* 2.830; and Bright, *Jeremiah,* 281.

28. See I. M. Kikawada, "Two Notes on Eve," *JBL* 91 (1972) 35–37, who compares this passage to an Atrahasis text where the goddess Mami creates life with the help of the god Enki. He argues that one should translate the preposition '*et* "together with," i.e., "with the help of."

gives a future. So the Jeremianic text, when viewed in its poetic context, announces that the way into the future is opened by Yahweh, who, in a miracle of creation, gives the people new life by restoring them to their land and giving them a posterity, a future (cf. "the seed of man," 31:27). The old age, symbolized by Rachel weeping for her lost sons, will be superseded by a new age when Virgin Israel will be fruitful.

The theme of Yahweh's "rebuilding" Virgin Israel is found also in the poem about "Grace in the Wilderness" (31:2-6), especially the central part where the language shifts from the masculine to the feminine and introduces a threefold emphatic "again" (*'ôd*): *again* you shall be built up, *again* you shall take timbrels and go forth in the dance of the merrymakers,[29] *again* there will be fertile vineyards in the land (31:4-5). Outside the book of Jeremiah, the theme resounds in the poetry of so-called Second Isaiah, where barren Zion, who had no hope for children, is comforted with the promise of a miracle of fertility that will result in more inhabitants than the land has room for (Isa. 49:14-23):

> The children born in the time of your bereavement
>   will yet say in your hearing:
> "The place is too crowded for me,
>   make room for me to settle."
> Then you will say in your heart,
> "Who has borne me these?
> I was bereaved and barren,
>   exiled and put away—
>   so who has reared these?
> I was left alone—
>   where then have these come from?" (vv. 20-21, NRSV)

The contrast between the old and the new is suggested by a wordplay in the final verse of Jeremiah's poem. On the one hand, the Woman is addressed as a "faithless one" (*haššôbēbâ*, v. 22a); but, on the other hand, she will "encompass" or "enfold" (*těsôbēb*) a man. The latter verb seems to have been chosen because of its assonance with the adjective describing God's Daughter (*haššôbēbâ* / *těsôbēb*). The poetic juxtaposition of the two words draws a sharp contrast between Israel's faithlessness, which led to divine judgment (exile from the land), and God's faithfulness to the peo-

---

29. The motif of Virgin Israel taking timbrels and leading in "the dance of the merrymakers" (31:4) is possibly a poetic allusion to the time of the exodus when Miriam "took a timbrel in her hand, and all the women went out after her with timbrels and dancing" (Exod. 15:20—as suggested by Holladay, *Jeremiah: Spokesman,* 114). The motif of the new exodus and the new entry into the land is prominent in the Book of Consolation, as it is also in the poems of Second Isaiah. See my essay, "Exodus Typology in Second Isaiah," in *Israel's Prophetic Heritage: Essays in Honor of James Muilenburg* (ed. Bernhard W. Anderson and Walter Harrelson; New York: Harper & Row, 1962) 177–95.

ple, despite their infidelity. In a miracle of divine grace, Rachel will receive her son back. The new life in the land, therefore, will be a gift of God, a new creation.

I called attention earlier to Weiser's illuminating suggestion that the final line of this poem is reminiscent of the creation story, where God created (*bārā'*) *'ādām,* consisting of "male [*zākār*] and female [*něqēbâ*]," in God's image and endowed them with the power of procreation and dominion over "the earth" (Gen. 1:27-28). If, however, the creation tradition is reflected here, the poet has reinterpreted it in a novel manner. For one thing, the word *'ereṣ* no longer means "the earth" but "the land" of the promise. Further, here the emphasis is not on the equality of male and female in God's creation; rather, the poet boldly affirms that the Woman, in some sense, is the initiator. There is no basis for the notion, often expressed by commentators, that *něqēbâ* symbolizes weakness—"femininity" in a pejorative sense. On the contrary, in the new age the Woman will be the agent of new life, new hope for a despairing, sorrowing people. But in the context of the poem, the Woman is Israel, typified by Rachel who wept for her lost sons and, through a juxtaposition of imagery, by the Virgin/Daughter who is invited to return and, in the grace of God, to rebuild Israel. "The woman will enfold a man"—contextually this sentence means that the bereaved Virgin Israel will have a son, a posterity, and therefore a future in the land promised to Israel's ancestors.[30]

---

30. I am indebted to William Holladay for reading this essay with a critical eye. Subsequent to the completion of the study, I received Phyllis Trible's illuminating essay, "The Gift of a Poem: A Rhetorical Study of Jeremiah 31:15-22," *Andover Newton Quarterly* 17 (1977) 271–80. Although her interpretive slant is different, she too agrees on the rhetorical unity of the poem. Her rhetorical study of the passage also appears in her book, *God and the Rhetoric of Sexuality* (OBT; Philadelphia: Fortress Press, 1978) 40–50.

CHAPTER 12

The Slaying of the
Fleeing, Twisting Serpent:
Isaiah 27:1 in Context[*]

This study focuses on a single verse found in the so-called Apocalypse
of Isaiah, which the JPSV translates:

> In that day the Lord will punish
> With His great, cruel, mighty sword
> Leviathan the Elusive Serpent—
> Leviathan the Twisting Serpent;
> He will slay the Dragon of the Sea. (Isa. 27:1)

Footnotes to the translation indicate that the meaning of the Hebrew words
translated "Elusive" (*bāriaḥ*) and "Twisting" (*ʿăqallātôn*) is uncertain.

The approach to this study is methodological. I will attempt to illumi-
nate Isa. 27:1 through various approaches, including the study of the
history of religions; a form-critical analysis of the pericope; stylistic or
rhetorical criticism of the verse in its literary context; the placement of the
passage within the structure of Isaiah 24–27; and finally, determination of
the function of the Isaiah Apocalypse—which contains this crucial verse—
within the canonical whole of the book of Isaiah. In this manner it will be
possible to move around the verse in concentric hermeneutical circles, as it
were. Each of these steps, I hope to show, is important in the exegetical
process.

* *Author's Note:* I gratefully dedicate this essay, originally presented in a graduate seminar
at Boston University School of Theology, to my esteemed colleague, Neil Richardson, who
would have enjoyed participating in the discussion.

THE MYTH OF THE *CHAOSKAMPF*

In his seminal work *Schöpfung und Chaos in Urzeit und Endzeit* (1895), Hermann Gunkel drew scholarly attention to the significance of the serpent motif in the history of religions.[1] In 1873 a copy of the Babylonian creation story was found during the excavation of the library of Ashurbanipal at the site of ancient Nineveh. This story traces the origin of the cosmos to a fierce duel between the divine warrior Marduk and the monster of chaos Tiamat, in consequence of which the victorious god was crowned king in the heavenly council. Gunkel drew attention to echoes of the dragon myth and traditions regarding the primeval sea in the Old Testament. Israel's interpreters, he observed, used mythical language to portray a typological correspondence between, on the one hand, the divine triumph over the forces of chaos in the beginning and, on the other hand, the new creation at the consummation of time. Thus *Urzeit gleich Endzeit* ("primeval time corresponds to eschatological time").

Gunkel maintained that this myth of the conquest of the powers of chaos had its source in Babylonia. Since the discovery of the Ugaritic texts, however, it has become evident that the Israelites inherited this mythical view more directly from the Canaanites, in whose midst they dwelled. These texts tell about a victory over a serpent *ltn,* usually vocalized *Lotan*[2] and identified with biblical *liwyātān,* Leviathan. In one case the victory is attributed to the goddess Anat on behalf of Baal. The passage is redolent of imagery used of the Divine Warrior Yahweh in various biblical texts: "rider of clouds," "sea" (*yām*), "river, flood" (*nāhār*), the "seven-headed crooked serpent." H. L. Ginsberg translates:

What enemy's ris[en] 'gainst Baal,
     What foe 'gainst the Rider of Clouds [*rkb 'rpt*]?
Crushed I not El's Belov'd Yamm?
     Destroyed I not El's Flood [*nhr*] Rabbim?
Did I not, pray, muzzle the Dragon [*tnn*]?
I did crush the crooked serpent [*btn 'qltn*],
     Shalyat the seven-headed.[3]

---

1. Hermann Gunkel, *Schöpfung und Chaos in Urzeit und Endzeit* (Göttingen: Vandenhoeck & Ruprecht, 1895); abbreviated translation by Charles A. Muenchow, "The Influence of Babylonian Mythology upon the Biblical Creation Story," in *Creation in the Old Testament* (ed. Bernhard W. Anderson; IRT6; Philadelphia: Fortress Press, 1984) 25–52.

2. However, J. A. Emerton proposes *litanu,* going back via *liyatanu* to an original *liwyatanu* ("Leviathan and *LTN:* The Vocalization of the Ugaritic Word for the Dragon," *VT* 32 [1982] 327–31).

3. H. L. Ginsberg, "Poems about Baal and Anath," *ANET,* 137, D:34–39. For the Ugaritic text, see *UT,* ᶜnt III:34–39; *KTU,* 1.3.III.37–42; and John Gray, *The Legacy of Canaan* (VTSup 5; 2d ed.; Leiden: Brill, 1965) 27–30.

Another text that has even closer linguistic affinities with Isa. 27:1 attributes the triumph to Baal:

> If thou smite Lotan, the serpent slant [*ltn bṯn brḥ*]
> Destroy the serpent tortuous [*bṯn 'qltn*]
> Shalyat of the seven heads.[4]

John Gray translates:

> Though thou didst smite Ltn the Primaeval Serpent,
> And didst annihilate the Crooked Serpent,
> The Close-coiling One of Seven Heads,
> The heavens will dry up, yea, languish;
> I shall pound thee, consume thee, and eat thee,
> Cleft, forspent, and exhausted.
> Thou shalt indeed go down into the throat of Mt
>   the son of El.[5]

The similarity between Isa. 27:1 *(liwyātān nāḥāš bāriaḥ / liwyātān nāḥāš 'ăqallātôn . . . hattannîn 'ăšer bayyām)* and the Ugaritic texts is very close. The passage, observes William R. Millar, "is almost a direct quote from Ugaritic text 5.1.1-5."[6] The close affinity, however, does not necessarily indicate that the poet had the Ugaritic texts at hand. It seems, rather, that the Ugaritic myth influenced the Israelite poetic tradition from early times, perhaps as early as the Song of the Sea (Exod. 15:1-18), and in all likelihood by the time of the cultic recitations connected with the acclamation of Yahweh as king in Zion (e.g., Psalm 93). In a community lament (Psalm 74), a hymnic interlude occurs:

> Yet God my King is from of old,
>   working salvation in the earth.
> You divided the sea by your might;
>   you broke the heads of the dragons in the waters.
> You crushed the heads of Leviathan,
>   you gave him as food for the creatures of the wilderness.
> (Ps. 74:12-14, NRSV; cf. Ps. 89:9-13 [10-14])

Outside cultic contexts the myth of the serpent appears, for instance, in an apostrophe to the victorious arm of the Divine Warrior in Isa. 51:9 and in a meditation on the power of the Creator in Job 26:12-13 (NRSV):

---

4. Translation by Ginsberg, *ANET*, 138. See *UT*, 67:I:1-3; *KTU*, 1.5.I.1-3.
5. Gray, *Legacy*, 30 n. 3.
6. William R. Millar, *Isaiah 24–27 and the Origin of Apocalyptic* (HSM 11; Missoula, Mont.: Scholars Press, 1976) 55.

By his power he stilled the Sea;
    by his understanding he struck down Rahab.
By his wind the heavens were made fair;
    his hand pierced the fleeing serpent *[nāḥāš bārîaḥ]*.

In all these biblical texts, the issue is not whether Israel was influenced by the myth of the *Chaoskampf*, of which there were variations in the ancient world; rather, the question is how the myth was interpreted in the poetry of Israel's religion. I turn then from the context of history of religions to a consideration of Isa. 27:1 in its own literary context.

DELIMITATION OF THE LITERARY UNIT

In the exegesis of a biblical text, the first task is to determine the literary unit. Following the method of form criticism, one usually first determines the scope of the literary genre, then seeks to determine its *Sitz im Leben*, and finally, compares it with other genres of the same sort, either in biblical or extrabiblical literature.

Some commentators maintain that in this case the literary unit is Isa. 27:1-5, but that is questionable on form-critical grounds. There is much to be said for regarding this verse as a literary unit that "stands by itself," as Ronald Clements remarks.[7] The verse has a decided beginning, the cliché "in that day," and is bounded by the beginning of v. 2, "in that day." Moreover, 27:1 has its own thematic integrity: the victory of the Divine Warrior over the monster of chaos. The ensuing unit, 27:2-5 (6), does not treat that theme at all but is a separate literary genre with another theme: a vineyard song announcing an eschatological reversal of the Song of the Vineyard found in Isa. 5:1-7. It is tempting to analyze the literary parallels between this eschatological song and the earlier one: in both, the vineyard is regarded as potentially fertile (5:1; 27:2); in both, the vineyard is threatened by "thorns" and "briars" (*šāmîr [wā]šāyit*, the same word pair in both cases: 5:6; 27:4); and in both, Yahweh is the Keeper of the Vineyard, though in 27:4 with this difference: "Of wrath I have none." But all of that is beyond the scope of this essay. Suffice it to say that the Song of the Vineyard is not intrinsically related to the announcement of the victory of the Divine Warrior. As I shall seek to prove, the victory of the Divine Warrior (27:1) connects with the foregoing poem at the end of chapter 26.

Isaiah 27:1 is often regarded as prose but, if it is prose, it is a prose that is close to poetry and is so regarded in the NJPSV translation.[8] In the past, some commentators have interpreted the text prosaically to refer to three

---

7. Ronald E. Clements, *Isaiah 1–39* (NCB; Grand Rapids: Eerdmans, 1981) 218.
8. Millar notes that the verse should be read "either as prose or as long poetic lines, run on" (*Isaiah 24–27*, 54–55).

monsters, each of which symbolizes an oppressing nation such as Egypt, Babylon, or Greece—the three domains of Alexander the Great.[9] A similar historicizing view is found in the commentary by John D. Watts, who, though translating as poetry, maintains that the monster refers to Tyre.[10] But the linguistic parallels with ancient Ugaritic poetry are sufficient to invalidate a prosaic interpretation. The subject of Isa. 27:1 is not three monsters but one, a monster who symbolizes the powers of evil at work in human history, manifest in any of the oppressive nations.

In Ugaritic texts the weapon of the divine warrior is apparently a club or mace that crushes the heads of the sea monster, whereas in the Isaiah text, Yahweh wields a mighty sword (see also the apocalyptic passage, Isa. 34:5-6). This is true also in Isa. 51:9, where the poet gives an appeal to the mighty "arm" of the Divine Warrior:

> Awake, awake, clothe yourself with splendor,
> O arm of the Lord!
> Awake as in days of old,
> As in former ages! (Isa. 51:9, JPSV)

The poet goes on to speak of Yahweh's victory over (the) Sea, over the *těhôm rabbâ*, "Great Deep." While the text of Isa. 27:1 varies the myth slightly, the poetic parallelism is retained: Leviathan the fleeing serpent, Leviathan the twisting serpent. Although the *Ketib* of the first modifier is unusual for an adjectival form (which ordinarily is spelled with a *yod*), the *Qere* may call for that form. The participial reading in the 1QIsa[a] manuscript (*bôrēaḥ*) and LXX *pheugonta*, "fleeing," also suggests that the archaic word describes some characteristic of the serpent. W. F. Albright's proposal of "prehistoric" or "primeval"[11] does not offer an appropriate parallel to the archaic term *'ăqallātôn*, "crooked, twisting, coiling."

THE LARGER LITERARY UNIT

Form criticism, however, has its limitations. For one thing, Isa. 27:1 does not seem to reflect the requisite *Sitz im Leben*, unless it is indirectly related to the cultic situation of the enthronement of Yahweh celebrated in some of the psalms. Furthermore, form criticism tends in the direction of dividing material into smaller literary units rather than perceiving larger literary wholes. It is difficult to believe that this single verse of Scripture really stands alone, as Clements maintains. It seems to me that this situa-

---

9. So Otto Procksch, *Jesaia I* (KAT 9; Leipzig: W. Scholl, 1930) 334–35.

10. John D. Watts, *Isaiah 1–33* (WBC 24; Waco, Tex.: Word, 1985) 345, 348–49.

11. W. F. Albright, "Are the Ephod and the Teraphim Mentioned in Ugaritic Literature?" *BASOR* 83 (1941) 39–42.

tion substantiates further the claim that the approach to the literature of Scripture must be "form criticism and beyond," to cite the title of a presidential address to the Society of Biblical Literature by James Muilenburg.[12] Even Clements apparently senses this need to go beyond the immediate literary unit when he states that this verse was "almost certainly" added "in order to sum up the message of assurance given in 26:19" (promise of victory over the power of death), and that "it is, therefore, a further response to the lament of 26:7-18."[13]

What lies "beyond" form criticism, though not repudiating its gains, is rhetorical criticism. This mode of criticism is concerned with *Sitz im Text,* as one of my students, Edgar Conrad, puts it: the function of the text in its literary context, the style and pattern of the literary unit, and the various devices that bind the whole together (*inclusio,* chiasmus, wordplays, alliteration, assonance, etc.).[14]

Consider now the possibility suggested earlier that Isa. 27:1 belongs with the poetic material at the end of chapter 26 rather than with the ensuing eschatological Song of the Vineyard. The presence of the words "in that day" does not necessarily argue against this proposal. An examination of the uses of that cliché reveals that it is not confined solely to introductory oracles; it may introduce a concluding eschatological promise, or it may be found in the middle of an oracle.

In his commentary Edward J. Kissane connected this verse with the foregoing verse (26:21).[15] In his poetic analysis William Millar made the same connection.[16] This association is suggested by the text, since the announcement (introduced by "for behold," *kî-hinnēh*) that Yahweh is prepared to go forth from his heavenly citadel or sanctuary (*māqôm*) connects nicely with the assertion that "in that day" the Divine Warrior will triumph over the power of evil. The poetic unit may even begin at 26:20, just after the announcement that death does not have the final verdict:

Come, my people, enter your chambers,
    and shut your doors behind you;
hide yourselves for a little while
    until the wrath is past.

---

12. James Muilenburg, "Form Criticism and Beyond," *JBL* 88 (1969) 1–18.

13. Clements, *Isaiah 1–39,* 218.

14. Edgar W. Conrad, "The Community as King in Second Isaiah," in *Understanding the Word: Essays in Honor of Bernhard W. Anderson* (ed. James T. Butler, Edgar W. Conrad, and Ben C. Ollenburger; JSOTSup 37; Sheffield: JSOT, 1985) 99–111.

15. Edward J. Kissane, *The Book of Isaiah* (rev. ed.; 2 vols.; Dublin: Browne and Nolan, 1960) 1.284.

16. Millar, *Isaiah 24–27,* 54–55.

For the Lord comes out from his place
to punish the inhabitants of the earth for their iniquity;
the earth will disclose the blood shed on it,
and will no longer cover its slain.
On that day the Lord with his cruel and great and strong sword will punish
Leviathan the fleeing serpent, Leviathan the twisting serpent, and he will kill
the dragon that is in the sea. (Isa. 26:20—27:1, NRSV)

Notice that the linkage of 27:1 to the foregoing poetic strophe is established by a rhetorical device, namely, the repeated use of the verb *pāqad* "visit, punish" (see 27:3, "harm"). The motif of divine visitation is found in the earlier passage introduced by "in that day" (24:21-23), where Yahweh will punish "the host of heaven" and "the kings on earth." According to 26:1 Yahweh will go forth from his celestial bulwark to punish the inhabitants of the earth for their iniquity; and according to 27:1 the Divine Warrior will punish with his mighty sword the powers of evil at work in human history. What is the relation between "the iniquity" (*'āwōn*) of the earth's inhabitants and the power of evil symbolized by Leviathan? When read in the larger context of the Isaiah Apocalypse, this iniquity is the violence that has oppressed the poor and helpless. Yahweh the Warrior comes to "punish" the power of evil. Notice too that the exhortation to the suffering people to hide "until the wrath is past" (26:20) anticipates the time of eschatological reversal when the day of judgment is past and Yahweh says, "I have no more wrath" (27:4), thereby suggesting that interconnecting motifs run through the larger literary whole.

THE LITERARY PATTERN OF THE ISAIAH APOCALYPSE

I turn now to a rhetorical study of the cluster of chapters in the book of Isaiah, 24–27, which for many years scholars have regarded as a separate section interpolated between the oracles against the nations (chaps. 13–23) and the conclusion of the original book of Isaiah (chaps. 28–32/33). Some doubt whether this section is apocalyptic in the same way that Daniel and similar literature are, but it is surely prophecy that is well on the way toward apocalyptic. At this point one may supplement form criticism and rhetorical criticism with redaction criticism *(Redaktionsgeschichte)* in attempting to trace the genesis of the Isaiah Apocalypse. Commenting on the key text, Isa. 27:1 (which he regards as standing alone), Clements observes that this piece was "added to the Groundwork of chs. 24–27 at a late stage," as is evidenced by the redactional formula "in that day."[17]
Since the approach of this study is primarily methodological, it is unnecessary to summarize all the debates surrounding the study of Isaiah 24–

---

17. Clements, *Isaiah 1–39,* 218.

27.[18] Suffice it to say that one of the noteworthy features of the Isaiah Apocalypse is the interspersing of the oracles of impending divine judgment with lyrical poems or liturgical songs:

24:13-16a	Hymnic Praise of Yahweh's Majesty
25:1-5	Psalm of Thanksgiving
26:1-6	Eschatological Song
26:7-19	Community Lament
27:2-6	Eschatological Song of the Vineyard

Some scholars have argued on form-critical grounds that eschatological poems and lyrical poetry should be separated into two groups.[19] This is true but arbitrary and gives insufficient attention to the poetic pattern and vigor brought to light by stylistic criticism (see W. Millar's metrical analysis). A more convincing criterion for analysis is the distinction between poetic strophes and the prose of passages bounded by the phrase "in that day." Even this criterion fails in that often "prose" borders on the verge of poetry, and further, these passages for the most part are inseparable from the tissue and marrow of the whole literary work.

I skirt the whole question of the genesis of the Isaiah Apocalypse and satisfy myself with the recognition that in its final form these four chapters display an overall structural unity.[20] The unit is composed of four poems, which may be outlined as follows:

1. *Isaiah 24:1-20:* the first poem, introduced by *hinnēh,* announces Yahweh's impending display of wrath (judgment), which threatens to reduce the earth to precreation chaos (cf. Jer. 4:23-28), because its inhabitants have violated the laws of "the everlasting covenant" (*běrît 'ôlām*).

2. *Isaiah 24:21—25:12:* the second is introduced with an "in-that-day" cliché and concludes with another "in-that-day" oracle (25:9-12). The subject of this poem is Yahweh's enthronement on Zion as cosmic king and judge, who in a victory banquet "at this mountain" offers security and peace to Israel and the nations.

3. *Isaiah 26:1—27:1:* the third poem opens with a song, introduced with the eschatological formula "in that day" (26:1-6), and—following the analysis given above (also W. Millar)—concludes with the "in-that-day" passage about the

18. See G. W. Anderson, "Isaiah XXIV–XXVII Reconsidered," in *Congress Volume: Bonn 1962* (VTSup 9; Leiden: Brill, 1963) 118–26; Benedikt Otzen, "Traditions and Structures of Isaiah XXIV–XXVII," *VT* 24 (1974) 196–206.

19. J. Lindblom, *Die Jesaja-Apokalypse: Jesaja 24–27* (LUÅ, N.S. 1/34/3; Lund: Gleerup, 1938).

20. The Moab passage, 25:10b-12, is suspect to some scholars; but note that "on this mountain" refers back to 25:6 and 24:23.

eschatological conquest of the Serpent (27:1). Here the question of theodicy is raised, and the people are assured that Yahweh will soon come to break the grip of evil, including the threat of death.

4. *Isaiah 27:2-13:* the fourth poem also opens with a song (Song of the Vineyard) introduced by the eschatological formula "in that day" (27:2-5) and concludes with two "in-that-day" oracles. Here the theme is the eschatological reversal of Yahweh's wrath against the vineyard Israel and the return of the dispersed people to Zion.

Whatever prehistory the Isaiah Apocalypse may have had, these four poems display an overall unity and dynamic. Indeed, when read in their present form and sequence, the effect is almost overpowering, especially at a time when the return of the earth to chaos is an existential possibility. The mythical motif of the slaying of the serpent Leviathan fits nicely into the literary whole. From the outset the theme is Yahweh's judgment, which threatens to return the earth to chaos:

> Now the Lord is about to lay waste the earth,
> and make it desolate,
> And he will twist its surface
> and scatter its inhabitants. (Isa. 24:1, NRSV)

The poet draws on the Priestly primeval history, which moves from creation-out-of-chaos to the near return to precreation chaos, owing to "violence" (*ḥāmās*).[21] The "inhabitants of the earth" have broken the laws of the Noachic *běrît 'ôlām* based on reverence for the life (*nepeš ḥayyâ*), both animal and human, that God has created.

> The earth lies polluted
> under its inhabitants,
> for they have transgressed laws,
> violated the statutes,
> broken the everlasting covenant.
> Therefore a curse devours the earth,
> and its inhabitants suffer for their guilt;
> therefore the inhabitants of the earth dwindled,
> and few people are left. (Isa. 24:5-6, NRSV)

In the manner of literary *inclusio,* the poem ends by returning to the chaos theme announced at the beginning:

> For the windows of heaven are opened,
> and the foundations of the earth tremble.

21. See chap. 9 above.

The earth is utterly broken,
   the earth is torn asunder,
   the earth is violently shaken.
The earth staggers like a drunkard,
   it sways like a hut;
its transgression lies heavy upon it,
   and it falls, and will not rise again. (Isa. 24:18b-20, NRSV)

In this poetic context, Yahweh is the Divine Warrior who comes to conquer the sinister powers in human history that cause oppression and death. Along with the theme of the *Chaoskampf,* a second motif is developed contrapuntally: the typological contrast between two cities. One is called variously "the city of chaos" (24:10), "the fortified city" (25:2; 27:10), "the lofty city" (26:5); the other city is "the strong city" into which the righteous enter, according to the processional psalm in 26:1-6, and which, according to another song, is a stronghold for the poor and oppressed (25:1-5). The former city is left unnamed; it may have been Babylon, or it could be any city that is a center of oppressive power. Marie-Louise Henry observes rightly that the description of the destroyed city, reminiscent of the fall of Babylon, is stylized and portrays "something typical, something of universal validity."[22] The latter city is clearly identified as Zion, situated in "the midst of the earth" (Isa. 24:13; cf. Ps. 74:12), the omphalos or *axis mundi.* Zion is the city where creation began and where the new age, the new creation, will start—as in the eschatological poem that opens the book of Isaiah concerning the ultimate pilgrimage of all peoples to the elevated mountain of Zion (Isa. 2:1-4). Apocalyptic (or protoapocalyptic) thought is universal in outlook, but it never surrenders the centrality of Zion or the vindication of God's people.

THE ISAIAH APOCALYPSE IN
CANONICAL CONTEXT

I turn finally to the question of the place of the Isaiah Apocalypse (which highlights the chaos myth) within the canonical context of the book of Isaiah. Earlier commentators have largely ignored this question. For instance, Walther Eichrodt in his two-volume commentary, *Der Heilige in Israel* (Isaiah 1–12) and *Der Herr der Geschichte* (Isaiah 13–23, 28–39), completely omitted these chapters, for he was concerned with the original prophecy of Isaiah of Jerusalem.[23] Eliminating chapters from the discus-

---

22. Marie-Louise Henry, *Glaubenskrise und Glaubensbewährung in den Dichtungen der Jesajaapokalypse* (BWANT 5/6; Stuttgart: Kohlhammer, 1967) 20–34.
23. Walther Eichrodt, *Der Heilige in Israel: Jesaja 1–12* (BAT 17/1; Stuttgart: Calwer, 1960); idem, *Der Herr der Geschichte: Jesaja 13–23* (BAT 17/2; Stuttgart: Calwer, 1967).

sion is unnecessary, however, for even though these two chapters were not composed by Isaiah, they belong to the Zion theological tradition in which the eighth-century prophet stood.

It is impossible to treat here the large issue of the theological unity of the book of Isaiah as a whole and the movement from prophecy to apocalyptic that one can trace within the book. My own view, set forth in various essays,[24] is that the final form of the book exhibits an apocalyptic rereading of the Isaianic tradition. This apocalyptic *relecture* is made evident in a number of ways: (1) the eschatological editing of chapters 2–33, which are punctuated with "in-that-day" refrains; (2) the insertion of the Isaiah Apocalypse into the heart of the basic Isaiah collection in chapters 1–33, thereby providing a context for understanding the oracles against the nations; (3) the placement of "the little apocalypse" (chaps. 34–35) before the poems of Second Isaiah, thereby providing a transition from prophetic to apocalyptic perspective; and last, (4) the addition of the so-called Third Isaiah, which reflects the apocalyptic or protoapocalyptic view of the early years of the restoration. Viewed in this canonical context, the Isaiah Apocalypse of chapters 24–27 has an important function in the total composition.

What happened in this movement from prophecy to apocalyptic was that Israel's interpreters grappled with the radical power of evil at a different level—some would say at a more profound level—than the prophets who preached repentance and spelled out the consequences of covenant infidelity. The notion that evil is wrongdoing for which the people are responsible was tried in the balance of suffering and found wanting. People are often not just the perpetrators of evil but victims of it. Evil manifests itself as an insidious, perhaps one should say "demonic," power in history. It manifests itself typically as a colossal military power that sweeps inexorably over small peoples, as Habakkuk perceived Babylonian imperialism to be (Hab. 1:2—2:5). It manifests itself in structures of power that crush the poor and helpless in society. In short, evil manifests itself as "violence"—the theme of Habakkuk's lament (Hab. 1:2) and the motive for the great flood (Gen. 6:11).

The question with which apocalyptic wrestles is not how the human heart can be changed (the question of *šûb* or repentance), but rather how

---

24. See my essay, "The Apocalyptic Rendering of the Isaiah Tradition," in *The Social World of Formative Christianity and Judaism: Essays in Tribute to Howard Clark Kee* (ed. Jacob Neusner et al.; Philadelphia: Augsburg Fortress, 1988) 17–38; idem, "'God with Us'—in Judgment and in Mercy: The Editorial Structure of Isaiah 5–10 (11)," in *Canon, Theology, and Old Testament Interpretation: Essays in Honor of Brevard S. Childs* (ed. Gene M. Tucker, David L. Petersen, and Robert R. Wilson; Philadelphia: Fortress Press, 1988) 230–45; idem, "The Holy One of Israel," in *Justice and the Holy: Essays in Honor of Walter Harrelson* (ed. Douglas A. Knight and Peter J. Paris; Atlanta: Scholars Press, 1989) 3–19.

history can be exorcised of the demonic evil that holds terrible sway and even threatens the sovereignty of God. In answer to questions of theodicy or laments of "how long, O Lord?" apocalyptic writers stir the imagination with the vision of the imminent advent of God in power to overcome the tyranny of evil or, in the language of the myth, to slay Leviathan the fleeing, twisting serpent. The theme of victory over the Serpent is picked up in the Apocalypse of John, which speaks of the seven-headed monster (Rev. 12:3), identified with Satan (12:9), who emerges out of the sea (13:1; cf. 21:1).

Brevard Childs is right, in my judgment, in observing that the canonical placement of the Apocalypse of Isaiah after Isaiah's oracles against the nations—and, I may add, just before Isaiah's message about God's "strange work" in chapters 28–30—enables the reader to interpret the prophetic message in a transhistorical setting.[25] Babylon is not just a political power but a symbol of a sinister force of evil that corrupts human history, and the same is true of other nations that take part in the great power game. Moreover, Jerusalem is not just a Palestinian city victimized in the power struggle but rather a symbol of the City of God, the *axis mundi,* where the power of God's kingdom and the power of evil clash. In the visionary's religious imagination, the outcome of the battle is sure: God will ultimately—indeed, will soon—overcome the forces of evil concentrated in "the city of chaos" and symbolized by Leviathan, and will free human beings from captivity to evil and even from the fear of death that shadows military aggression. The Israelite people are a paradigm of all poor and helpless victims of evil everywhere; they too are invited to Zion, the center of the earth, where God's kingly power is manifest. Jerusalem, the city of God, is the theme of the psalm of thanksgiving, occasioned by the destruction of "the city of chaos" or "the fortified city":

> For you have been a refuge to the poor,
>   a refuge to the needy in their distress,
>   a shelter from the rainstorm and a shade from the heat. (Isa. 25:4, NRSV)

---

25. Brevard S. Childs (*Introduction to the Old Testament as Scripture* [Philadelphia: Fortress Press, 1979] 330–33), on "the theological shaping of First Isaiah," observes: "The redactional connection between chs. 13 and 24 points to Babylon's representative role among the nations, which function is not to be lost by an over-historicizing of the material" (332).

CHAPTER 13

Creation Faith in Its
Setting of Worship

Some years ago Bishop Hanns Lilje, in answer to a question about the condition of the church in East Germany, portrayed to a conference of American students a great *Kirchentag* held in Leipzig, to which city some six hundred thousand people had gathered for discussion, fellowship, and worship. The great gathering took place in the very shadow of a communist building, at the top of which was the Red Star. In front of the building was a statue of Stalin, a detail that dates this story well before the time when Stalin was "demythologized." "Right under Stalin's nose," as the bishop whimsically put it, a sermon was preached on the opening words of Psalm 24:

> The earth is the Lord's and all that is in it,
>   the world, and those who live in it;
> for he has founded it on the seas,
>   and established it on the rivers. (Ps. 24:1-2, NRSV)

One would think that the text, with its affirmation that God established the earth upon waters, would have been completely irrelevant in the sophisticated twentieth century, when any grammar school student knows that the earth orbits in space. The statement in v. 2 that God founded the earth upon the "seas" (*yammîm*), established it upon the "rivers" (*nĕhārôt*), clearly reflects the ancient view of the earth as an island suspended over the primeval ocean (see diagram above, p. 21) and faintly echoes the myth of the divine victory over the hostile powers of chaos, explicitly named Sea (*Yamm*) and River (*Nahar*) in Canaanite mythological texts. But in that situation of worship the intention of the text was probably more evi-

207

dent than in the usual arguments about science and religion. For the creation faith's insistence that the earth belongs to God is a challenge to modern self-understanding. Doctrinaire communism has to deny the biblical meaning of creation, not just for the spurious reason that it conflicts with a scientific worldview but for the deeper reason that it is existentially unacceptable to modern peoples. Pious persons may be allowed to say that "heaven" belongs to the Lord; but one thing is clear to this-worldly "realists" for whom scientific knowledge is power: the earth belongs to human beings and is subject to their control.[1]

THE CALL TO WORSHIP

The setting of the creation faith within worship is clearly evident in Psalm 24, which undoubtedly was once used in connection with a processional bearing of the ark into Jerusalem during a great pilgrimage festival celebrating Yahweh's kingship. The psalm has three sections: an introit announcing that Yahweh is Creator (vv. 1-2), an "entrance Torah" in question-and-answer form (vv. 3-6) like the one in Psalm 15, and finally an "entrance liturgy" that was sung antiphonally in the presence of the ark, the throne-seat of "Yahweh of hosts" (cf. 1 Sam. 4:4; 2 Sam. 6:2), as the company of worshipers stood before the gates of Jerusalem.[2] In this liturgical setting the function of creation language is to give the *grounds* for praising God. The worshiping community confesses that the earth, and all the creatures it contains, belong solely to Yahweh, for Yahweh is Creator and King. God's power upholds the world, and God's purpose gives meaning to existence. Thus in the book of Psalms the affirmation that God is the Creator is a Venite, a call to worship.

> O come, let us sing to the Lord;
>   let us make a joyful noise to the rock of our salvation!
> Let us come into his presence with thanksgiving;
>   let us make a joyful noise to him with songs of praise!
> For the Lord is a great God,
>   and a great King above all gods.
> In his hand are the depths of the earth;
>   the heights of the mountains are his also.
> The sea is his, for he made it,
>   and the dry land, which his hands have formed. (Ps. 95:1-5, NRSV)

---

1. Elements of this chapter are taken from chap. 1 above.

2. See Hans-Joachim Kraus, *Worship in Israel* (trans. Geoffrey, Buswell; Richmond, Va.: John Knox, 1966) 208–18, for an attempt to delineate the structure of the festival cult at Jerusalem, with special reference to Psalm 24. The "entrance Torah" included the question of the right to enter (24:3), the declaration by the priests of the laws binding upon the people (vv. 4-5), and the response of the pilgrims (v. 6).

To the psalmist the greatness of God is shown in the fact that even the extremities of the world—from the heights of the mountains (in popular thought the abode of the gods) to the depths of the earth (the realm of the powers of darkness and death)—are under God's control (cf. Amos 9:2-3; Ps. 139:7-12). The sea and the dry land, the lofty mountains and the abysses of the earth belong to God, not because God extended the Deity's domain to include them, like a king who enlarges his empire, but because God made them and they belonged to God from the first.

In the succeeding lines of Psalm 95 the Venite is repeated, though this time it is grounded upon the creation of Israel.

> O come, let us worship and bow down,
>   let us kneel before the Lord, our Maker!
> For he is our God,
>   and we are the people of his pasture,
>   and the sheep of his hand. (Ps. 95:6-7, NRSV)

Here the people of God are described under the image of the shepherd and his flock (cf. John 10). Creation implies *belonging to God* on the analogy of the sheep who are constituted as a flock by belonging to their shepherd. Israel affirms that Yahweh is "our Maker," the One who created a people *ex nihilo,* and therefore Yahweh is *our* God and we are *his* people (see Ps. 100:3, which makes the same affirmation). To believe in God the Creator is to acknowledge that the Creator is Lord absolutely.

In the 1920s, when a storm of controversy broke out over the doctrine of evolution, people passionately took sides in the "science-versus-religion" battle, some attempting to demonstrate that the biblical doctrine of creation is good science and others rejecting it as bad science. Now that the smoke of battle has lifted, one can see more clearly what the real issue is. The conflict does not lie fundamentally in the realm of scientific hypothesis about *how* the universe began or *how* humans evolved. That false determination of the battlefront resulted from a failure to understand the intention of Israel's language of worship. Rather, the announcement that God is the Creator concerns primarily the source and basis of life's meaning. Negatively, it rebukes the notion that the world is at the disposal of human beings—susceptible to the meaning they impose and subject to the purposes they devise. The earth is not ours, it is the Lord's; hence the meaning of human life is not derived from the world. Positively, the doctrine evokes in human beings an understanding of who they really are: transient and contingent beings who, together with all that exists, are dependent on the God who alone is Lord. Human life on earth derives its meaning from relationship to the God whose creative purpose has initiated the whole historical drama.

More and more we are coming to realize that the word *creation* belongs to a language that has a vocabulary and syntax of its own, a theological language whose affirmations one should not confuse with statements made in the context of scientific language.[3] The creation faith has to do with the meaning of human life—not only the meaning of *my* life in the world here and now but also the meaning of the whole historical process that unfolds between the horizons of beginning and end. Therefore theologians and scientists are coming to admit that they may not be talking about the same thing when each speaks of "creation" or "the beginning." Indeed, a British scientist, Reginald O. Kapp, reportedly advised his scientific colleagues to avoid using the theological word *creation* to avoid semantic confusion.[4]

Considering the special character of the biblical language, Claus Westermann is justified in suggesting that to understand the creation stories at the beginning of the Bible we ought to divest our minds of scientific and philosophical preconceptions and begin with the psalms that praise God as the creator. "Praise of God, the Creator, does not presuppose the creation story, but quite the reverse: praise of God is the source and presupposition of the creation story. The present narrative is, in fact, a developed and expanded confession of faith in God as Creator."[5] If I understand this statement correctly, Westermann is not suggesting that one start from a position of worship that is detached from Israel's sacred history (*Heilsgeschichte*); rather, he is saying, the psalms of Israel help one to understand that the story of creation is told *confessionally,* that is, to express faith in God, not to engage in prescientific, prephilosophical reflections about nature. In other words, the story of creation is related theologically to God's redemptive activity, which is the ground of Israel's praise.

This is certainly the case with the Priestly story of creation with which the Bible opens. In its present *position,* this creation account is the opening of the whole historical drama and accordingly is the prelude to the story of God's special dealings with the people Israel, represented by Abraham and Sarah. The *form* of the story, however, suggests that it was shaped by liturgical usage over a period of many generations, perhaps in connection with one of the great pilgrimage festivals of Israel, and thus it is told confessionally, to glorify the God of Israel. This is the way Paul Humbert wants to read the story. After comparing the close similarities between

3. In *The Logic of Self-Involvement* (London: SCM, 1963), Donald Evans discusses the function of theological language about creation from the standpoint of modern philosophy of language.

4. Cited by Carl Michalson, *The Rationality of Faith* (New York: Charles Scribner's Sons, 1963) 47. In his discussion of creation (p. 42–48) this theologian pushes provocatively to the extreme of saying that creation deals *only* with history and has no application to the sphere of "nature" at all. See chap. 6 above.

5. Claus Westermann, *A Thousand Years and a Day: Our Time in the Old Testament* (trans. Stanley Rudman; Philadelphia: Muhlenberg, 1962) 3.

Genesis 1 and Psalm 104 (see the comparisons below, p. 217–19), he concludes that both are *liturgical* texts associated with the Israelite New Year festival—the fall harvest festival known as the Feast of Tabernacles. In this respect Humbert has taken a step that Hermann Gunkel did not think of taking. Gunkel had pointed out that Genesis 1 echoes motifs from the Babylonian creation story, which was designed to be read on the occasion of the *akitu* (New Year) festival; but he did not consider Genesis 1 to be a *Festlegende* or cultic text designed for use at the Israelite New Year festival. Humbert, however, suggests that the Genesis story is structured in a seven-day scheme not to accommodate an ordinary week but to reflect the *festal week,* the seven days of the Feast of Tabernacles with which the New Year begins.[6]

Later on I shall return to the question of the New Year feast, especially to the so-called enthronement psalms, which acclaim Yahweh as king of the universe. Quite apart from the question as to whether Genesis 1, on the analogy of the Babylonian creation story, is a festal legend, there should be general agreement on the fundamental point: the Priestly account of creation, like the creation psalms of the Psalter, is a sublime expression of Israel's praise. The creation story is most at home in a setting of worship.

THE AWARENESS OF BEING

This leads to an important point. Interpreting the creation faith within the context of worship tends to shift the accent from creation as the event in the beginning to a relationship in the present, from the initiating act of the Creator to the creature's dependence on the Creator. Here the vertical dimension (the relationship between God and humanity) is more important than the horizontal one (the movement of events from beginning to end). An excellent illustration occurs at the beginning of Augustine's *Confessions,* where he utters the prayer: "O Lord, thou hast made us for thyself and our hearts are restless until they find their rest in thee." In this famous prayer the creation faith is understood in its vertical dimension: human being is constituted by relationship with God. Outside that relationship, which defines human nature or "personhood," one leads an unauthentic and finally meaningless existence.

In our time the existentialist interpretation of creation has found considerable support. For instance, Alan Richardson advocated this interpretation in his commentary on Genesis 1–11.[7] Richardson objects to calling the

---

6. Paul Humbert, "La relation de Genèse 1 et du Psaume 104 avec la liturgie du Nouvel-An israélite," *Opuscles d'un hébraïsant* (Neuchâtel: Université de Neuchâtel, 1958) 60–82.

7. Alan Richardson, *Genesis I–XI* (Torch Commentary; London: SCM, 1953). See also the essays on creation by Rudolf Bultmann, "Faith in God the Creator" and "The Meaning of the Christian Faith in Creation," in *Existence and Faith* (trans. and ed. Schubert M. Ogden; New York: Meridian, 1960) 171–82 and 206–25, respectively.

creation stories "myths" because, in popular parlance, this term suggests that there was no real act of creation at all. "God *did* create the world: this is no myth. Similarly man's condition *is* fallen: there is, alas, no question of myth here."[8] Nonetheless, the language used in Genesis 1–11 differs completely from that of a scientific textbook.

> The truth with which [the creation stories] deal is not of the same order as the truth with which history and geography, astronomy and geology, deal; it is not the literal truth of the actual observation of measurable things and events; it is ultimate truth, the truth which can be grasped only by the imagination, and which can be expressed only by image and symbolism.[9]

Therefore, he proposes to consider these stories as "parables," to be read as poetry, not prose. Although one might object that, from a form-critical perspective, this is a loose usage of the genre "parable," one must see that the central point Richardson makes regarding religious language is important. Even those, like Karl Barth, who advocate a *heilsgeschichtliche* view of creation as the first of God's historical acts would have to acknowledge that this first event, which lies at the remote boundary of history, can be portrayed only in symbols of religious imagination. In this case, however, Richardson seems to put the accent in a different place than *Heilsgeschichte.* The parables of Genesis, he says, contain a special kind of truth: "the truth of religious awareness." It is the kind of truth that cannot be expressed in philosophical, theological, or psychological terms, for that, he says, "would be to transpose it into one of the other orders of truth, to de-personalize it."[10]

The intention of the parables of the *Urgeschichte,* according to this view, is to express the existential awareness that my origin, my being, my destiny are subject to the will of God, not governed by my own will. As some existentialist theologians would put it, the self is "a derived self."

> The parables of Creation do not offer us a theory, a philosophical hypothesis, of how the world came into existence; nor does the parable of the Fall offer us a scientific analysis of human nature. On the contrary, they offer me personal knowledge about my existence, my dependence upon God, my alienation from [God], my need of reconciliation to [God].[11]

Richardson goes on to say that implicit in this existential knowledge of

8. Richardson, *Genesis,* 28.
9. Ibid., 30.
10. Ibid.
11. Ibid.

"myself-in-relation-to-God" are certain "general truths"—truths about the universe, about the earth, about human nature. But these general truths are inferences from the truth of *my* existence.

Only if I have *first* perceived that this existential truth applies to *me,* shall I comprehend that such general truths for philosophy and theology are involved in the Genesis stories. I must first understand that I am Adam, made in God's likeness, rebelling against his purpose, desiring to be "as God." The Genesis parables certainly carry many and deep implications concerning mankind in general, but I shall not understand this until I have first come to know that they are addressed to the particular Adam which is myself.[12]

 So interpreted, the creation stories are not just about the past but about the present. *Urgeschichte* refers not merely to *primeval* history but to *primal* history, to the historicity that is constitutive of the human person. The element *Ur-* ("original," "primal") is a description of human historical being—the being of the person who knows existentially that one's life originates with God, even as one also knows that sin is original with him or her. While one may question whether this interpretation does full justice to the view expressed in the creation faith, one surely cannot deny that contemporaneity is an important dimension of the biblical stories. These stories purport to be our story. It is well known that the Hebrew word *'ādām* is a generic term for "man, humankind." As the old Jewish proverb says, everyman is Adam.[13] Accordingly, Helmut Thielicke, whose dynamic preaching in a Hamburg cathedral has reverberated far beyond his own city and country, is justified in regarding the language of Genesis 1–11 (the primeval history) as fundamentally "parabolic symbolism" and in interpreting these stories as a searching exposé of human life itself. Commenting on the first two verses of Genesis, which portray an earth without form and void and the beginning of God's creative work, he remarks that the interest of this story could hardly have been scientific;

> otherwise we would surely see in it the attempt to drive the drill still deeper into the bedrock of the world and go back behind the world of creation.

> These first pages of the Bible have a totally different interest. Their purpose is to show what it means for me and my life that God is there at the beginning and at the end, and that everything that happens in the world—my little life with its

12. Ibid., 30–31.
13. "Adam is therefore not the cause, save only of his own soul, but each of us has been the Adam of his own soul" (*2 Apoc. Bar.* 54:19). See *Apocrypha and Pseudepigrapha of the Old Testament* (ed. R. H. Charles; 2 vols.; Oxford: Clarendon, 1913) 2.512.

cares and its joys, and also the history of the world at large extending from stone-age man to the atomic era—that all of this is, so to speak, a discourse enclosed, upheld, and guarded by the breath of God.[14]

This is in line with Luther's Shorter Catechism, where he states that the creedal affirmation that God is Maker of heaven and earth boils down essentially to this: I believe that God is *my* creator.

It is not difficult to move from the creation story, so interpreted, to biblical psalms that express wonder about one's being alive and the greater wonder that God is mindful of the existing person. Psalm 8, which is related to the Priestly creation account of Genesis 1, is an eloquent witness to the meaning of the creation faith in the liturgy of Israel's worship. This hymn begins and ends with an exclamation of praise to God's glory and majesty that, to the eye of faith, are evident in the beauty of the world and in the astonishing order of the universe. The psalmist knows that while adults come to take this world for granted, the little child responds with spontaneous and elemental joy to the works of God. This poet knows too that praise is the sign that one is alive, that one is fully human; for a person lives vis-à-vis God, his or her creator.

> When I look at thy heavens, the work of thy fingers,
>   the moon and the stars which thou hast established;
> what is man that thou art mindful of him,
>   and the son of man that thou dost care for him? (Ps. 8:3-4, RSV)

Here the creation faith focuses on the relationship between God and the human person. It is not just that human beings, in contrast to the God who has spread out the star-studded canopy of the heavens, are transient and finite. As the book of Ecclesiastes shows, the awareness of the gulf fixed between Creator and creature can prompt a melancholy feeling of insignificance and emptiness. Rather, the creation faith awakens an understanding of one's existence—the awareness that one's "relationship with God is that of an *incomprehensible grace*."[15] The wonder of wonders, which evokes the psalmist's praise, is that the Almighty God who spread out the heavens and created the innumerable starry host is actually mindful of this small creature and, even more astounding, that God confers upon a human being the honor of exercising dominion over the earth as God's representative, as

---

14. Helmut Thielicke, *How the World Began* (trans. John W. Doberstein; Philadelphia: Muhlenberg, 1961) 13–14.

15. Artur Weiser, *Psalms* (trans. Herbert Hartwell; OTL; Philadephia: Westminster, 1962) 143.

one who is made but a "little less than God." Praise rises to a climax as the psalmist draws on the old cultic tradition found also in the Priestly creation story:[16]

> Yet thou hast made him little less than God,
>   and dost crown him with glory and honor.
> Thou hast given him dominion over the works of thy hands;
>   thou has put all things under his feet. (Ps. 8:5-6, RSV)

In this psalm, God's giving human beings dominion over the earth means specifically to subdue the animals and to use them for human benefit. But it is surely appropriate to understand this dominion in a larger sense: the conquest of nature by human science and the exploration of the realms of space that lie beyond the earth. The modern age has accentuated one's sense of smallness. A human being is a faceless individual in a vast and lonely industrial crowd, a mere infinitesimal speck on the surface of the dust globule called the earth. Today one can ask the psalmist's question with great passion: Can it be that the God whose glory fills the universe is *really* interested in this tiny creature? If this question is answered affirmatively, as it is in this psalm and in the whole Bible, then praise should manifest itself in one's work, whatever it is, whether turning a nut in an assembly line, plowing the soil with a tractor, mending clothes, or manning a spaceship.

This sense that a person is not only creaturely but dependent on God's grace is, by extension, the basis of "general truths" concerning the world, the animals, and the creatures in the universe. Therefore in the Psalter the invitation to praise God reaches out beyond human beings, in whom praise becomes articulate, to all of God's creatures. Thus in Psalm 148 the sun, moon, and stars; the sea monsters and the deeps; lightning and hail, snow and frost; mountains and hills, beasts and cattle—everything and everyone join in the great anthem of praise to the glory of God.

> All your works shall give thanks to you, O Lord,
>   and all your faithful shall bless you. (Ps. 145:10, NRSV)

Thus the understanding of one's own existence as God's creature is mirrored in and confirmed by what one sees all around in the world. All creatures exist within the relationship of God's incomprehensible grace.

---

16. Cf. Gen. 1:26-28. There the "image of God" also conveys the idea of a special relationship with God that entitles humans to exercise dominion as God's representatives. On this point, see Gerhard von Rad, *Genesis* (trans. John H. Marks; OTL; rev. ed.; Philadelphia: Westminster, 1972) 57–61. See also chap. 7 above.

THE SENSE OF WONDER

In view of what has been said about the "vertical" or existential dimension of creation one should not be surprised to find that the psalms usually designated as "creation psalms"—Psalm 8 (which I have already considered) and Psalm 19A, and Psalm 104—display no interest in *Heilsgeschichte,* Israel's sacred history. The first part of Psalm 19 (part A = vv. 1-6[2-7]) is a good illustration. Although the psalm in its present form is firmly anchored in Israel's faith, owing to the praise of the Torah with which it concludes (part B = vv. 7-14[8-15]), the first part is neutral in regard to the historical faith of Israel.[17] It even employs the old Semitic word for deity, El—not the special name of Israel's God, Yahweh.

> The heavens are telling the glory of God [*'ēl*];
>   and the firmament proclaims his handiwork.
> Day to day pours forth speech,
>   and night to night declares knowledge.
> There is no speech, nor are there words;
>   their voice is not heard;
> yet their voice goes out through all the earth,
>   and their words to the end of the world. (Ps. 19:1-4a, NRSV)

It is important to notice that here the psalmist does not say that God is revealed in nature; rather the heavens are *witnesses* to God's glory. As Henri Frankfort reminds us, Psalm 19 intends to emphasize the transcendence of God, and therefore it "mocks the beliefs of Babylonians and Egyptians" who conceived the divine as "immanent in nature."

> The heavens, which were to the psalmist but a witness of God's greatness, were to the Mesopotamians the very majesty of godhead, the highest ruler, Anu. To the Egyptians the heavens signified the mystery of the divine mother through whom man was reborn. In Egypt and Mesopotamia the divine was comprehended as immanent: the gods were in nature. The Egyptians saw in the sun all that a man may know of the Creator; the Mesopotamians viewed the sun as the god Shamash, the guarantor of justice. But to the psalmist the sun was God's devoted servant who "is as a bridegroom coming out of his chamber, and rejoiceth as a strong man to run a race." The God of the psalmists and the prophets was not in nature. [God] transcended nature—and transcended, likewise, the realm of mythopoeic thought.[18]

---

17. In its present form, however, Psalm 19 seems to reflect a late stage in Israelite faith when God's revelation was identified with the gift of the Torah, in contrast to the earlier emphasis on Yahweh's historical acts; and at this stage Torah theology and wisdom theology tended to blend together. See J. C. Rylaarsdam, *Revelation in Jewish Wisdom Literature* (Chicago: University of Chicago Press, 1946). Another psalm of this type is Psalm 1.

18. H. and H. A. Frankfort, *The Intellectual Adventure of Ancient Man* (Chicago: University of Chicago Press, 1946) 363; repr. as *Before Philosophy* (Baltimore: Penguin, 1973) 237.

In the psalmist's faith the creation points beyond itself to the Creator, upon whom all things and all beings depend. The light that suffuses the creation is God's *kābôd* ("glory"), the refulgent radiance that shields God's being. The marvelous order of the universe bears witness to God's artistry, to God's handiwork. Throughout the creation rings nature's silent anthem of praise, which is repeated from day to day and night to night without cessation. With poetic freedom the psalmist draws on pagan mythological motifs, such as the view that the sun god has his abode in the sea, where at night he rests in the embrace of his lover, only to emerge from the bridal chamber in the morning with youthful vigor and radiant splendor. This mythical imagery, however, is converted to the metaphorical language of praise.

> In the heavens he has set a tent for the sun,
>> which comes out like a bridegroom from his wedding canopy,
>> and like a strong man runs its course with joy.
> Its rising is from the end of the heavens,
>> and its circuit to the end of them;
>> and nothing is hid from its heat. (Ps. 19:4b-6, NRSV)

To the psalmist the sun is only one of God's creatures that obediently performs its appointed task and thereby joins the heavenly anthem of praise to the sublime majesty of the Creator.

The same accent is found in Psalm 104, a prayer addressed to Yahweh the God of Israel that is strikingly similar in spirit and wording to Akhenaton's hymn to the Aton as the sole creator and renewer of life.[19] The psalmist is filled with a profound sense of wonder when surveying the whole range of God's creation. The scope of thought is matched by the creation story of Genesis 1. Indeed, the sequence is so similar that one should probably assume that both passages reflect the liturgical practice of the Jerusalem Temple.[20] Notice how the seven strophes parallel the Genesis account:

Strophe 1

104:1-4	In traditional language the psalmist speaks first of the creation of the heavens. God's heavenly palace has been firmly established upon the cosmic ocean above the firmament. Light, clouds, wind, and fire display God's cosmic majesty.	Cf. Gen. 1:6-8

---

19. The Egyptian Hymn to the Sun is translated by John A. Wilson in *ANET,* 369ff.

20. See further Humbert's article dealing with the relation of Genesis 1 and Psalm 104 to the New Year festival (*Opuscules d'un hébraïsant,* 60–82). In view of its affinities with the Egyptian Hymn to the Sun, Psalm 104 may be relatively early and prior to Genesis 1 in literary formulation, in which case perhaps the Priestly account is dependent on it.

Strophe 2

104:5-9   God has firmly established the earth by   Cf. Gen. 1:9-10
            pushing back the waters of chaos and
            establishing bounds for them, so that chaos
            would not engulf the earth. The old myth of the
            Creator's victory over the rebellious powers of
            chaos is used more freely in Psalm 104 than in
            the Genesis account. Note the conflict language:
            "At thy rebuke they [the waters of chaos] fled" (v. 7).

Strophe 3

104:10-13   The waters of chaos, having been   Implied in Gen. 1:6-10
            tamed, are converted to beneficial use.
            The water gushes up from underground
            springs and rains down from heaven.

Strophe 4

104:14-18   The result is that vegetation grows, which   Cf. Gen. 1:11-12
            in turn makes life possible for birds, beasts,
            and humans.

Strophe 5

104:19-23   God created the moon and the sun to reckon   Cf. Gen. 1:14-18
            the times, so that the beasts may find their
            food in the night and human beings may
            perform their work during the day.

Strophe 6

104:24-26   The psalmist reflects on the remnant of   Cf. Gen. 1:20-22
            watery chaos, the sea, with its teeming
            creatures great and small. Leviathan is no
            longer the dreaded monster of chaos but
            God's "plaything" (cf. Job 41:5[40:29]).

Strophe 7

104:27-30   The dependence of humans and animals on   Cf. Gen. 1:24-30
            God for life.

While the Genesis story culminates with God's creation of human beings in the divine image (cf. Ps. 8:5[6]: "lacking but a little") and investing them with dominion over the earth, Psalm 104 moves toward an exclamation of wonder about the dependence of life—animal and human—upon the Creator.

These all look to thee,
    to give them their food in due season.
When thou givest to them, they gather it up;
    when thou openest thy hand, they are filled with good things.

When thou hidest thy face, they are dismayed;
  when thou takest away their breath, they die
  and return to their dust.
When thou sendest forth thy Spirit [lit., "breath"], they are created;[21]
  and thou renewest the face of the ground. (Ps. 104:27-30, RSV)

The Hebrew verbs (imperfects) describe actions that continue, thus indicating that God's creation is a continual sustaining and renewing activity. The intention of Psalm 104, Gerhard von Rad observes, is "to show how the whole world is open to God—in every moment of its existence it requires to be sustained by God, everything 'waits' on him (vs. 27); and it also receives this sustenance all the time. Were Yahweh to turn away from the world even for just one moment, then its splendour would immediately collapse (vs. 29)."[22]

In his oratorio *The Creation,* Haydn appropriately placed a paraphrase of these verses at the point of the sixth day of creation (Gen. 1:31), when God saw everything that he had made and called it very good.

THE CRY FOR DELIVERANCE

As mentioned above, these creation psalms show no interest in *Heilsgeschichte.* They may have entered Israelite tradition by way of the wisdom schools, which, at least from the time of Solomon, increasingly influenced Israelite life and worship. It is noteworthy, however, that in other psalms that have the theme of deliverance from death, the old creation imagery is used to portray the *redemptive* activity of God. In these cases, too, one may say that creation is understood existentially, but the thought shifts from an awareness of the creature's dependence on the Creator to an existential cry "out of the depths" to the God who alone can save. In other words, the interest is *soteriological.*

Here one may recall the various psalms in which a suppliant portrays personal distress in the imagery of being engulfed by "deep waters" or as a descent into the waters of the deep.[23] This is the case in the psalm inserted into the book of Jonah, which portrays a sojourn in the belly of a fish (Jonah 2:2-9[3-10]).

I called to the Lord out of my distress,
  and he answered me;

21. The verb translated "they are created" is a form of the same verb used in Gen 1:1 (*bārā'*). This verb is used only of God's creative activity and its accusative is always the product of God's action, never the material out of which something is formed.
22. Gerhard von Rad, *Old Testament Theology* (trans. D. M. G. Stalker; 2 vols.; New York: Harper & Row, 1962–65) 1.361.
23. For this type of water imagery, see such passages as Pss. 18:4-5 (5-6); 32:6; 42:7 (8); 69:1-2, 14-15 (2-3, 15-16); 88:6-7 (7-8); 124:3-5; 144:7; Job 38:16-17; cf. Isa. 43:2.

out of the belly of Sheol I cried,
and you heard my voice.
You cast me into the deep,
into the heart of the seas,
and the flood surrounded me;
all your waves and your billows
passed over me. (Jonah 2:2-3, NRSV)

Here Sheol is pictured as a pit beneath the earth, surrounded by the waters of the subterranean ocean. One should not, however, convert this picture into a literal spatial location. In the ancient way of thinking, since water signified the dimension of the chaotic (we would say, perhaps, "non-being"), it was appropriate to conceive of death, the great threat to life, as having its abode within the deep.

These descriptions presuppose a view of life and death that is strange to the modern world. We tend to diagnose the difference between life and death in physical terms. Death, we think, occurs in that instant when bodily functions cease and consciousness goes out like a light. The Israelite, however, viewed death as a weak form of life, as a decrease in "the vitality of the individual."[24] Any threat to a person's *šālôm* ("welfare"), whether from sickness, weakness, imprisonment, or attack by enemies, was felt to be an encroachment of death into the land of the living. The Israelite view of the universe, as Johannes Pedersen reminds us, is a dramatic conception of "the fight for life against death."

> The land of life lies in the centre, on all hands surrounded by the land of death. The wilderness lies outside, the realm of death and the ocean below, but they send in their tentacles from all sides, and make the world a mixture of life and death, of light and darkness. But life *must* be the stronger. The great terror of the Israelite is that some day evil shall get the upper hand, and chaos come to prevail in the world of man.[25]

Thus the Israelite knew existentially that the domain of death could extend into "the land of the living," the realm of history. Above all, in the Israelite view death means separation from God. "Death begins to become reality," observes von Rad, "at the point where Jahweh forsakes a man, where he is silent, i.e., at whatever point the life-relationship with Jahweh wears thin."[26]

Therefore the psalmists often describe their experience of the absence

---

24. See Aubrey R. Johnson, *The Vitality of the Individual in the Thought of Ancient Israel* (2d ed.; Cardiff: University of Wales Press, 1964).

25. Johannes Pedersen, *Israel: Its Life and Culture* (4 vols. bound in 2; London: Oxford Univ. Press, 1926–40) 1-2.470–71.

26. Von Rad, *Old Testament Theology,* 1.388.

of God, of God-forsakenness, as a descent into Sheol, where there is no life precisely because in that dark region the "shades"[27] do not praise God. Psalm 88 is a typical lament. The psalmist speaks as "one who has no strength" (v. 4b[5b]), who is reckoned among those who go down to the Pit (Sheol).

> You have put me in the depths of the Pit,
> in the regions dark and deep.
> Your wrath lies heavy upon me,
> and you overwhelm me with all your waves. (Ps. 88:6-7, NRSV)

To the suppliant the bitterness of dying is that death means separation from God, for in Sheol there is no proclamation of Yahweh's saving work in history.

> Do you work wonders for the dead?
> Do the shades rise up to praise you?
> Is your steadfast love declared in the grave,
> Or your faithfulness in Abaddon?
> Are your wonders known in the darkness,
> or your saving help in the land of forgetfulness? (Ps. 88:10-12, NRSV)

Since death, or its imminence, is a threat to the meaning of human life in history, it was appropriate for psalmists to turn to creation-versus-chaos imagery—the imagery of Genesis 1 that contrasts the darkness and confusion of chaos with the ordered world of light and life.[28] It is interesting as well to see how psalmists employed this same creation imagery, even with its mythical features, to describe "the epiphany of God" for deliverance— a prominent motif in many psalms.[29] A psalmist tells how, when the snares of death were all around, Yahweh came to the rescue in an earthshaking epiphany (Psalm 18 par. 2 Samuel 22). So violent was the storm that accompanied God's coming that the creation was shaken to its very foundations. The vivid description (Ps. 18:7-15[8-16]) includes these lines:

> The Lord also thundered in the heavens,
> and the Most High [^{c}elyôn] uttered his voice.
> And he sent out his arrows, and scattered them;

---

27. A shade is a person's ghost, that is, the person reduced to the weakest form of vitality. The Old Testament rejects the view prevalent in the ancient Near East that the shades had sufficient vitality to do good or evil, a belief that was the basis of necromancy. Notice, however, the tradition that Saul, though having banished mediums, clandestinely consulted the witch of Endor, who summoned Samuel's shade from Sheol (1 Samuel 28).

28. See Aubrey R. Johnson, "Jonah 2:3-10: A Study in Cultic Phantasy," in *Studies in Old Testament Prophecy* (ed. H. H. Rowley; Edinburgh: T. & T. Clark, 1950) 89.

29. See Claus Westermann, *Praise and Lament in the Psalms* (trans. Keith R. Crim and Richard N. Sowlen; 2d ed.; Atlanta: John Knox, 1981) 93–101.

he flashed forth lightnings, and routed them.
Then the channels of the sea [*yām*]³⁰ were seen,
and the foundations of the world were laid bare
at your rebuke, O Lord,
at the blast of the breath of your nostrils. (Ps. 18:13-15, NRSV)

Here the poet draws heavily on traditional storm-god symbolism, such as the portrayal of Baal's battle against Sea (*Yamm*) and River (*Nahar*) or Marduk's mounting his storm chariot and using the winds and the lightning as his weapons.³¹ According to the psalmist, the purpose of the coming of Elyon, the Creator, was to redeem from the "strong enemy."

He reached down from on high, he took me;
he drew me out of mighty waters.
He delivered me from my strong enemy,
and from those who hated me;
for they were too mighty for me. (Ps. 18:16-17, NRSV)

The expression "many waters" (or "mighty waters"), here and often in the psalms of Israel, refers to the insurgent waters of chaos, as Herbert May has shown; and the imagery is used here to show the divine triumph over enemies that threaten the king and the people (see v. 50[51]).³² Thus the subterranean waters through which one must pass in the descent to Sheol are identified with the hostile waters of chaos. The victory over menacing death comes from Yahweh, who triumphs over the waters.

The motif of "the epiphany of God" is developed in a striking manner in the psalm of Habakkuk (chap. 3), a passage that echoes mythological elements found in Ras Shamra texts. After an initial address (3:2), the psalm presents a vivid description of a divine epiphany for the purpose of obtaining victory for Yahweh's people and Yahweh's "anointed," the king (vv. 3-15). From afar Yahweh came to the rescue, accompanied by such a violent storm that the everlasting mountains supporting the earth were leveled. God's coming on a storm chariot to vanquish the enemies threatening the people is portrayed as a dramatic conflict with the waters of chaos.

Was your wrath against the rivers [*nĕhārîm*], O Lord?

---

30. Psalm 18 at this point has "waters," but the parallel text in 2 Sam. 22:16 has "sea" (without the article), which is unquestionably correct. See Frank M. Cross and David N. Freedman, "A Royal Song of Thanksgiving," *JBL* 72 (1953) 26.

31. See Herbert G. May, "Some Cosmic Connotations of *Mayim Rabbîm,* 'Many Waters,'" *JBL* 74 (1955) 14. He also draws attention to the parallel of the Hittite myth in which the storm god defeats the dragon Illuyankas; see Albrecht Goetze in *ANET,* 125–26.

32. "The 'many waters' are the chaotic, disorderly, insurgent elements which must be controlled" (May, *JBL* 74[1955] 10).

Or your anger against the rivers,
   or your rage against the sea [yām],
when you drove your horses,
   your chariots to victory? (Hab. 3:8, NRSV)

The poet says that when Yahweh charged forth in the heavenly chariot, with lightning arrows poised to shoot and a glittering spear flashing, the mountains supporting the earth writhed and *těhôm* ("deep") cried out in panic (v. 10). Here the dependence on the Canaanite myth of Baal's fierce battle with Prince Sea and Ruler River is so obvious that originally the Hebrew text must have read "Sea" rather than "the sea" (with the definite article, as in RSV):

Thou didst trample Sea with thy horses,
   the surging of mighty [or "many"] waters. (Hab. 3:15, modified RSV)

This psalm, however, appropriates the chaos imagery to show Yahweh's historical victory for the people (cf. Ps. 89:9-10[10-11]) as in the days of old—the time of the exodus—when he marched from the region of Sinai toward Edom (Hab. 3:7).[33]

In fury you trod the earth,
   in anger you trampled nations.
You came forth to save your people,
   to save your anointed. (Hab. 3:12-13a, NRSV)

Therefore the psalmist, recollecting Yahweh's saving acts of old, can wait in quiet confidence for divine deliverance from foes and can trust God absolutely.

Though the fig tree does not blossom,
   and no fruit is on the vines;
though the produce of the olive fails
   and the fields yield no food;
though the flock is cut off from the fold
   and there is no herd in the stalls,
yet I will rejoice in the Lord;
   I will exult in the God of my salvation. (Hab. 3:17-18, NRSV)

---

33. In his illuminating discussion of Habakkuk 3 and related passages, May (*JBL* 74[1955] 13), draws attention to the fact that Yahweh's domination of the dragon of chaos (Rahab, "the sea," "the rivers" ["floods"], "many waters") is synonymous with triumph over Israel's or Yahweh's enemies at the Reed Sea or in subsequent historical crises.

COSMIC KINGSHIP: THE ENTHRONEMENT PSALMS

It is clear from these psalms that the creation faith is not just the awareness of the creature's radical dependence on the Creator; it is also an expression of confidence in the Creator's power to save, of God's rule over the tumultuous forces of history. Creation faith in this dynamic sense is expressed in a number of psalms whose central motif is the kingship of Yahweh over the nations and the whole cosmos. Yahweh is not only praised as "maker of the heavens" (Ps. 96:5) but also acclaimed as enthroned triumphantly over the restless and rebellious waters of chaos. According to Psalm 93, which is typical of these so-called enthronement psalms,[34] Yahweh's throne was established primordially—"from of old."

> The Lord [Yahweh] reigns [or "Yahweh is King!"]; he is robed in majesty;
>   The Lord [Yahweh] is robed, he is girded with strength.
> Yea, the world is established; it shall never be moved;
>   thy throne is established from of old;
>   thou art from everlasting. (Ps. 93:1-2, RSV)

Then the psalmist praises Yahweh for his victory over the chaotic powers of the cosmos:

> The floods [*nĕhārôt*][35] have lifted up, O Lord [Yahweh],
>   the floods have lifted up their voice,
>   the floods lift up their roaring.
> Mightier than the thunders of many waters,
>   mightier than the waves of the sea,
>   the Lord [Yahweh] on high is mighty! (Ps. 93:3-4, RSV)

According to another enthronement psalm, the waters of chaos have become so tamed and transformed that, instead of being hostile to Yahweh, they roar their acclaim of the cosmic king.

> Let the sea roar, and all that fills it;
>   the world and those who live in it.
> Let the floods clap their hands;
>   let the hills sing together for joy
> at the presence of the Lord, for he is coming
>   to judge the earth.
> He will judge the world with righteousness,
>   and the peoples with equity. (Ps. 98:7-9, NRSV)

34. Scholars differ in the number of psalms to be placed in this category, but at least the following should be included: Psalms 47, 93, 96, 97, 98, 99.

35. This is the feminine plural of "river," a word that appears in the masculine plural (*nĕhārîm*) in Hab. 3:8. The singular (*nāhār*) is the same as one of the names of the adversary of Baal in the Ugaritic mythology, namely, "Ruler *River*."

The enthronement psalms are the product of the Jerusalem cult, which was a crucible in which Israel's ancient historical faith was blended with elements of Canaanite, Babylonian, and Egyptian mythology. The Canaanite element in these psalms is attested by another psalm that begins by summoning the members of the heavenly council ("the sons of God") to praise Yahweh, God of storm. The storm described in this psalm is not just the phenomenon known in Palestine, for the "thunder" (voice) of Yahweh is upon "many waters."[36]

> The voice of the Lord is over the waters;
>   the God of glory thunders,
>   the Lord, over mighty waters.
> The voice of the Lord is powerful;
>   the voice of the Lord is full of majesty. (Ps. 29:3-4, NRSV)

The psalm reaches a climax by proclaiming that Yahweh, having won his victory over the chaotic waters, sits enthroned over the flood.

> The Lord sits enthroned over the flood;
>   the Lord sits enthroned as king forever. (Ps. 29:10, NRSV)

This is clearly an old Canaanite hymn that Israel took over and converted to the Yahweh faith.[37] Since this appropriation must have taken place early in the period of the monarchy, it is unnecessary to say, as have some scholars (e.g., Kraus, Westermann), that the enthronement psalms come from the postexilic period when they were influenced by Second Isaiah.

Following the lead of Sigmund Mowinckel, many scholars have assigned these psalms to a cultic *Sitz im Leben,* namely, the Feast of Tabernacles or the New Year feast in Jerusalem, when Yahweh's kingship was celebrated by rehearsing his victory over the waters of chaos. Some have even proposed that the cultic shout *Yahweh mālak,* found, for instance, in 93:1 and 96:10 (NRSV: "The Lord is king"), should be translated "Yahweh has become king,"[38] which would parallel the Babylonian New Year festival, when Marduk's elevation to supreme rulership in the assembly of the gods prompted the shout "Marduk has become king!" or perhaps a similar ceremony in Canaan (Ugarit) when the cry "Let Baal reign!" was raised.

---

36. In this connection, May (*JBL* 74[1955]16) calls attention to Nah. 1:3-4, where Yahweh, coming in whirlwind and storm, "rebukes the sea" and dries up "all the rivers" (*nĕhārôt*).

37. On the Canaanite character of the psalm, see for instance articles by Louis Ginzberg, "Ugaritic Studies and the Bible," *BA* 8 (1945) 41–58; and Frank M. Cross, "Notes on a Canaanite Psalm in the Old Testament," *BASOR* 117 (1950) 19ff.

38. So Sigmund Mowinckel especially. See his work *The Psalms in Israel's Worship* (trans. D. R. Ap-Thomas; 2 vols.; Nashville: Abingdon, 1962), esp. 1.106–92, "Psalms at the Enthronement Festival of Yahweh"; see also his earlier *Psalmenstudien* (6 vols.; Oslo.: 1921–24), which opened a new phase in the study of the Psalms.

While it is possible to translate the Hebrew verb (a Hebrew perfect) in this sense ("Yahweh has become king"), this translation is exegetically dubious; for in contrast to Marduk's or Baal's dominion, Yahweh's kingship is not subject to the seasonal cycle of summer barrenness and fertility, of death and resurrection. The exclamation should undoubtedly be rendered "Yahweh is king!"

Nevertheless, these psalms show that Israel appropriated mythological elements from the pagan environment and reinterpreted them to express Yahweh's cosmic kingship and universal sway over the nations. Some scholars believe that during the period of the monarchy an annual festival was held in Jerusalem in the fall at the turn of the year, when pilgrims celebrated Yahweh's kingship as well as the founding of Zion and the election of the Davidic king. An echo of this great pilgrimage festival is heard in a late (postexilic) passage in the book of Zechariah that states that those who survive the final battle of history "shall go up year after year to worship the King, Yahweh of hosts, and to keep the Feast of Booths [Tabernacles]," and that the penalty for failure to observe this custom would be no rainfall (Zech 14:16-17).[39]

It is likely that the Jerusalem festival to which these psalms belonged was infused with royal covenant theology. There the anointed Davidic king was regarded as the agent and representative of the King who was enthroned "high and lifted up"—as Isaiah perceived in a vision in the temple, possibly in connection with an enthronement festival (Isa. 6:1-5). According to this belief, the order created at the beginning, when Yahweh established the world on its foundation so that it would never be moved (cf. Ps. 96:10), is mediated through the king to society. The king, like God who has elected him, performs the role of a judge (*šōpēṭ*), that is, he upholds order by administering justice and by defeating Israel's enemies, the two major functions of rulership.[40] Thus in the so-called royal psalms, such as Psalms 2 and 110, the king is assured of victory over enemies, and this victory was apparently understood as a repetition of the divine victory in the beginning. In Israel's cult the "cosmic drama" of creation, as Paul Ricoeur discerningly observes, has become a "messianic drama" of history, in which the anointed (the "messiah," i.e., the reigning king) battles the enemy, who is none other than the primordial enemy in historical

---

39. The holding of this festival on the eve of the coming of the winter rains suggests to John Gray (*The Legacy of Canaan* [VTSup 5; 2d ed.; Leiden: Brill, 1965] 21, 33–34) that at Ugarit too an enthronement festival was celebrated, when Baal was worshiped as lord of storm and rain.

40. The Hebrew verb *šāpaṭ* (e.g., Ps. 98:9) often has a broader meaning than English *judge*—as in the book of Judges. This is true also in the Ras Shamra texts, where the adversary is known as Ruler ("judge") River or where Baal is acclaimed as ruler: "Our King is Baal the Mighty, Our ruler [judge] above whom there is none." Cited in Gray, *Legacy*, 49.

guise.[41] Yahweh says to the anointed: "I will set his hand on the sea and his right hand on the rivers" (Ps. 89:25, NRSV). In a time of distress the Davidic king prays to Yahweh to come in an epiphany of storm and deliver him "from the many waters, from the hand of aliens" (Ps. 144:5-8).

CREATION AS HISTORY: THE REED SEA

In pagan festivals the events that occurred "in the beginning" were cultically contemporized. The victory over the waters of chaos was not a liturgical metaphor; this was, in the faith of archaic society, an event in which worshipers participated. The divine victory was reenacted, with the king playing a central role in the ritual combat. In view of the striking parallels between Israel's psalms and ancient mythological texts it may well be that the Israelite celebration of Yahweh's kingship had a similar sacramental significance. This is the view of Helmer Ringgren, who takes up the suggestion of Johannes Pedersen that for an Israelite "to remember a thing" meant that it "becomes an active reality in the life of the believer."[42] Ringgren draws attention to various passages in the Psalter that refer to *seeing* God's mighty deeds. For instance,

Come and see what God has done:
he is awesome in his deeds among mortals. (Ps. 66:5, NRSV)

Come, behold the works of the Lord;
see what desolation he has brought on the earth. (Ps. 46:8, NRSV)

Whatever one makes of the notion of a "cultic drama," he says, there must have been a cultic actualization of God's ḥesed ("faithfulness") through the remembrance of the past. One does not have to subscribe to the theory of an enthronement festival celebrated at the turn of the New Year to recognize that the book of Psalms reflects cultic experiences of the worshiping people. "It is very probable that there were cultic ceremonies, in which the Lord was celebrated as the Creator, the King, and the Judge of the world, and that the mythological or historical events connected with these concepts were symbolically represented or enacted in some way."[43] In other words, the creation imagery of the victory over the waters of chaos was something more than metaphorical language to express Yahweh's absolute lordship and the dependence of the whole creation upon

41. See Paul Ricoeur, *The Symbolism of Evil* (trans. Emerson Buchanan; New York: Harper & Row, 1967), the entire discussion of the role of the Hebrew king, pp. 191–206.
42. Helmer Ringgren, *The Faith of the Psalmists* (Philadelphia: Fortress Press, 1963), esp. p. 19.
43. Ibid., 19.

God's sovereign will. This language, at least in some of the psalms, points to *events* that were cultically remembered.

Since the 1960s scholars have given a great deal of attention to *Vergegenwärtigung* (often translated "re-presentation" or "actualization"), that is, making the past present.[44] These discussions are based on the recognition that it is not enough to say that biblical faith finds expression in the telling of a story, the recitation of a *Heilsgeschichte*. If an event has significance for faith, if it is a crucial event for the believing community, it should be possible to contemporize it, especially in the context of worship. An excellent illustration is the cultic celebration of the Eucharist or Holy Communion, when worshipers relive and reenact the sacrifice of Christ. In Jewish worship the redemptive event of the exodus is one in which every generation is involved. The Passover Haggadah says:

> In every generation one must look upon himself as if he personally had come forth from Egypt, in keeping with the Biblical command, "And thou shalt tell thy son in that day, saying, it is because of that which the Lord did to *me* when I went forth from Egypt." For it was not alone our fathers whom the Holy One, blessed be He, redeemed, but also us whom He redeemed with them, as it is said, "And *us* He brought out thence that He might lead *us* to, and give *us*, the land which He swore to our fathers."[45]

The question is, What would be meant, within the context of Israelite faith, by the announcement that Yahweh's victory over the powers of chaos was an event—a crucial event—in which the worshiping community participated? One should probably answer this question by saying that within the Israelite cult a great shift took place from a mythical event to a historical event "in the beginning." Paul Ricoeur understands this "demythologizing" well:

> A purely historical combat takes the place of the theogonic combat. The Exodus—that is to say, the departure from Egypt—the key event of the whole Biblical theology of history, has acquired a consistency of its own, a new signification with regard to the primordial creation; it is an event without any reference in principle to any drama of creation. . . . It is History, and no longer the drama of creation, that becomes the active center of symbolism.

44. See, for instance, Martin Noth, "the 'Re-presentation' of the Old Testament in Proclamation" (trans. James L. Mays), in *Essays on Old Testament Hermeneutics* (ed. James L. Mays; Atlanta: John Knox, 1963) 76–88.

45. *The Haggadah of the Passover* (ed. David and Tamar de Sola Pool; Bloch, 1953) 51. See also Will Herberg, "Beyond Time and Eternity: Reflections on Passover and Easter," *Christianity and Crisis* 9/6 (1949) 41–43; repr. in *Faith Enacted as History* (ed. Bernhard W. Anderson; Philadelphia: Westminster, 1976) 66–71.

The consequence of this shift from the drama of creation to the drama of history, he continues, is that the enemy is no longer primeval chaos in the mythical sense but "undergoes a sort of reduction to the purely historical."[46]

One can see the evidences of this drastic shift of emphasis in the literature of Israel. The creation faith of Israel, though heavily dependent on mythological and cultic traditions of the ancient world, witnesses to a decisive, nonrepeatable *historical event* of the past that marked a new beginning. It is not surprising, then, that in various psalms Yahweh's victory over the waters of chaos is historicized, as in the prayer in Habakkuk 3 or Psalm 114 ("When Israel went forth from Egypt"). This creative event was identified with the *crucial event* of Yahweh's victory at the Reed Sea, the event that marked the beginning of Israel's history. In an early tradition about the crossing of the sea, the Song of the Sea in Exodus 15, Yahweh's enemies are the hosts of Pharaoh. The sea is merely the passive instrument by which Yahweh won the victory on behalf of Israel. But in other poems of a later origin the waters of the Reed Sea are none other than the waters of chaos. Yahweh's battle was fought not in the timeless realm of mythology but in the arena of history—namely, at the beginning, when Israel was created as a people. Thus Psalm 77, a lament that recalls those "mighty deeds" of old when Yahweh redeemed the people, says that:

> When the waters saw you, O God,
>   when the waters saw you, they were afraid;
>   the very deep trembled.
> The clouds poured out water;
>   the skies thundered;
>   your arrows flashed on every side.
> The crash of your thunder was in the whirlwind;
>   your lightnings lit up the world;
> the earth trembled and shook. (Ps. 77:16-18, NRSV)

But the concluding verses of this lament indicate when the victory was won: it was at the crossing of the Reed Sea.[47]

> Your way was through the sea,
>   your path, through the mighty waters;
>   yet your footprints were unseen.
> You led your people like a flock
>   by the hand of Moses and Aaron. (Ps. 77:19-20, NRSV)

---

46. Ricoeur, *Symbolism of Evil,* 204.

47. May (*JBL* 74[1955] 12–13) discusses the literary parallels between Psalm 77 and Habakkuk 3.

Mythical imagery also appears in Psalm 74, a lament composed in the shadow of a great national disaster, presumably the destruction of Jerusalem in 587 B.C.E. The psalmist appeals to God to remember the congregation that God "created" (NRSV: "acquired") of old and Mount Zion, which was chosen as God's dwelling place (v. 2). The lament shifts to a new key, as God is addressed as king in hymnic tones:

> Yet God my King is from of old,
>> working salvation in [the midst of] the earth.
> You divided the sea [*yām*] by your might;
>> you broke the heads of the dragons [*tannînîm*] in the waters.
> You crushed the heads of Leviathan;
>> you gave him as food for the creatures of the wilderness.[48]
> You cut openings for springs and torrents;
>> you dried up ever-flowing streams.
> Yours is the day, yours also the night;
>> you established the luminaries and the sun.
> You have fixed all the bounds of the earth;
>> you made summer and winter. (Ps. 74:12-17, NRSV)

Here there are distinct allusions to the myth—known especially from Ugaritic texts—of the god who slays Leviathan (Ugaritic: *Lotan*), the dragon with seven heads.[49] The psalmist clearly intends to extol the Creator, who has demonstrated power over chaos by cleaving open springs and brooks and drying up the "ever-flowing rivers" (*nahărôt 'êtān*; cf. Ps. 104:10). But the connection of this mythical symbolism with Israel's *Heilsgeschichte* is not so clear as in Psalm 77, which I have considered above. Crucial for interpretation is v. 12, especially the clause translated "working salvation [Hebrew: 'doing deeds of salvation'] in the midst of the earth." Does this refer to the divine deeds at the beginning when, according to the creation myth, the monster of chaos was slain? Or does the psalmist allude to Israel's *Urzeit*, when Yahweh delivered the people by "dividing" or "drying up" (vv. 13a, 15b) the sea? In the last analysis one is not forced to choose between these alternatives, for the psalmist's use of creation imagery carries overtones from Israel's historical experience: the victory at the Reed Sea, the crossing of the Jordan, and the entry into the promised land. When one considers these hymnic verses in the context of the psalm as a

---

48. The translation "for the creatures of the wilderness" is uncertain. The Hebrew has this: "for the people, for the dwellers of the wilderness [?]." Later the view arose that Leviathan would be food for the messianic banquet; cf. *2 Apoc. Bar.* 29:4.

49. Perhaps "dragons" in v. 13 should be singular: "Dragon." See Isa. 27:1. Cyrus H. Gordon stresses the relation of these passages to Ugaritic mythology in "Leviathan: Symbol of Evil," in *Biblical Motifs: Origins and Transformations* (ed. Alexander Altmann; Cambridge: Harvard Univ. Press, 1966) 1–9. See further chap. 12 above.

whole, the psalmist's concern is unmistakably historical: to express "the unshakable belief that God, who has shown himself in the creation of the universe to be Lord over the chaos, now also has the power to suppress the revolt of the chaotic powers."[50]

This historicizing of a mythical motif, which was probably accomplished within the Jerusalem cult, was carried to completion by Second Isaiah. Recalling the old myth of creation, the poet appeals to Yahweh to arouse "as in days of old" when the sea dragon Rahab was slain and the sea was dried up. That time of Yahweh's creative action, says the prophet, was the historical time when Yahweh created the people: when the Divine Warrior cut a path through the great deep (i.e., the Reed Sea) in order that the redeemed could pass over. It was also a typological anticipation of the new creation, when Yahweh would make a path through the chaotic waters so that the redeemed people could pass over into the promised land:

Awake, awake, put on strength,
    O arm of the Lord!
Awake, as in days of old,
    the generations of long ago!
Was it not you who cut Rahab in pieces,
    who pierced the dragon [tannîn]?
Was it not you who dried up the sea [yām],
    the waters of the great deep [těhôm rabbâ];
who made the depths of the sea a way
    for the redeemed to cross over?
So the ransomed of the Lord shall return,
    and come to Zion with singing;
everlasting joy shall be upon their heads;
    they shall obtain joy and gladness,
    and sorrow and sighing shall flee away. (Isa. 51:9-11, NRSV)

We stand here on the threshold of the understanding that creation has an eschatological dimension. If it was within the cult that the cosmological myth was historicized to refer to the divine victory when Yahweh created the people Israel, it was also in the same setting of worship that Israel caught the vision of Yahweh's eschatological kingdom—the day of Yahweh when all the powers of death and darkness would be vanquished and Yahweh's lordship would be unchallenged by any enemy, historical or cosmic. The community of faith may put its trust in life's meaning in spite of the chaotic threats of history because the whole historical drama, from beginning to end, is enfolded within the purpose of the God who is wor-

---

50. Weiser, *Psalms*, 520.

shiped as creator and redeemer. As the theme of Yahweh's kingship over the rebellious waters of chaos was transposed out of the cult into the language of prophecy and apocalyptic, the full implications of this comprehensive view became increasingly apparent.

CHAPTER 14

Creation and
New Creation

From the second century on persons who sought baptism into the Christian community learned the meaning of the Christian faith by reciting and studying a version of the creedal statement known as the Apostles' Creed, beginning: "I believe in God the Father Almighty, maker of heaven and earth." Down through the centuries to the present day, this creed, which puts creation first on the theological agenda, has been recited throughout the world church as a sign of Christian unity and commitment.[1]

Especially in our time it is urgent for the Christian community to give priority to the doctrine of creation. In a pluralistic society faith seeks for a theological understanding of "a wideness in God's mercy," to echo the words of Frederick W. Faber's hymn.[2] On a threatened planet faith seeks for an understanding of our ecological task to preserve the earth and to conserve its resources.[3] As science rapidly advances our technology, faith seeks for an understanding that is adequate for the new horizons of the space age. In this situation it is important for the church to realize and affirm that the Christian Bible consists of two volumes, the first of which we call the Old Testament.

When speaking about creation in the cosmic sense, the church depends primarily on the Scriptures of Israel. Christians turn to the Old Testament

---

1. See Robert C. Neville, *A Theology Primer* (Albany; SUNY Press, 1991) 156–59.

2, See the discussion by a leading "evangelical" theologian, Clark H. Pinnock, *A Wideness in God's Mercy: The Finality of Jesus Christ in a World of Religions* (Grand Rapids: Zondervan, 1992).

3. Al Gore, *Earth in the Balance: Ecology and the Human Spirit* (Boston: Houghton Mifflin, 1992).

in the conviction that the God of the Bible, the true and only God who created the heavens and the earth, is the God of Jesus Christ. In a recent essay on "Theology and Science," Wolfhart Pannenberg observes that

> the situation may be somewhat different in the case of the Jews to whom God is their God primarily because of his covenant with their forbears. For Christians, however, who came from the Gentiles to believe in the God of the Jews, the reality of this one God is based on the belief that it is [God] from whom the world and all humankind took their origin.[4]

CREATION IN THE NEW TESTAMENT

Given our Christian dependence on the theocentric faith of the Old Testament, it is rather strange that the New Testament has so few references to God as creator of heaven and earth. Christian writers refer to the doctrine of creation rather casually, as something taken for granted. Concordance entries under "create, creator, creation" are sparse. In connection with a question about divorce, Jesus says (according to Mark 10:6, NRSV): "From the beginning of creation, 'God made them male and female'"—a clear reference to the paradise story of Genesis 2–3. There is also the famous passage in Paul's Epistle to the Romans (Rom. 1:20), which has become controversial in discussions of sexual ethics, that the Gentiles, like the Jews, are subject to the judgment of God, for "ever since the creation of the world God's eternal power and divine nature, invisible though they are, have been understood and seen through the things he has made" (NRSV). Otherwise, with the exception of christological passages to which I shall turn later, a few casual references occur, as in:

1 Tim. 4:4 (NRSV):	"For everything created by God [referring to foods] is good."
1 Pet. 4:19 (NRSV):	"Let those suffering in accordance with God's will entrust themselves to a faithful Creator, while continuing to do good."

Doxological passages occur in the Apocalypse of John:

> You are worthy, Our Lord and God,
> to receive glory and honor and power,
> for you created all things,
> and by your will they existed and were created (Rev. 4:11, NRSV).

4. Wolfhart Pannenberg, "Theology and Science," *Princeton Seminary Bulletin* 13 (1992) 299–310; quotation from 299.

Similarly in Rev. 10:6 (NRSV) the ascription of praise to the God who lives forever:

> who created heaven and what is in it, the earth and
> what is in it, and the sea and what is in it.

Anticipating what is to come in this essay, one should pay special attention to passages that view creation in the apocalyptic perspective that was characteristic of early Christianity. In the "Little Apocalypse" of Mark we read:

> In those days there will be suffering, such as has not been from the beginning of the creation that God created until now, no, and never will be. (Mark 13:19, NRSV)

Then there is that marvelous passage, Rom. 8:18-25, in which Paul announces that the whole creation (including what we would call nature and history) is involved in God's redemptive purpose that is hastening toward consummation. Here the discussion definitely has an apocalyptic ring, as we shall see.

Given the paucity of references to God as creator of heaven and earth in the New Testament, it is no wonder that early interpreters of Christianity—especially those in the Gnostic camp—tried to establish a deep discontinuity between the two Testaments, or, more accurately, between the two ages, the old age and the new.

J. Christiaan Beker calls attention to a striking statement by Leo Baeck in his work *Judaism and Christianity.* "Gnosticism is Christianity without Judaism and, in that sense, pure Christianity. Whenever Christianity wanted to become pure in this way [that is, separated from Judaism and the Old Testament], it became Gnostic."[5] Gnosticism was a powerful movement in the ancient world into which the gospel of Jesus Christ was introduced. Gnosticism is a generic term encompassing various religious movements that shared the common view that material existence (our life "in the flesh") is illusory and evil. Salvation was offered to the individual through *gnōsis* ("knowledge") disclosed by a revealer, in this case, Jesus Christ.

The degree to which this movement challenged Christianity has become evident from the Nag Hammadi texts, such as *The Gospel of Thomas,* which were discovered in Upper Egypt in December 1945. The texts were written in the fourth century, but the originals were written earlier, in the second or third century, and in some cases possibly the first. Gnosticism, in updated form, is still a powerful challenge to Christianity. In a recent

---

5. See J. Christiaan Beker, "Paul's Letter to the Romans as a Model for Biblical Theology," in *Understanding the Word: Essays in Honor of Bernhard W. Anderson* (ed. James T. Butler, Edgar W. Conrad, and Ben C. Ollenburger; JSOTSup 37; Sheffield: JSOT, 1985) 359.

book entitled *The American Religion,* Harold Bloom maintains that much American spirituality, with its individualistic piety and one-to-one relation to God "up there," or "out there," is essentially Gnostic.[6]

According to church historians, in the early centuries of creedal discussion Christian interpreters relied heavily on their Jewish colleagues for theological support.[7] That is understandable, for the Old Testament, with its doctrine of creation and its monotheistic announcement that this world in which we live and move and have our being is good and ultimately meaningful, provided an antidote to Gnostic dualism. In this respect, Christianity and Judaism were allies, not adversaries. Considering the intensity of the conflict with Gnosticism, one should not be surprised that the Apostles' Creed begins theocentrically, by placing the doctrine of creation first, even before a christological affirmation: "I believe in God the Father Almighty, maker of heaven and earth."

CONTINUITY AND DISCONTINUITY

In the early Christian community, the question of the authority of Scripture was formulated primarily in terms of the claim that the Old Testament (that is, the Torah and the Prophets) is revelation of God. The emphasis was on the texts of Scripture that presented, as Paul put it (Rom. 3:2), the "words [*logia*] of God." Inspiration was attached to the texts, not—as we would be inclined to say—to "authors." Perhaps it is legitimate to extend inspiration to the whole process by which the texts came into being or, in our terms, the history of the redaction of the text. Nevertheless, it is the text in its final form that functioned as the "words of God" in the early Christian community.

In the second century, the challenge to the Christian church came in the form of a controversy over the contents of a Christian canon of Scriptures. The leader of this controversy was Marcion, an influential Christian who was expelled from the church of Rome about 144 C.E. Marcion proposed a Christian canon that included a few Christian writings, mainly selections from Pauline epistles. In his work *Antitheses,* he construed Paul's contrast between the law and the gospel, the flesh and the spirit, the old age and the new, to mean that Jewish Scriptures were antithetical to God's revelation in Jesus Christ. Hence his canon excluded the Old Testament. He agreed that the Old Testament is revelation, but not the saving revelation of the God of Jesus Christ.[8]

6. Harold Bloom, *The American Religion* (New York: Simon & Schuster, 1992).

7. I refer to a paper for the American Theological Society by Robert L. Wilken, "Religious Pluralism and Early Christian Thought" (1992).

8. Elements of this discussion are taken from my introduction to *The Old Testament and Christian Faith* (ed. Bernhard W. Anderson; repr. New York: Herder and Herder, 1969) 1–7.

To be fair to Marcion, one must keep in mind that he was trying to take Paul's teaching seriously. After all, Paul had said that the Jewish law was holy, that it was given by God; but the law was weak in that it could not rescue human beings from sin and bring them into right relation with God. Deliverance from sin had come not by the law but by God's gracious action in Jesus Christ. In the heat of controversy, however, Marcion went much further, owing to the influence of Hellenistic (Gnostic) dualism upon his thinking. The God of the Old Testament, he said, is another God, inferior to the God of Jesus Christ. In the language of the time, the God of the Old Testament is a demiurge, a term used in Plato's philosophy for the deity as creator of the material world, and in Gnostic philosophy as a deity, subordinate to the supreme deity, who was sometimes regarded as the creator of this evil world. Thus the two Testaments are antithetical to each other. The God of the Old Testament, Marcion said, is the creator of this transient world; the God of Christ is the God who redeems us from this world. The God of the Old Testament is the God of wrath and justice; the High God is the loving Father who is apprehended only through faith in Christ. Following this line of thinking, the discontinuity between the two revelations is absolute. The gospel "fulfills" Jewish Scripture only in the sense that it supersedes and abrogates it. Even though Christian theologians repudiated Marcion's view, Marcionism continued to be a temptation. Indeed, many Marcionites are still hiding in the bushes, poised to ambush the unsuspecting preacher.

The Christian apocalyptic perspective—as well as Gnostic influence—undoubtedly made Christian interpreters vulnerable to this kind of antithetical thinking. Apocalyptic eschatology drew a sharp contrast between the "old" and the "new." As found in the poetry of so-called Second Isaiah, prophecy announced the "new thing" that God was on the verge of doing to carry out the divine plan for Israel and the nations. The *Novum* would be so marvelous that, at times, a sharp line was drawn between "the former things" and "the things to come." A poet hears God speaking:

Do not remember the former things,
    or consider the things of old.
I am about to do a new thing;
    now it springs forth, do you not perceive it? (Isa. 43:18-19, NRSV)

As prophecy moved into apocalyptic, for instance in the last part of the book of Isaiah, the disjunction between the old and the new was described as "new heavens and a new earth"—a complete transformation of the creation in which "the former things shall not be remembered" (Isa. 65:17-19).

In full-blown Jewish apocalyptic, interpreters announced that the corruption of evil had affected not only the historical realm on earth but the heavenly realm as well. Hence, there must be a radically new beginning, a new creation, symbolized by a new heaven and a new earth. When consistent and thoroughgoing, apocalyptic stresses the discontinuity between the two ages—"the present evil age" and "the age to come," the old world and the new. In this sense, apocalyptic has affinities with Gnostic thought, which in its own way offered salvation from this evil, transitory world.

Early Christian witnesses, whose writings are preserved in the New Testament, were enthusiastically aware of the new thing that God had done in Jesus Christ. The new age was nothing less than a new creation, as Paul announced:

> So, if anyone is in Christ, there is a new creation; everything old has passed away; see, everything has become new. (2 Cor. 5:17, NRSV)

New Testament witnesses do not make a sharp, absolute separation between the two ages. That is perhaps the major difference between the preaching of Jesus ("Repent, for the kingdom of God is at hand") and the preaching of John the Baptist, whose message must have been akin to the apocalyptic community of Qumran, on the shore of the Dead Sea. Unfortunately, lengthy disputes over the sectarian "Dead Sea" scrolls from Qumran, first discovered in 1947, have so far almost obscured their apocalyptic contents.

Disagreeing with Jewish apocalyptic visionaries, the early Christian community broke with the sharp separation between the two ages. These two ages are not like two circles that touch each other only tangentially; rather, the two circles overlap. For already in the old age, people may taste the power of the age to come; already in the old age the leaven of God's kingdom is at work; already in the time of the old creation a new creation is beginning. Thus, the relation between the two ages or two Testaments is neither a straight-line continuity nor a disjunctive discontinuity. Rather, it is continuity and discontinuity. People are called to live in the zone where the circles overlap—where there is discontinuity with the old age even while the old age continues. This kind of "two-age" theology received a profound expression in the thinking of the apostle Paul, for whom Jesus' resurrection "signalled the intrusion of the age to come into the present."[9]

THE OLD TESTAMENT DOCTRINE OF CREATION

This unusual situation—living in the new age while the old age continues—has many implications and ramifications. For instance, from this

---

9. See the illuminating discussion of Paul's "ex post facto thinking" by Leander E. Keck, "Paul as Thinker," in *Int* 47 *(Essays in Honor of Paul J. Achtemeier)* (1993) 27–38, esp. 29–34.

vantage point one can better understand the ambiguities of ethical decisions that are made in the perspective of the kingdom of God yet in a society that has not become the kingdom of God. This essay, however, is concerned primarily with how the Christian community rereads the Old Testament, particularly the book of Genesis, which speaks about the God who is Creator of heaven and earth. Since the relation between the Testaments must be seen in the dimensions of continuity and discontinuity, my first task will be to consider elements of continuity. In a profound sense, the Christian gospel is grounded upon God's originating purpose: as it has been "from the beginning of the creation that God created" (Mark 13:19). The proper place to begin is with a consideration of the nature and purpose of the creation account found in Gen. 1:1—2:3. One immediately confronts a literary question: What kind of literary unit (or genre) is this? Is it history, myth, cultic poem, story, or what?

For many centuries it was supposed that the opening chapters of Genesis present straightforward history, beginning with the creation of the world (which some fixed in 4004 B.C.E.), moving to the great flood that covered the whole earth, and on to the history of Israel's ancestors: the exodus from Egypt, the covenant of Sinai, wanderings in the wilderness, and so on. In this view, the first chapter of Genesis presented a "historiographical" account of creation. It was believed that information about the creation of the world was given to the first parents of humanity and was passed down through a chain of oral tradition until it was eventually written down by Moses in the book of Genesis. On this assumption, a war between science and religion was inevitable. The conflict has become fierce at times, as evidenced in the legal battles over so-called creation science or creationism.

We may be moving into a new situation where this warfare will no longer be necessary (see chap. 6 above). There is increasing agreement that the creation account belongs to the genre of story, not history. Even conservative "evangelical" scholars are moving in this direction, if one can rely on the testimony of a recent book, *Portraits of Creation,* by scholars at the Calvin Center for Christian Scholarship in Grand Rapids, Michigan. The Genesis account, they say, "presents a storied rather than a historiographical account of creation."[10] Those who have followed my writings on this subject know that I would prefer to say that this is a mythopoeic account, in which imagery known in the ancient world (e.g., the myth of the creator god's victory over the powers of chaos) was used

---

10. Howard J. Van Till et al., *Portraits of Creation: Biblical and Scientific Perspectives on the World's Formation* (Grand Rapids: Eerdmans, 1990), esp. John H. Stek, "The Nature and Purpose of Genesis 1:1—2:3," 221–42; quotation from 238. See also Clark H. Pinnock, "Climbing out of a Swamp: The Evangelical Struggle to Understand the Creation Texts," in *The Best in Theology* (ed. J. I. Packer; Carol Stream, Ill.: Christianity Today, 1990) 4.39–50.

to present an imaginative portrayal of creation. An inspired literary artist has given an impressionistic painting of creation, not a photograph. It is something like Monet's painting of his garden, for instance the Japanese bridge or the lily pond, which differs from the literal photographs taken by visitors to his home in Giverny, France.

Similarly we have two "portraits" of creation, one biblical and the other scientific, which may be placed side by side but are not necessarily at odds with one another. The literary artistry of the portrayal in Gen. 1:1—2:3 is exhibited in several respects.[11] Briefly, the whole account is structured in a series of paragraphs based on command and execution. God speaks and the executive command is executed. This structure is like that in the Priestly Sinai narrative, where God gives commands on the mountaintop (Exodus 25–30) and Moses executes them (Exodus 35–40). Also, this impressionistic picture has symmetry and balance. The account is divided into two triads of three days, each day of the first triad corresponding to a day in the other:

Day 1:   the creation of light and the separation of day and night, corresponds to

Day 4:   the creation of luminaries to govern the day and night.

Day 2:   the creation of the firmament to separate the waters above (the heavenly ocean) from the waters below (the earthly ocean), reflecting the ancient cosmology. This corresponds to

Day 5:   the creation of living beings (marine creatures) to fill the earthly waters and birds to fly beneath the firmament.

Day 3:   the creation of dry land by pushing back the waters, and the greening of the earth with vegetation. This corresponds to

Day 6:   the creation of land animals to roam the earth and live on its vegetation, and the creation of humankind to have dominion over the earth and all living creatures.

Finally, the whole story has a heptadic structure, culminating in Day 7— the day that stands outside of the triadic pattern of days. The number seven, a sacred number, signifies the mystic harmony and perfection of the whole and anticipates the Sabbath day that was instituted at Sinai.

---

11. See further chap. 3 above.

Literary Parallelism in the Genesis Creation Story

HEAVEN

Day 1: Light to separate day and night

Day 4: Heavenly lights to govern day and night

Day 2: Firmament to separate upper and lower waters

Day 5: Living beings to soar under the firmament and to swim in the waters

EARTH

Day 3: (a) Dry land called the "earth"
(b) Vegetation on earth

Day 6: (a) Animals to roam the surface of the earth
(b) Humans to rule the earth

Day 7: SABBATH REST[12]

One could spend a long time on the nature and purpose of the Genesis account. Suffice it to say, in agreement with Howard Van Till and others, that this is story, composed with aesthetic design for the purpose of giving "teaching" (*tôrâ*) or "doctrine" about creation in a cosmological sense. Here I call attention to several aspects of his teaching concerning creation.

First is the teaching that the universe had its origin in the creative purpose of God. To be sure, Genesis 1 speaks of creation out of chaos, not creation "out of nothing" (a later doctrine; cf. 2 Macc. 7:28). Yet it is the clear teaching that God created the world in freedom, with no restraint or necessity. As Pannenberg observes,

> To be created does not only mean to depend on some cause, but also to be an utterly non-necessary product of a completely free action . . . a creature, in the strict sense of the word, did not come to exist by any necessity. It would never have come into existence, except for the free act of God the creator. If the entire world is a creation of God, that means that its existence is completely and thoroughly contingent. There could have been no world at all.[13]

As a psalmist exclaims:

---

12. Other scholars stress this symmetry as well, including John H. Stek in *Portraits of Creation*, 238. See the similar chart in chap. 3 above, p. 50.
13. Pannenberg, *Princeton Seminary Bulletin* 13 (1992) 301.

> Let all the earth fear the Lord,
>   let all the inhabitants of the world stand in awe of him.
> For he spoke, and it came it to be;
>   he commanded, and it stood firm. (Ps. 33:8-9, NRSV)

Second is the teaching that the glory of God is displayed in the marvelous order of the cosmos, wherein every creature has its place in an interconnected whole, or, as we would say, an ecosystem. The harmonious order of God's creation is not only physical order but also moral order—a point that is stressed in Psalm 19, which begins by announcing that the heavens display God's glory and reaches a climax in praising God, who orders life with the "law" or *tôrâ*. Moreover, God's creation also preserves and maintains the order that was created in the beginning. In this sense, God engages in a continuous creation, as Psalm 104 attests. In contrast to the Genesis creation story, to which it is related, this magnificent poem stresses continuing creation, not creation in the beginning. In the Hebrew the verbs, translated in the English present, refer to frequentative action and reach a climax with the theme of God's re-creation:

> When you send forth your spirit, they are created;
>   and you renew the face of the ground. (Ps. 104:30, NRSV)

It is worth noting, too, that some biblical passages, especially in Second Isaiah, portray God's historical deeds as creative acts (Isa. 43:12, 19; 45: 7-8). The combination of these two ideas—constant preservation and new acts in history—paves the way for the idea of a continuous creation in the proper sense, that is, creation as "an act of the eternal God . . . relating to the universe in its *entire process,* in its history throughout time." Christian theology, Pannenberg observes, should not be limited to creation as the origin of the cosmos that continued unchanged from the beginning. "Thinking of creation as incomplete at the beginning corresponds more fully to the Christian conception of God's action in history as culminating in Jesus Christ."[14] Again, the Genesis creation story teaches that human beings are called to an important role in God's cosmic administration, namely, to act as God's representatives by helping to maintain peace on earth—a peace in which animals and humans share the earthly house and the earth is cared for properly. According to the climax of the story, this is what it means to be made "in the image of God," A psalmist puts it beautifully: human beings are elevated above the earthly realm toward the realm of the angels of God's heavenly court:

14. Ibid., 302.

You have made them a little lower than God [or "angels"]
and crowned them with glory and honor. (Ps. 8:5, NRSV)

That coronation of humankind is for the purpose of ruling over the earth, not as an autonomous being but as God's royal steward. Finally, the Old Testament teaching of the doctrine of creation summons us to a healthy this-worldliness. The life that God has given us on this earth is basically good; it is not a material realm from which to seek escape through Gnostic illumination or from which to withdraw in apocalyptic otherworldliness. Even in times of perplexity and distress, we expect to taste the goodness of the Lord in the land of the living, as psalmists said in their prayers. Dietrich Bonhoeffer was deeply impressed with the this-worldliness of the Old Testament and advised Christians not to come to the New Testament too soon or too directly, lest they miss the full meaning of the cross and resurrection.[15]

CHRIST AND GOD'S NEW CREATION

These are some of the positive teachings that the Christian church receives from reading the Scriptures of Israel, or the Old Testament. In the Christian rereading of the Old Testament, however, some discontinuities arise, owing to the inbreaking of the new age through the life, death, and resurrection of Jesus Christ.

First of all, in Christ God has created a new community. Second Isaiah had spoken of the community of Israel as God's creation:

Now thus says the Lord,
   the one who created you, O Jacob,
   who formed you, O Israel:
"Fear not, for I have redeemed you;
   I have called you by name, you are mine." (Isa. 43:1)

The New Testament picks up this theme of the creation of a community and gives it new meaning. Through Christ, God has formed a new community in which all social and ethnic barriers are overcome. To be "in Christ" or to be "baptized into Christ" is to be incorporated into this new community in which, according to an old baptismal formula, "There is neither Jew nor Greek, there is neither slave nor free, there is neither male nor female; for you are all one in Christ Jesus" (Gal. 3:28, RSV). Even yet we speak of the church as God's new creation when singing the hymn, "The Church's One Foundation."

15. Dietrich Bonhoeffer, *Prisoner for God: Letters and Prayers from Prison* (New York: Macmillan, 1953) 79. See also Martin Kuske, *The Old Testament as a Book of Christ: An Appraisal of Bonhoeffer's Interpretation,* trans. S. T. Kimbrough, Jr. (Philadelphia: Westminster Press, 1976) 96ff.

Second, the creation motif of the image of God is transferred in a primary sense to Jesus Christ, who represents God's royal rule on earth. Believers partake of that royal image as they share the resurrection life of Christ (Rom. 8:29), "being changed into his likeness from one degree of glory to another" (2 Cor. 3:18). But "image" and "likeness" are primarily attributes of Jesus Christ. In this regard, notice how the Epistle to the Hebrews reinterprets Psalm 8 messianically. Understanding the psalm to be a royal psalm, and following the Septuagint rather than the Hebrew text, the writer acclaims Jesus as the royal steward of God's cosmic kingdom who "for a little while [Greek *brachy,* rather than Hebrew *mĕ' aṭ,* 'a little bit'] was made lower than the angels" (Heb. 2:5-9). To the eye of faith, Jesus is the ruler, the messianic agent of God, the one who takes part in God's cosmic administration seated at God's right hand, although the full exercise of his royal rule on earth is temporarily postponed.

Above all, one must emphasize that the New Testament has been influenced by the apocalyptic message that already the kingdom of God has dawned, even though the present evil age lingers. That is evident, for instance, in the wonderful passage in Rom. 8:18-25, referred to earlier, in which Paul says that the creation is "in bondage to decay" and—along with the children of God in history—waits in hope for liberation. Indeed, "the whole creation has been groaning in travail together until now," as though in birth pangs, struggling to give birth to a new creation.

Finally, the radically new element in the New Testament is that creation is viewed christologically. Some New Testament writers announce boldly that in the beginning God created all things in and through Christ. This is found especially in deutero-Pauline passages, such as the statement in Colossians:

> He is the image of the invisible God, the firstborn of all creation; for in him all things in heaven and on earth were created, things visible and invisible, whether thrones or dominions or rulers or powers—all things have been created through him and for him. He himself is before all things, and in him all things hold together. (Col. 1:15-17, NRSV)

According to this tremendous statement, the whole creation centers in, and is grounded upon, God's revelation in Jesus Christ. This christological view of creation is especially evident in the prologue to the Fourth Gospel. Like the book of Genesis, it opens with "in the beginning"; and like the portrayal of Wisdom in Prov. 8:22-31, it speaks of an agent that was present with God at the creation. Here, however, is a radically new note: the incarnation of God's creative word:

> He was in the beginning with God. All things came into being through him, and without him not one thing came into being. (John 1:2-3, NRSV)

Before such lofty statements, one is inclined to say with the psalmist: "Such knowledge is too wonderful for me; it is high, I cannot attain unto it" (Ps. 139:6, KJV). Here, I think, we find the deepest discontinuity between the Old Testament and the New. For in this incarnational Christology Christian interpretation moves into another dimension. If I may rely on the distinction drawn by Clark Pinnock, no longer do we find the functional Christology inherent in the Old Testament word "Messiah" (or "Christ")—the agent of God. Rather, we have an ontological Christology, one that deals with the *being* of Christ in relation to God.[16] This profound shift in emphasis leads beyond the Bible to the trinitarian discussions and the creedal formulations of the Christian church in the first centuries of its history.

16. Pinnock, *Wideness in God's Mercy*, 62–63.

Index of

Biblical References

Index of

Modern Authors